BETWEEN THE BULLET AND THE LIE

ESSAYS ON ORWELL

KRISTIAN WILLIAMS

Foreword by David Goodway

Praise for *Between the Bullet and the Lie*:

"Rather than provide literary criticism or biography, Kristian Williams is most concerned in this felicitous collection to derive George Orwell's method—the process he used to translate personal experiences and worldly explorations into democratic anti-capitalist principles, and convey them to broad audiences in an irresistible fashion. A bit of Orwell's literary élan has rubbed off on Williams's own clever, precise prose. I'm left convinced of the urgency in studying Orwell, despite his acknowledged flaws, as a guide to living ethically in our ominous present moment."
— Andrew Cornell, author of *Unruly Equality: U.S. Anarchism in the Twentieth Century*

"As a writer of the Twentieth Century, George Orwell requires a careful rereading and reinterpretation for the Twenty-First. Kristian Williams goes beyond sheer reflections toward providing an engaging, politically relevant, and useful Orwell for our contemporary period. *Between the Bullet and the Lie* emerges from the malaise of the moment and enrolls the reader in a political project: the left must return to clear writing, clear thinking, and common decency; it must return to Orwell."
— Kevin Van Meter, author of *Guerrillas of Desire: Notes on Everyday Resistance and Organizing to Make a Revolution Possible*

"Kristian Williams reminds us of the importance of George Orwell when it comes to our conversations and actions. Orwell is the awkward one, the one who chips away at our smugness by suggesting that matters may be a little more contradictory and complex than we want them to be. He's both irritating and intelligent, intellectual and emotional. In short, Williams presents Orwell as a complicated human being who insists on grounding his ideas in what constitutes the realities that make up everyday life for most people. As far as Orwell was concerned our ideas and thoughts have to engage with that awkward, messy, and quite disturbing actuality. Influenced by Orwell's impatience with cliché and the laziness of political thought, Williams's writing is as clear as crystal—both in his own reflections and his engagements with Orwell's writings. The latter, especially, reflect Williams's impressive knowledge and understanding of all areas and periods of Orwell's work. We regularly talk about books being essential reading. This one just might be for those of us looking to build a movement of some kind, rather than maintain a cult."

—Barry Pateman, Kate Sharpley Library

"Millions of words have been written about George Orwell since his tragically early death, but amazingly, it took many decades for us to get a serious study of 'Orwellism.' Now we have one. Kristian Williams's *Between the Bullet and the Lie* is the first substantial exploration of Orwell's thought and it's thorough, acute, and astonishingly contemporary. Orwell's key concerns—with the mechanics of state power and its abuse, with 'decency,' with the failings of the Left and the promise of socialism (broadly defined)—are ours. (If you need convincing, just read Williams's update of Orwell's classic essay, 'Politics and the English Language.') Williams gives us the best summation to date of this remarkable English writer's political philosophy, and in doing so, he reawakens an important source of understanding of our own time."

—Eric Laursen, author of *The People's Pension: The Struggle to Defend Social Security Since Reagan*

Between the Bullet and the Lie: Essays on Orwell
© 2017 Kristian Williams
Foreword © 2017 David Goodway

This edition © 2017 AK Press (Chico, Oakland, Edinburgh, Baltimore)
ISBN: 978-1-84935-290-1
E-ISBN: 978-1-84935-291-8
Library of Congress Control Number: 2017936238

AK Press
370 Ryan Ave. #100
Chico, CA 95973
USA
www.akpress.org
akpress@akpress.org

AK Press
33 Tower St.
Edinburgh EH6 7BN
Scotland
www.akuk.com
ak@akedin.demon.co.uk

The above addresses would be delighted to provide you with the latest AK Press
distribution catalog, which features books, pamphlets, zines, and stylish apparel
published and/or distributed by AK Press. Alternatively, visit our websites for the
complete catalog, latest news, and secure ordering.

Cover design by Josh MacPhee | https://antumbradesign.org/
Interior design by Margaret Killjoy | birdsbeforethestorm.net
Printed in the USA on recycled paper

Also by Kristian Williams

Our Enemies in Blue: Police and Power in America, third edition
(AK Press, 2015)

Fire the Cops: Essays, Lectures, and Journalism
(Kersplebedeb, 2014)

Hurt: Notes on Torture in a Modern Democracy
(Microcosm, 2012)

American Methods: Torture and the Logic of Domination
(South End Press, 2006)

Contents

Foreword

Williams's Orwell

OH, NO, NOT ANOTHER BOOK ABOUT ORWELL! HERE IS A WRITER whose expressed wish was that there was to be no biography, yet there are now half a dozen. An Orwell Society was founded in 2011 and has since launched a biannual academic journal, *George Orwell Studies*. The revelation in 2013 by Edward Snowden, National Security Agency contractor and whistleblower, of the scale of the global surveillance systems operated by the intelligence agencies of the USA and United Kingdom has led to their description as "Orwellian"—in reference to the controlling intrusion by the state detailed so nightmarishly in *1984*. Online sales of the novel mushroomed by 5,800 percent within a week of Snowden's action. The inanities, unfortunately usually malign, of the Trump presidency, also have one reaching for Orwell: what could be more Orwellian than the concept of "alternative facts"? Kellyanne

Conway's coinage caused *1984* to jump to the top of Amazon's best-seller list, an unprecedented achievement for a book first published sixty-eight years previously. As a friend informs me, "Orwell's now hot in the States, you know."

Concurrently, my reading has led me to appreciate how difficult the man could be in person. V.S. Pritchett, short-story writer and critic, who memorably called him "the wintry conscience of a generation," not only described him as "complex, straying, and contradictory" but seems to have regarded him as an "eccentric … crank, and … thorn in the flesh," commenting that to become his friend you first had to undergo "the usual quarrel." Herbert Read rightly considered that he had raised journalism to the status of literature and "felt nearer to him than to any other English writer of our time," yet was all the same irritated by "some aspects of his personality," including "his proletarian pose in dress." Read might also have mentioned the ostentatious drinking of tea from his saucer, slurping it noisily, one of the habits that greatly irked John Morris, a wartime colleague at the BBC Eastern Service.

Morris, a conventional man who disliked Orwell, surprises by observing:

> Although he wrote so well, he was a poor and halting speaker; even in private conversation he expressed himself badly and would often fumble for the right word. His weekly broadcast talks were beautifully written, but he delivered them in a dull and monotonous voice. I was often with him in the studio and it was painful to hear such good material wasted: like many other brilliant writers, he never really understood the subtle differences between the written and the spoken word, or, if he did, he could not be bothered with them.

Although Orwell remains controversial in many ways, there is extensive recognition that his work was indeed "beautifully written," even that he is one of the masters of English prose.

Any writer, I am convinced, writes as well as they read. Kristian Williams knows his Orwell inside out—there is nothing pertinent with which he does not appear familiar—and so the prose of this exceptional book, which I am privileged to introduce, is exquisitely straightforward. Attention to the quality of writing is not to be dismissed as a mere artistic or aesthetic fad, irrelevant to the major issues of the day, to the fundamental concerns of life. On the contrary, Kristian and myself, and Orwell, too, passionately believe in the writer's responsibility to make accessible to the ordinary intelligent reader ideas and analysis however strange or difficult.

It is the duty of the communicator to communicate, not to revel in obscurantist, even if supposedly technical, language that only "experts" pretend to understand. As Kristian remarks in his introduction:

> Orwell is not renowned as a deep thinker, partly because deep thinking has become confused with difficult writing—that is to say, with writing that is difficult to read. It is in fact harder to produce smooth, clear prose, but readers are prone to assume that if they do not struggle over a passage then the writer must not have either. They are just as likely to suppose—or a certain type of reader is, anyway—that if a piece of writing is obscure it is also necessarily profound.

It was probably G.K. Chesterton who apologized to an editor for submitting an overlong article, explaining that he had not had time to write a shorter piece. Kristian explains that Orwell wanted his prose to be "like a window pane," so transparent one forgets that it's there.

Between the Bullet and the Lie collects essays several of which have been previously published. The second part applies Orwell's outlook to a range of contemporary issues, whereas the first, especially rich and impressive, discusses both decency (always his touchstone) and human imperfection and compares at some length the homophobic Orwell with Oscar Wilde. With typical unpredictability and contradiction, Orwell insisted that he had "always been very pro-Wilde."

Kristian describes himself as an "anarchist with social-democratic sympathies," whereas Orwell was—and this is extremely well put—a "democratic socialist with anarchist sympathies." His appeal, however, is remarkably broad, and he can not unreasonably be claimed by a variety of incompatible ideologies: state socialism as well as libertarian socialism, of course, but in addition conservatism, nationalism, liberalism, even Trotskyism. Notably absent from this spectrum of admiration are most Marxists, apologists, whether past or present, for the Soviet Union, and advocates of utopian communism. They continue to hate him for "spilling the Spanish beans" in *Homage to Catalonia*, for his fable of revolutionary degeneration *Animal Farm* and above all, I believe, for the dystopia of *1984*. The Bolsheviks, he had argued in 1941, sought to create "a Rule of the Saints, which, like the English Rule of the Saints, was a military despotism enlivened by witchcraft trials."

I have already directed attention to Orwell's contradictions and the impossibility of much of his behavior. Recognizing how imperfect, how flawed he himself was, philosophically he was an anti-perfectionist, and this entailed an anti-utopianism. In a central passage Kristian ably summarizes:

> Orwell wrote against Utopia, not merely because he believed it impossible, and not simply because it might become perverted, but also because he found the very *idea* of perfection repulsive and even oppressive. In his essay on Jonathan Swift, Orwell worries over "the totalitarian tendency which is implicit in the anarchist or pacifist vision of society"….The problem, as Orwell saw it, is that Utopias, by definition, are perfect and that human beings—also by definition—are not. Always the realist, he concludes that the fault lies with Utopia: that these dreams of a perfect society are not only impossible, but inhuman and therefore, by human standards, undesirable. Were they realized, the practical result could only be a narrowing of the scope of human life.

The problem then lies not just in a dystopia like *1984*, but also in seemingly benign utopias such as Wells's *A Modern Utopia* and Huxley's *Island*: the quest for perfection makes us all less human.

This disquisition appears in the chapter on Wilde; and Kristian concludes that his utopianism and Orwell's anti-utopianism are equally necessary, that we do not need to choose between them. Wilde memorably maintained: "A map of the world that does include Utopia is not worth even glancing at, for it leaves out the one country at which Humanity is always landing." Yet the continuation—"And when Humanity lands there, it looks out, and, seeing a better country, sets sail"—Kristian considers as tragic as Orwell's position. Indeed throughout his book, his stance is almost always the same as that of Orwell, fruitfully applying the approach the older writer arrived at in the unhappy second quarter of the twentieth century to the probably even more desperate second decade of the twenty-first. Thus he applauds Orwell's "reverence for fact, his sense of decency, his respect for intelligence, his faith in the common people, his courage (moral, intellectual, and physical), and his refusal to mock traditional virtues for the sake of looking sophisticated," commenting that "these are qualities disastrously lacking in our present discourse—political and cultural, Left and Right, popular and intellectual." Kristian stresses that it is essential for radical ideas to address the world as it actually is, "as we find it in our lives rather than in our daydreams or our theories." He rejects the "sense of ideological purity" in which "alleged" radicals luxuriate:

> Any revolution worth the name must be the work of many millions of people. For that very reason it will fail to please the more orthodox revolutionaries who specialize in finding fault and view any idea with genuinely broad appeal as ideologically suspect.

Kristian never mentions Rojava, but I have been shocked by the relish with which anarchists highlight the extent to which what has been achieved there falls short of doctrinal blueprints—and ideological purity—instead of celebrating and supporting the libertarian success of Syrian Kurdistan and its inspiring social innovations. On the one hand, there is the self-satisfaction of radicals and their sense of superiority over the population at large; on the other, they "become locked in a vicious cycle of purism and defeat, convinced that since no victory is ever total, no victory is ever real...."

In total, Kristian believes, more important than Orwell's ideas is "his example in handling these ideas—the clarity of expression, the resistance to dogmatism, the 'power of facing unpleasant facts'": "And further back, behind that approach, there stands Orwell himself, who ought not to be revered as any kind of saint, but who may instead serve as an example of a flawed, often unhappy individual, doing his best to preserve his integrity and nudge the world, however slightly, toward a more sane and decent future."

For his day job Kristian operates drawbridges. I am reminded of the British poet Peter Reading (1946–2011), who worked for twenty-two years as a weighbridge operator at an animal-feed mill, leaving him free to write highly original verse which he published prolifically. (He was ultimately sacked for refusing to wear a uniform required by the new owners of the firm.) When I remarked to Kristian that his job went far to explain his independence and clarity of mind, "far from the intellectual restraints and absurdities of academia," his interesting response was: "I don't really know if my defection from academia explains the clarity of my thinking; I suspect it may be the other way around." That is, he considers plausibly that it was the clarity of his thought that was responsible for his shunning academia. Whatever, I have no doubt that Orwell would have approved of Kristian's paid work. George Woodcock recalled of their first meeting:

> At that time I was running a market garden in Middlesex, and Orwell questioned me about it; he seemed to approve of the fact that I was engaged in manual work and that my hands were chapped and ingrained with soil.

Similarly Pritchett remembered "standing for a long time in a doorway off Piccadilly while he told me about the advantage of keeping goats in the country with full details of cost and yield—for he was a born small-holder and liked manual work."

Between the Bullet and the Lie is a notable work, which belongs with the best books written about Orwell. In this foreword I have quoted extensively from it, relishing three features: the quality of Kristian's prose, Orwell's gritty independence and insight, and Kristian's own intellectual penetration and lucidity of thought.

David Goodway

Acknowledgements

NUMEROUS PEOPLE OFFERED COMMENTS ON ONE OR SEVERAL OF THE essays included in this collection. Thanks are owed to Amelia Cates, Emily-Jane Dawson, Eleanor Jones, Chris Knudtsen, Eric Laursen, Peter Little, Jerusha McCormack, Geoff McNamara, Paul Messersmith-Glavin, Tabatha Millican, Gabriel Ryder, Josef Schneider, Todd Stewart, M. Treloar, Kevin Van Meter, Adam Warner, Dolores Williams, Robert Williams, and Emily Winokur.

Introduction

"An Age Like This"
Orwell in His Time, and Ours

GEORGE ORWELL, LIKE RUDYARD KIPLING, IS ONE OF THOSE WRITERS whom one quotes without meaning to.[1] "Cold War," for example, was his coinage, albeit without the capitals.[2] So were the more commonly recognized "Big Brother" and "Thought Police"—both from *1984*, a number that continues to signal a dystopian future more than thirty years after the date has passed.[3] "Orwellian" is of course used to signify the very things the writer warned against—as is sometimes, less forgivably, simply "Orwell."

Orwell remains a recognizable figure—even if there is some confusion about what he was a figure of.[4] I remember before the 2004 election seeing ironic, ill-conceived "Bush/Orwell" bumper stickers, intended to compare the reigning administration with the fictitious totalitarian regime of *1984*. A friend of mine suggested that "Bush/ O'Brien" would be more accurate, which is true, though far fewer people would recognize the name of the novel's Inner Party inquisitor.[5] "Bush/Big Brother," in contrast, would border on the too-obvious-for-humor. "Big Brother," as a term, has in some ways outgrown its literary origins and become simply an everyday phrase—not to mention a popular television show about the joys of voyeurism and control in an artificial environment entirely lacking privacy.

Now, as we drift through the second decade of the seemingly permanent War on Terror, Orwell's place in the political lexicon is if anything more secure—especially in connection to ubiquitous surveillance. In 2011, US Supreme Court Justice Stephen Breyer worried that warrantless GPS-tracking could "suddenly produce what sounds like *1984*."[6] And two years after that, when Edward Snowden revealed the true range of the National Security Agency's electronic surveillance programs, online sales of *1984* shot up 3,000 per cent in just a few days.[7] The book hit the best-seller lists again in 2017, after an advisor to President Trump characterized the administration's blatant falsehoods as "alternative facts."[8] Meanwhile, two hundred theatres nationwide responded with simultaneous screenings of a film version of *1984*.[9] It is remarkable that any writer might maintain such currency nearly seventy years after his death. It is more astonishing still for a writer whose work so specifically addressed the affairs of his time.

Orwell's work—most obviously his journalism, but almost equally his novels—supplies a kind of running commentary on world events unfolding during the period of his writing. The thirties and forties supplied the atmosphere of his fiction and nonfiction alike, even when current events did not directly dictate the subject matter. The preoccupations of the age—socialism, fascism, poverty, war—worked their way into every crevice, and colored every phrase: "Every line of serious work that I have written since 1936," Orwell explained, "has been written, directly or indirectly, *against* totalitarianism and *for* democratic Socialism, as I understand it."[10] Essays on subjects as remote as comic postcards or Jonathan Swift follow an arc drawn by the gravitational force of these most central concerns. Much of Orwell's work retains a historical interest, less for the facts it records (those are available elsewhere) than for his vivid portrayal of what things were *like.* His work helps us to understand the Depression, for instance, in *The Road to Wigan Pier* and essays like "The Spike," not merely through the enumeration of government policies and economists' statistics, but in descriptions of the homes of unemployed miners and the prison-like shelters offered to tramps in the name of Christian charity. In *Burmese Days*, the corruption of the Empire is revealed in the depiction of a provincial controversy and the moral ruin of an insignificant timber merchant. The long moment of dread before the inevitable World War is voiced in *Coming Up for Air*, not by newspaper editors or parliamentarians, but by an overweight insurance salesman who only wants to go fishing. The worm's eye view, Orwell thought, can be as revealing as the eagle's.[11]

Orwell's approach was characteristically that of an engaged outsider. He did not try to speak for the Burmese peasants, the Wigan miners, or the revolutionaries in Spain. He did not even pretend that he could always sympathize with their feelings, agree with their views, or approve of their habits. What he did do, however, was to go where such people were and record what he found there.

He did not cast himself as a neutral observer; he was a partisan and sometimes a participant. Yet he was not at home amid the events or among the people he so carefully described. It was a source of some frustration for Orwell that the miners at Wigan, among whom he lived for weeks, could never regard him as precisely an equal, and that "it needed tactful maneuverings to prevent them from calling me 'sir.'"[12] Later, writing in *Homage to Catalonia*, recalling Barcelona suddenly immersed in revolution—the buildings "draped with red flags," walls "scrawled with the hammer and sickle," "loudspeakers … bellowing revolutionary songs"—Orwell commented first on the very strangeness of it: "All this was queer and moving. There was much in it that I did not understand, in some ways I did not even like it, but I recognized it immediately as a state of affairs worth fighting for."[13] Fight he did do, and as his reward he was shot through the throat by a fascist sniper, forced to flee the Communist secret police, and alternately ignored and libeled by the socialist press in England. The ordeal only strengthened his resolve. It solidified *both* his belief in socialism and his independence of mind.[14] His critical distance did nothing to diminish his moral commitment; nor *vice versa*. Orwell proved himself willing to fight, to die if necessary, but he would not cease probing, questioning, judging by his own standards. He was ready to follow orders, but not to swallow absurdities.[15]

Like his protagonists George Bowling, Gordon Comstock, and Winston Smith, Orwell felt himself out of place in the modern world. He nurtured a fantasy of a quiet life in "a peaceful age," writing "ornate or merely descriptive books,"[16] untroubled by politics and war. "A happy vicar I might have been, Two hundred years ago," he begins one poem; it concludes: "I wasn't born for an age like this: Was Smith? Was Jones? Were you?"[17] Though Orwell wrote of the events of his time, though he did his best to take part and to shape them, he was not, by character or disposition, a figure *of* his time. His friend, the anarchist writer George Woodcock, called him a "nineteenth-century liberal."[18] Another friend, Cyril Connolly, described him as "a revolutionary in love with 1910."[19] As Orwell readily acknowledged, the world that seemed his own was one that no longer existed—a world with warm beer and horse carts, and no V-1 rockets crashing into London.[20]

It is precisely this old-fashioned quality that accounts for his endurance as a cultural figure. Just as a conservative suit will age better than a flashy one, Orwell's preference for plain-speaking over artistic experimentation, common sense over high theory, and common decency over fashionable cynicism has made him one of the twentieth-century writers who remains not only readable but worth reading.

That this conservative disposition would align with radical politics is exceptional and interesting but by no means a contradiction. As I will argue, Orwell's radicalism developed as an extension of these traditional values, and these values helped to ground his politics in messy, discomforting, unreasonable reality, rather than in cozy fantasies, too-neat propaganda points, or Marxian scholasticism. As a consequence, he has come to represent intellectual honesty rather than intellectual depth. That assessment relies on a misunderstanding, one with which he himself was complicit.

Orwell is not renowned as a deep thinker, partly because deep thinking has become confused with difficult writing—that is to say, with writing that is difficult to read. It is in fact harder to produce smooth, clear prose, but readers are prone to assume that if they do not struggle over a passage then the writer must not have either. They are just as likely to suppose—or a certain type of reader is, anyway—that if a piece of writing is obscure it is also necessarily profound. (This premise can be readily disproved by referring to any document produced by the Internal Revenue Service.) Furthermore, if it is a struggle to interpret some piece of dense and challenging prose, then when one arrives at the meaning one is liable to find oneself persuaded just by virtue of having put in the work to decipher it. The reader becomes invested in the ideas by confusing a hard-earned understanding of the *text* with an important discovery about the *world*. A great many theorists have thus built towering reputations on foundations of fog.

Orwell, of course, took the opposite approach. He labored to make the written word sound as natural as the spoken. He wanted his prose to be "like a window pane"—so transparent, one forgets that it is there.[21] That too is a trick, however. One looks *through* the glass, not *at* it, and thus one forgets that the window frames and colors what one sees. Additionally, Orwell liked to issue shocking, startling, outrageous pronouncements, but with a tone suggesting that they must be obvious to anyone with the courage to admit it. Sometimes they *are* obvious, if only after they've been pointed out to us. Other times, however, they are simply baffling. "Why on earth would he say *that?*" we wonder. And his style, at once casual and dramatic—like that of a stage magician who refuses to be impressed by his own trick—hides the mental work that went into forming his conclusions.

Many of my essays here began with just such a moment of puzzlement. I would come across a line—for example, "you do less harm by dropping bombs on people than by calling them 'Huns'"—and my brow would crease.[22] My first thought is, of course, that that cannot possibly be right. I would re-read the sentence to see if a word had perhaps been omitted by mistake. And then I would start to wonder *why* he would say such a thing. I'd look for similar statements, related observations, common themes. Beginning with the points visible at the surface, it is sometimes possible to excavate the arguments connecting them. In Orwell's work, these arguments often proceed in stages, spread across several publications, sometimes separated by years.

This collection, resulting from such investigations, is highly idiosyncratic. The agenda throughout is wholly my own. The questions I have tried to answer and the issues I seek to address are taken up here simply because I find them interesting and important. Roughly the first half of the book is occupied with my efforts to understand various aspects of Orwell's outlook—his ethics, his patriotism, his emotional life. The second half attempts to apply his thought to a range of political (and, to a lesser degree, literary) questions that trouble us today.[23] My aim has not been to treat him as an oracle issuing sacred decrees, but instead to see how his thought can help us to understand the circumstances in which we find ourselves.[24] In other words, the question I pose is not what he *would* say given present conditions, but how we might use what he *did* say. Naturally my perspective is in some important respects very different from Orwell's own, and both the subjects I address and the conclusions I draw necessarily reflect these differences. I am writing more than half a century after his death, from the US rather than the UK, and I approach politics as an anarchist with social-democratic sympathies, rather than as a democratic socialist with anarchist sympathies.

Furthermore, much of my work here reads against the grain of the text, or at least, against the usual interpretations—for instance, by emphasizing the aestheticist element of Orwell's thought or detecting an optimistic note in both *Homage to Catalonia* and *1984*. And in the process, I relate Orwell to a surprising range of other figures—CrimethInc and Camus, Wilde and Dickens, Henry Miller and James Burnham, Charlie Chaplin and Nietzsche.

I should stress that I am particularly interested with what Orwell consciously *thought*, not with his deepest psychological drives and motives. And I am only really concerned with what he *did* to the degree that it might illuminate his thinking. Thus this collection is in no sense a biography, though it does at points make use of biographical materials. I likewise deal only sparingly with the critical literature on Orwell, citing it when it has informed my reading but not engaging the arguments directly. My chief source, therefore, is the body of Orwell's published work. As Orwell said of his own essay on Dickens, "I have never really 'studied' him, merely read and enjoyed him, and I dare say there are works of his I have never read."[25]

I take it for granted that the reader will have some familiarity with Orwell's writing, though I do not expect her to be any sort of expert. I have tried to provide sufficient context for the bits that I quote, but except where it is necessary to make some definite point I have also sought to spare the reader the tedium of paraphrase. At the same time, I have done my best to make my meaning clear without demanding lengthy study beforehand.[26] Most of these essays were not written for this book or even with the thought that they would eventually appear together. The resulting collection is necessarily a bit fragmentary. I have made no effort to be comprehensive—to recount all the major events of Orwell's life or to carefully dissect every book—and there is no single, unifying argument. But the essays do fit together, I think, connected by some common themes that recur throughout and even develop as the volume progresses. Among them are: the relationship between aesthetics, ethics, and politics; the difference between honesty and integrity; the role of courage in the face of defeat; the corruption of language; the importance of observation and evidence; and the shortcomings of the Left.

On the last point, we should remember that, despite his criticisms of the Socialist movement, Orwell felt that he "belong[ed] to the Left and must work inside it."[27] His criticisms were intended, not to undermine the Left but to strengthen it, not to stifle its progress but to preserve its ideals and to advance its cause. It is in that same spirit, in these essays, that I voice criticisms of my own, and my harshest words are generally reserved for those with whom I sympathize most fully. One can examine an enemy's follies somewhat clinically or with an ironic distance, but the errors and inequities of one's own side weigh on the mind more urgently and insistently.

Orwell remains useful to us now—and by "us," I mean especially the anti-capitalist Left—because what we most desperately need is to bring radical ideas into touch with reality. That is true in two respects. First, the problems facing our world—climate change, inequality, permanent war—are very serious and will surely not be solved through minor adjustments in policy. They require solutions commensurate to the danger, changes fundamental to society. Equally, it is absolutely imperative that radical ideas address the world as it actually exists, as we find it in our lives rather than in our daydreams or our theories.

Many of Orwell's observations and especially his criticisms—whether of the cruelty of imperialism, the vulgarity of capitalism, or the inanities of the Left opposition—maintain their force and still hit their targets. And yet, *what* he tells us about politics, culture, and mid-century England may ultimately be less important than his approach, even his style. His reverence for fact, his sense of decency, his respect for intelligence, his faith in the common people, his courage (moral, intellectual, and physical), and his refusal to mock traditional virtues for the sake of looking sophisticated—these are qualities disastrously lacking in our present discourse—political and cultural, Left and Right, popular and intellectual. What we have instead is a culture of self-satisfied sadism, of ratings-driven pseudo-controversy, of talking points in place of facts, of smug cynicism and slavish conformity, of dismissal instead of critique, and of disdain for anyone who isn't exactly as glib and soul-dead as we are ourselves.[28]

The Left is as bad as the Right, in this regard. "Particularly on the Left," as Orwell so incisively put it, "political thought is a sort of masturbation fantasy in which the world of facts hardly matters."[29] What is most striking are the lengths to which alleged radicals will go to preserve their narcissistic feelings of superiority—preaching a gospel that they believe, with one part of their minds, to be unrealizable, thus preserving their outsider status, the freedom of irresponsibility, and a sense of ideological purity, while also believing with a different part of their minds that the ideals they espouse are, miraculously, embodied in their own actions and manifest in their own lives. The result is a Left that somehow manages to simultaneously take itself far too seriously and never seriously enough. The petty dramas, the sectarian bickering, the insular "scenes," and ineffectual "actions" are all elevated to crucial, symbolic, epoch-defining, world-historical heights, while at the same time invoking, but never really coming to grips with, the scale of the challenges before us—including the possibility, and perhaps likelihood, of human extinction. For too long the Left has sought to preserve its idealism by mentally fleeing any possible doubts or objections. In the short term, such a strategy may preserve any number of outdated, contradictory, or merely ridiculous orthodoxies, much as certain chemical elements can only exist inside a laboratory; but in the long term the attempt to avoid challenges to one's own assumptions, testing our ideas against experience, and revising our theories in light of new information can only prove self-defeating.[30] As Orwell warned, "sooner or later a false belief bumps up against solid reality, usually on a battlefield."[31]

Orwell's work, I believe, models another approach. More important, even, than his ideas is his example in handling these ideas—the clarity of expression, the resistance to dogmatism, the "power of facing unpleasant facts."[32] And further back, behind that approach, there stands Orwell himself, who ought not be revered as any kind of saint, but who may instead serve as an example of a flawed, often unhappy individual, doing his best to preserve his integrity and nudge the world, however slightly, toward a more sane and decent future.

Part One

Reflections on Orwell

Chapter One

"Imperfect Creatures"
Letters and Diaries

A Series of Defeats

GEORGE ORWELL IS REMEMBERED TODAY CHIEFLY FOR HIS COMMENTARY on the major developments of the mid-twentieth century—on unemployment, socialism, war, and the rise of totalitarian states. It is often overlooked how entwined the events of his life were with the political conflicts on which his work focused. Put differently, despite the first-person perspective of his nonfiction, we sometimes forget how deeply personal his published writing was.

Yet his private papers—his letters and diaries—tell us little of the most dramatic episodes of his life.[1] The collection *A Life in Letters*, for example, contains no notes from his years policing Burma, none from his time "down and out" in Paris, just one from his "adventure as an amateur tramp" in England,[2] very few from his excursion to Wigan, and hardly any from the war in Spain. The excerpts appearing in his *Diaries*, meanwhile, constitute mainly a record of the quaint and quotidian: a recipe for fruit loaf, an illustration of a donkey cart, summaries of newspaper articles.[3] Sometimes trivial and often mundane, these documents nevertheless help us to view Orwell's story, as it were, from the inside—and, as Orwell himself remarked "any life when viewed from the inside is simply a series of defeats."[4]

With such a symbolic figure, it is useful from time to time to pause and consider the purely human aspects of his story—the unwritten books, the canceled travels, the spoiled attempts at romance, the illness, the money woes, the difficulty finding shoes that fit. That sense of failure and frustration may help us see past the accumulated decades of posthumous praise. That Orwell's reputation was already taking hold during his life and found proponents among people who knew him well suggests that it was in some important ways deserved; but it is also necessarily a simplification and therefore a distortion.[5]

Inside Your Skull

Orwell the writer is present in his letters and diaries only as a kind of shadow figure. Orwell the man stands in the foreground. Much of the bulk of his journal is taken up with the details of gardening: what he planted, what was in bloom, eggs laid, sick animals, notes on the weather, birds spotted, wars to keep out the rabbits. In fact the only reference to his wife's death reads: "Polyantha roses on E[ileen]'s grave have all rooted well."[6] The progress of his two-year-old son's measles is recorded in exactly the same clipped, concise, unsentimental manner:

> April 23, 1947: "R[ichard] very poorly with feverish cold & cough, which started last night."
> April 25, 1947: "R's cough still bad, & temperature high during most of day."
> April 26, 1947: "R seems better—hardly any temperature at 6pm, & the rash, which was over most of him

including his legs a few hours earlier, had temporarily disappeared."

Later, same day: "It is now definitely established that R has measles. He will have to be in bed another week & stay indoors for a week after that."

April 27, 1947: "R. better. Tried to make jigsaw puzzle for him, but can only cut pieces with straight edges as my only coping saw blade is broken."[7]

The numerous letters from the end of Orwell's life, when he was confined to a sanatorium and dying from tuberculosis, are just as matter-of-fact, though lightened with a resigned and even sometimes a rather cheerful tone. For instance, having just arrived at University College Hospital, barely a month before his death, he wrote to David Astor: "I feel ghastly & can't write much, but we had a wonderful journey down yesterday in the most ritzy ambulance you can imagine."[8] He says little to others of his physical suffering; his main complaints were the illness's interference with his work and the distance it put between him and his son, as Richard could not visit "for fear of infection."[9] In his diary, however, the documentation of his maladies is more exhaustive, and also, therefore, more merciless. He describes the effects of streptomycin with horrific precision:

> My face became noticeably redder & the skin had a tendency to flake off, & a sort of rash appeared all over my body, especially down my back.... After abt 3 weeks I got a severe sore throat.... There was now ulceration with blisters in my throat & on the insides of my cheeks, & the blood kept coming up into little blisters on my lips. At night these burst & bled considerably so that in the morning my lips were always stuck together with blood & I had to bathe them before I could open my mouth. Meanwhile my nails had disintegrated at the roots.[10]

Similarly, the entry from March 30, 1948, would stand as a fairly good essay on how it feels to try to write when ill—and the realization "what a deterioration has happened inside your skull":

> At the start it is impossible to get anything on to paper at all. Your mind turns away to any conceivable subject rather than the one you are trying to deal with, & even the physical act of writing is unbearable and irksome. Then, perhaps, you begin to be able to write a little, but whatever you write, once it is set down on paper, turns out to be stupid & obvious.... In all this the striking thing is the contrast between the apparent normality of your mind, & its helplessness when you attempt to get anything on to paper. Your thoughts, when you think them, seem to be just like your thoughts at any other time, but as soon as they are reduced to some kind of order they always turn out to be badly expressed platitudes.[11]

What all these details and asides share and thus demonstrate is a powerful impulse toward direct observation. Orwell's ideas, his insights, and even sometimes his mistakes began, in nearly every case, with the look and the feel of things—and usually also the smell. That is true of his descriptions of the baths at St. Cyprian's, hotel kitchens in Paris, the mines at Wigan, a Spanish trench, and then, too, imaginary settings like Kyauktada, Knype Hill, and Air Strip One. Orwell's thought starts with a concern for the visual, sensual world:[12] "First of all the physical memories, the sounds, the smells and the surfaces of things."[13] Then, there is a collection of facts related to tangible events: eggs are laid, roses bloom, wounds bleed, and the earth goes around the sun. His own corporeal decline and even his perception of these various phenomena are treated as parts of the same natural processes. However broad and declarative his generalizations, he begins by *looking*, by investigating the world. And the resulting report is always, to a greater or lesser degree, self-consciously a report of how the world seems *to him*. A weaker writer might then assign absurd importance to his own sentiments and passing moods. Orwell instead treats them as just another observable fact in a world full of observable facts, and he employs his own idiosyncrasies, frailties, and blind spots to humanize the events he has witnessed, to find meaning in the well-noted detail.

The Key Doesn't Fit

Orwell's diaries accumulate such details, often without any definite purpose in mind beyond a "love [for] the surface of the earth" and a "pleasure in solid objects and scraps of useless information."[14] Thus he sets down some of the "scraps of nonsense poetry" that were "constantly coming into my mind" during the Blitz. One of these serves quite well as a satirical couplet capturing the mental atmosphere of wartime England:

> And the key doesn't fit and the bell doesn't ring,
> But we all stand up for God save the King.[15]

In a rare reference to his own feelings—tied, not coincidentally, to the journal itself—Orwell observes, "Looking back through this diary, I see that of late I have written in it at much longer intervals and much less about public events than when I started it. The feeling of helplessness is growing in everyone."[16] Orwell's diaries provide a cultural record of the home front—not the official culture of films and newspapers, but culture as it existed and was encountered at street-level. In this spirit he copies down the text from a "Huge advert. on the side of a bus: 'FIRST AID IN WARTIME, FOR HEALTH, STRENGTH AND FORTITUDE. WRIGLEY'S CHEWING GUM.'"[17] Likewise he repeats the occasional bit of scandalous gossip: "It appears from reliable private information that Sir O. Mosley is a masochist of the extreme type in his sexual life."[18] And he even includes a dirty joke circulating at the time:

> An A.T. [member of the women's Auxiliary Territorial Service] stops a Home Guard: "Excuse me, but your front door is open."

H.G. "Oh. And did you by any chance see a tall strong
sentry guarding the door?"
A.T. "No, all I saw was an old Home Guard lying on a
pair of sandbags."[19]

Interspersing bemusement with dread, he captures the intrusion of
the war into domestic life:

I was talking to E[ileen] over the 'phone. A sudden
pause in the conversation and a tinkling sound:
[George:] "What's that?"
[Eileen:] "Only the windows falling in."[20]

This perspective might not surprise us, on reflection, given that
many of Orwell's books—*Homage to Catalonia, Coming Up for Air,*
and *1984*, especially—are stories of common people caught in an un-
dertow of world events. From *Down and Out in Paris and London*
to *1984*, Orwell explored the ways large, inhuman systems of power
impinge on the lives of ordinary individuals. And his political views
were largely shaped by his personal experiences, from serving in the
Imperial Police in Burma, to working as a dishwasher in France and
picking hops in the English countryside, to fighting in the Spanish
Civil War. So it makes sense that his diary shows us history not as it
is told later in text books, but as it is lived by its unwitting partici-
pants—not the Great Men and Epic Events but the bit players, day
in and day out.

The truth is, as history unfolds it often feels sordid and tedious
rather than grand and dramatic. Orwell confessed that "when reading
The Battle of Britain and looking up the corresponding dates in this
diary" he was struck by "the way in which 'epic' events never seem
very important at the time." He explains:

I have a number of vivid memories of the day the
Germans broke through and fired the docks ... but
mostly of trivial things. First of all riding down in
the bus to have tea with [Cyril] Connolly, and two

women in the front insisting that shell-bursts in the sky were parachutes.... Then sheltering in a doorway in Piccadilly from falling shrapnel, just as one might shelter from a cloudburst. Then a long line of German planes filing across the sky, and some very young R.A.F. and naval officers running out of the hotels and passing a pair of field glasses from hand to hand.[21]

Orwell's journals assess events from the perspective of the past looking forward, rather than that of our present looking back. They refreshingly remind us of the uncertainty of the times, the contingency of history, and also the moral and political complexity so often lost to nostalgia.

A Compromising Possession

There are also important gaps in this record—stories dropped down the memory hole—and what is absent may be of interest in itself.

The evidence suggests that other diaries remain missing, most famously those from Spain for the period of the civil war. Those were seized by the Communists and (it is reported) now reside somewhere in the once-secret archives of the NKVD.[22] Perhaps this loss weighed on Orwell as he wrote *1984*, which opens with Winston Smith preparing to begin a diary, knowing that in doing so he is practically sentencing himself to death. From the totalitarian perspective, a diary, as a record of an individual's private thoughts, is doubly dangerous. First, it is dangerous because it necessarily implies that an individual *has* private thoughts, meaning that his mind is not entirely a receptacle for Party doctrine. Second, it supplies a personal record of the past, which suggests that the past *has an existence*, so to speak, independent of any subsequent orthodoxy.

As Orwell wrote in one of his essays:

To see what is in front of one's nose needs a constant struggle. One thing that helps toward it is to keep a diary, or, at any rate, to keep some kind of record of one's opinions about important events. Otherwise, when some particularly absurd belief is exploded by events, one may simply forget that one ever held it.[23]

It is for just such reasons that Winston Smith's diary, "Even with nothing written in it ... was a compromising possession."[24] One needn't record one's secrets, or share one's reservations about those in power. One need not even have such secrets, or harbor such doubts. Even with no heretical content or salacious detail, just by virtue of being what it is, a diary can be a kind of subversive literature. It survives as a document of human error, and so undermines all claims of perfection, omniscience, infallibility. As Orwell himself admits, "Looking back through the diary I kept in 1940 and 1941 I find that I was usually wrong when it was possible to be wrong." But then, he continues: "Yet I was not so wrong as the Military Experts."[25]

This observation, published in 1943, drew on an earlier conversation, recorded in his journal:

> Stephen Spender said to me recently, "Don't you feel that any time during the past two years you have been able to foretell events better than, say, the Cabinet?" I had to agree.... But where I feel people like us understand the situation better than so-called experts is not in any power to foretell specific events, but in the power to grasp what *kind* of world we are living in.[26]

The two notions are likely connected: To be right in general—"to grasp what *kind* of world we are living in"—it likely helps, indeed it may be vitally important, that one be capable of recognizing that "it was possible to be wrong."

Naming Names

Orwell was sometimes wrong. And what is more, he was sometimes *in* the wrong. Two incidents in particular might invite rebuke. In the first, at the age of eighteen, he made aggressive and unwanted sexual advances toward his friend, Jacintha Buddicom, leaving her bruised and shaken, her dress torn. In the second, a quarter-century later, he passed a list of suspected Communists to a government agent.

The latter case, which sounds so much like the "naming names" of the McCarthy period, turns out to be something very different. Orwell's friend Celia Kirwan was employed by the Information Research Department (IRD), which was looking for left-wing anti-Stalinists to help counter Soviet propaganda. She asked Orwell for an article, but he was too ill to oblige. A few days later, however, he wrote her to suggest some other writers who might be good for the job and, as a precaution, offered to "give a list of journalists & writers who in my opinion are crypto-Communists, fellow-travelers or inclined that way & should not be trusted as propagandists."[27] He had been for some time compiling in a notebook a list of 135 public figures, with notations as to their political leanings, national or ethnic backgrounds, and his evidence and doubts concerning their views. Of these, he excerpted thirty-eight names, which he forwarded to Kirwan.[28]

Whether this was wise (or fair) could of course be debated, but it is clearly something different than testifying before the House Un-American Activities Committee or (as his detractors would have it) joining the Thought Police.[29] Despite the IRD's active ties to the intelligence services, there is no evidence that Orwell's list was passed along to MI5, MI6, or anyone else.[30] As Kirwan herself later said of those named there, "The only thing that was going to happen to them was that they wouldn't be asked to write for the Information Research Department."[31] And, in fact, that *is* all that happened to them. Several on the list—including Tom Driberg, E.H. Carr, Isaac Deutscher, Naomi Mitchison, and J.B. Priestley all continued to enjoy successful and celebrated literary careers without interference from the government. The actor Michael Redgrave, ironically enough, went on to play the O'Brien character (renamed O'Connor) in the 1956 film of *1984*.[32]

From the perspective of poetic justice, one might also mention that the only figure Orwell named as "giv[ing a] strong impression of being some kind of Russian agent"—Peter Smollett, aka Peter Smolka—was in fact later shown to be a Soviet spy operating inside the Ministry of Information. He used that position to try to arrange the suppression of Orwell's anti-Stalinist satire, *Animal Farm*.[33]

What is perhaps most striking about Orwell's list, as opposed to (say) J. Edgar Hoover's, was his refusal to judge people by their acquaintances, or even to treat them as enemies for purely ideological reasons. He was instead deeply curious about their loyalties and conscious intentions; he wanted to know, so far as one could, whether they viewed *themselves* as instruments of Soviet policy. As he wrote to Richard Rees, on the very day he mailed his list to the IRD:

> It's of course true that "objectively" people like [Labour Party Chair Harold] Laski are a lot more useful to the Russians than the overt Communists.... But it seems to me very important to attempt to gauge people's *subjective* feelings, because otherwise one can't predict their behaviour in situations where the results of certain actions are clear even to a self-deceiver. Suppose for example that Laski had possession of an important military secret. Would he betray it to the Russian military intelligence? I don't imagine so, because he has not actually made up his mind to be a traitor, & the nature of what he was doing would in that case be quite clear. But a real Communist would, of course, hand the secret over without any sense of guilt, & so would a real crypto, such as [Independent Labour MP Denis] Pritt. The whole difficulty is to decide where each person stands, & one has to treat each case individually.[34]

This passage can be read, in retrospect, as Orwell pleading his own defense, urging us to consider not merely the uses made of his work by the anti-Communist forces—first, the IRD; later, the CIA (which was instrumental in producing the animated adaptation of *Animal Farm* and the first film version of *1984*)[35]—but also to take into account his motives, his intentions, and his deepest commitments. Whatever its ultimate effects, we can yet detect in this list, as in "Every line of serious work that I have written since 1936," Orwell's underlying purpose—not to defend capitalism or aid in repression, but to work "*against* totalitarianism and *for* democratic Socialism."[36] Both the act and the man must be judged with this desire in mind.

The incident with the list, however, was not the worst of his blunders.

Closely Intertwined

Nothing can be said to excuse Orwell's conduct toward Jacintha Buddicom.

"He had ruined what had been such a close and fulfilling relationship since childhood," Buddicom wrote in a letter, much later.[37] Orwell—or, at that date, Eric—had been close, not only with Jacintha, but with her siblings and mother as well, playing games with the other children, hunting with her brother, regularly staying with her family on their holidays. He was particularly attached to Jacintha, she being the one he felt he could talk to, and his romantic longings seem to have developed fairly early. Her feelings toward him, however, did not proceed along the same line.

This asymmetry is evident throughout their correspondence, and especially in the poems they exchanged. In 1918, when he was only just fifteen years old, Orwell had written her a poem beginning "Our minds are married, but we are too young." She later commented: "But that was Eric's idea, which was unfortunately and regrettably never mine. He was a perfect companion and I was very fond of him—as a literary guide-philosopher-and-friend. But I had no romantic emotion for him."[38]

Earlier that same year, he had sent her "the first more-or-less love poem I ever received, and … probably the first more-or-less love poem Eric ever wrote," titled "The Pagan."[39] It begins:

> So here are you, and here am I,
> Where we may thank our gods to be;
> Above the earth, beneath the sky,
> Naked souls alive and free.[40]

Jacintha wrote back to suggest that "naked" should be "unarmoured"—clearly a defensive maneuver and maybe even a pun on *amor* (if only a subconscious one).[41]

Later, again, Orwell wrote to her plaintively:

> Friendship and love are closely intertwined,
> My heart belongs to your befriending mind;
> But chilling sunlit fields, cloud-shadows fall—
> My love can't reach your heedless heart at all.[42]

She replied almost too graciously, also in verse:

> By light
> Too bright
> Are dazzled eyes betrayed;
> It's best
> To rest
> Content in tranquil shade.[43]

When this tension reached its dramatic peak, Orwell's sense of decency deserted him. It was but a moment, yet the consequences shaped the rest of their lives.

There was once a letter, dated September 4, 1921—"a furious letter from Jacintha to Eric, telling him of her disgust and shock that he should try and FORCE her to let him make love to her."[44] Her sister Guinevere destroyed it after Jacintha's death in 1993, so we are only left with the memory of what Guiny told their cousin Dione Venables—thirdhand information, recorded decades after the fact. Venables writes:

> During the course of one of their almost daily walks round the Rickmansworth lanes and fields Eric, it seems, had attempted to take things further and make SERIOUS love to Jacintha. He had held her down (by that time he was 6' 4" and she was still under 5') and though she struggled, yelling at him to STOP, he had

torn her skirt and badly bruised a shoulder and her left hip.[45]

Guiny was clearly unnerved by this discovery, and so Dione paused a moment before inquiring "whether [Guiny] thought it sounded as though Eric had raped Cini." Guiny didn't believe so: "No, she thought that had not happened because there was a reference to Jacintha screaming at Eric to stop—and he had." Jacintha had run back home then, and "Guiny said that she had a hazy memory of Jacintha rushing in with a torn skirt and a tear-stained face."[46]

Eric and Jacintha never saw one another again after that last disastrous visit. He tried, five years later, on leave from Burma. In fact he had brought a ring and intended to propose marriage. He stayed with her family at their Aunt Lilian's home but, as Jacintha later wrote, "completely unavoidable circumstances prevented me from joining the party."[47] Eric tried, then, to telephone her in London, pleading with her to see him. She refused any meeting. He must have assumed that she was still angry, and perhaps she was. She certainly had every right to be. But weighing on her more heavily at the time was a sense of grief and shame. While Eric was away in Burma, Buddicom had become pregnant and the child's father abandoned her. Just as Eric returned, she was making the arrangements for an adoption. *Those* were the unavoidable circumstances that kept them apart. Eric never learned the truth.

The final irony and tragedy is that Orwell always desperately wanted a child.[48] Ultimately he and Eileen adopted a little boy, Richard, whom they loved without reservation. It is likely, then, as Jacintha's sister Guinevere surmised, that had Cini confided in him, Eric "might well have welcomed the little girl as his own child."[49]

Practically an Assault

For literary purposes, Orwell's brutal treatment of Jacintha Buddicom is especially concerning because this lapse in personal conduct seems to correspond with a weakness, not merely in his character, but in his writing and his thought. Misogyny was one of the few prejudices present in himself that Orwell did not actively fight against, and in his work many otherwise insightful passages are marred by unnecessary and sneering references to feminists, birth control, or some brand of foolishness that struck him as peculiarly womanly.[50] His female characters, even at his best, rarely rise above the level of stereotype and regularly sink to that of caricature. Worse still, it appears that his very model for sexual relations was that of an animal attack. As he wrote in one journal, perhaps as a reminiscence, perhaps as a sketch for a story (hence the third person):

> [In childhood,] he derived a firm impression that women *did not like* men, that they looked upon them as a sort of large, ugly, smelly and ridiculous animal, who maltreated women in every way, above all by forcing their attentions upon them.... He knew that sexual intercourse has something to do with the man getting on top of the woman, and the picture of it in his mind was of a man pursuing a woman, forcing her down and jumping on top of her, as he had often seen a cock do to a hen.[51]

All of Orwell's male protagonists suffer from something of this outlook, and it spoils—or threatens to spoil—nearly every one of their romantic affairs. In *Burmese Days*, John Flory's efforts to impress Elizabeth Lackersteen are pathetic and self-defeating, not only because in his desperate loneliness he is blind to her real character, but also because he views her as an unattainable prize. Gordon Comstock's courtship with Rosemary Waterlow takes much the same form in *Keep the Aspidistra Flying*; if anything it is more abusive, though Rosemary proves more forgiving. In *1984*, Winston Smith fantasizes about raping and killing Julia before learning that she only wears her Anti-Sex League sash as a kind of protective camouflage.[52] And even good-natured George Bowling, in *Coming Up for Air*, seems to take it for granted that his wife's greatest pleasure lies in denying him his fun—though in that case the issue is money rather than sex.[53]

But isn't there a hint of self-reproach implicit in these portrayals? One wonders how much Orwell's shame at his treatment of

Buddicom lingered in the background and cast a shadow over his fiction. In *A Clergyman's Daughter*, his only book with a female protagonist, we read of Mr. Warburton, the town freethinker, who imagines himself a sort of Byronic rebel but is really only a middle-aged cad.[54] Soon after they first met, Dorothy Hare had gone to pay him a visit: "Mr Warburton had given her a delightful tea, talked amusingly about books, and then, immediately after tea, sat down beside her on the sofa and begun making love to her, violently, outrageously, even brutally. It was practically an assault." She resisted, he relented, and "[in] spite of this bad beginning, a sort of friendship had grown up between the two."[55] After another affront of the same kind—Orwell's original manuscript, altered at his publisher's insistence, stated frankly that Warburton "tried to rape Dorothy"—Dorothy suffers the mental break that provides the novel's premise.[56]

In nearly every case, misogyny proves to be mixed up with the man's sense of inadequacy. And the bitterness Orwell's men feel toward the female sex is typically treated as one of their flaws. It is part of what makes them unattractive—to the reader, if not always to the women in the story.

Less Imperfect

It wasn't until the last months of his life that Jacintha Buddicom discovered that her Eric Blair had become the writer George Orwell. Her diary of 1949 records:

> FEB. 8 Tuesday Letter from Auntie Lilian saying George Orwell was Eric Blair.
> 9 Wednesday Rang up [the publisher] Martin Secker to find out about Eric and write to him …
> 17 Thursday 2 letters from Eric Blair when I got home.[57]

Orwell's tuberculosis was by this stage very serious. He wrote her from the sanatorium, closing:

We are older now, & with this wretched illness the years will have taken more of a toll of me than of you. But I am well cared-for here & feel better than I did when I got here last month. As soon as I can get back to London I do so want to meet you again.

As we always ended so that there should be no ending.

Farewell and Hail,

Eric[58]

Decades after his death, Buddicom wrote a touching memoir of their time together as children. She confided in a letter that she was driven to do so after,

> a lifetime of ghosts and regrets at turning away the only man who ever really appealed on all levels.... How I wish I had been ready for betrothal when Eric asked me to marry him on his return from Burma.... It took me literally years to realize that we are all imperfect creatures but that Eric was less imperfect than anyone else I ever met.[59]

Though she had not forgotten that the fault was his, that "he had ruined" what they shared, Buddicom also remembered the qualities that made their friendship precious. She is left, then, decades later, with feelings of grief, "wishes" that their lives had gone differently, and "regrets" that their reconciliation came too late. Her willingness to forgive was, naturally, informed by her own tender memories of the boy he had been, eased by the passage of time, and, perhaps most of all, shaped by her own kind spirit. But that phrase—"less imperfect"—fits so well with Orwell's own outlook, his rejection of utopias, his distaste for sainthood and hero-worship, his pessimism about all varieties of perfection, and also his insistence that we accept dilemmas on their own terms and be willing to choose between greater and lesser evils. These features make up an attitude that is both realistic and humane, strict in its adherence to the truth, but for just that reason forgiving of human weakness.

Buddicom, with exceptional generosity, takes such a view toward Orwell himself. Reading his letters and diaries—especially alongside hers—may help us to do the same. Rather than hold him up as a symbol or a saint, these private writings show us something more: Orwell the imperfect creature, the mortal, the failure, the sinner, the human being—greater than his faults, smaller than his virtues.

Chapter Two

"Not Too Good"
Orwell, Wilde, and the Saints

Introduction:
Human Brotherhood and the Pansy Left

IN 1947, AS HE WAS BEGINNING HIS BOOK ON OSCAR WILDE, THE
anarchist George Woodcock received a note of encouragement from
his friend, George Orwell: "I'm glad ... that you contemplate writing
something on Wilde. I've always been very pro-Wilde."[1] It is a strange
thing to hear from Orwell, given his disdain for "Nancy poets,"[2] "pious
sodomite[s],"[3] and "the pansy left."[4] And by reputation, the two men
stand as almost antithetical figures: Orwell as modest, serious, and
stoic, Wilde as egotistical, frivolous, and extravagant; Orwell's politics
as practical, realistic, and grim, Wilde's as airy and utopian; Orwell

as moralist, Wilde as hedonist and aesthete. Yet some months later, when Woodcock's Porcupine Press reprinted Wilde's essay *The Soul of Man Under Socialism*, Orwell wrote a laudatory review, in which he argued: "Wilde's pamphlet and other kindred writings ... may demand the impossible ... but they do at least look beyond the era of food queues and party squabbles, and remind the Socialist movement of its original, half-forgotten objective of human brotherhood."[5]

Woodcock thought that "Orwell's liking for Wilde was based mainly on his natural sympathy for the defeated"—meaning, ironically, that Orwell's sympathy would rely precisely on the fact of Wilde's homosexuality, and the persecution he suffered because of it. "However," Woodcock continues, "he did realize, more than most people, that there was a very serious side to Wilde's character."[6]

Orwell nursed an interest in Wilde throughout his life. He loaned *Dorian Gray* to Cyril Connolly at Eton,[7] read at least two biographies (G.J. Renier's[8] and Hesketh Pearson's[9]), reviewed *The Soul of Man* for the *Observer* and *Lady Windermere's Fan* for the BBC, alluded to Wilde in *A Clergyman's Daughter* and *Coming Up for Air*, and told Woodcock that "I particularly like *Dorian Grey* [sic], absurd as it is in a way."[10] Among the last books he is known to have read, while confined to a sanatorium, were two accounts of Wilde's trials and his prison letter, "De Profundis."[11] Orwell criticized Wilde for his "cheap witticisms" that simply "disagree with the majority at all costs,"[12] yet he sometimes adopted a Wildean pose himself, producing such lines as: "people who lead strict lives have dirty minds";[13] "a novelist is not required to have good intentions, but to convey beauty;"[14] and, "All progress comes through heretics."[15]

As a young man, disgusted by his experience of imperialism in Burma, Orwell adopted what he later described as "an anarchistic theory that all government is evil, that the punishment always does more harm than the crime and, that people can be trusted to behave decently if only you will let them alone."[16] Again Wilde seems a likely influence. Compare Orwell's description of his youthful philosophy with these lines from Wilde's *Soul of Man Under Socialism*: "all authority is equally bad";[17] "All modes of government are failures";[18] "a community is infinitely more brutalised by the habitual employment of punishment than it is by the occasional occurrence of crime";[19] and, finally, "people are good when they are left alone."[20]

Chief among the commonalities between Orwell and Wilde are their recognition of the value of aesthetics and their opposition to all forms of Puritanism. The divergence in their philosophies, I will argue, turns out their different approaches to the problem of "moral saints."

Antinomians and Saints

In her provocative 1982 essay, "Moral Saints," the philosopher Susan Wolf defines the "moral saint" as "a person whose every action is as morally good as possible, a person, that is, who is as morally worthy as can be." She proceeds to detail numerous reasons why "moral perfection … does not constitute a model of personal well-being toward which it would be particularly rational or good or desirable for a human being to strive."[21] She thus "call[s] into question the assumption that it is always better to be morally better."[22]

Relating Wolf's view to Orwell's and Wilde's, it will be necessary for us to distinguish between several spheres of life or types of value— discerning between morality, aesthetics, and politics. In what follows, we will assume that morality is concerned with right and wrong, aesthetics with beauty, and politics with the organization of society.[23] It is sometimes also necessary to draw a distinction between morals and ethics.[24] For our purposes, *ethics* will refer to a philosophical system by which an individual deliberates about and evaluates conduct; *morality* is a conventional system of judgment that society brings to bear to censure or sanction its members' behavior.[25] Ethics can, in principle, be personal, professional, or situational; morality is by definition universal—applying to everyone under all circumstances—though in fact moral systems and moral standards vary by geography, culture, and historical tradition. A further and perhaps more fundamental distinction is that ethics are often understood to be constructions—that is, they are seen to be synthetic systems, created and developed by human beings, individually or collectively. Morality, in contrast, is generally thought of as existing in some fashion independent of us, inhering in the universe, or in nature, or existing in eternity as Divine Law.[26]

The possibilities for confusion are numerous. *Ethics* and *morals* are often used interchangeably, even by philosophers familiar with the distinction—and, in fact, by the authors under consideration here. In general, when one discusses obligations and prohibitions, especially where social expectations or religious edicts clash with individual desires, one is talking about morals. When considering issues of character or integrity, one is concerned with ethics. Wolf's saints, then, are specifically *moral* saints. Their outlook is characterized by a particularly strong sense of duty (or, perhaps, a hypertrophied altruism) and a seemingly bottomless capacity for self-sacrifice. They are specifically *not* motivated by ideals of excellence, depth of character, or personal attachment.[27] As a result, the saints are in one sense *too good*, but in another sense (and for the same reasons) they are *worse* than normal, decent human beings.[28]

Well before Wolf's article, both Orwell and Wilde struggled with this paradox and partly resolved it. Each writer described himself—Orwell at Eton and Wilde at Reading—not merely as a critic of morals, but as an "antinomian," a heretic who believes the moral law void.[29] An antinomian, more so even than an ordinary sinner, is the virtual opposite of a saint. However, between Orwell and Wilde, their approach to moral questions and the answers at which they arrived were often strikingly different. Orwell kept morality but gave up on perfection, while Wilde kept perfection and gave up on morality. One author reached conclusions that were idealistic and utopian; the other's politics were practical and *anti*-utopian. But both men, in their separate ways, advanced the cause of socialism and used their writing to develop a political vision that avoids either cynicism or moralism, that prizes decency over dogma, and that keeps in view, to repeat Orwell's phrase, the "half-forgotten objective of human brotherhood."

Part One:
Aesthetics—A Spiritual Sphere and the Common Toad

In his BBC commentary on *Lady Windermere's Fan*, Orwell offered this assessment of Wilde's work:

> Wilde is a difficult writer to judge ... because he himself

was never fully certain of what he wanted to say. Like many others of his time, Wilde professed to be a devotee of "Art for Art's sake"—that is, of the idea that Art has nothing to do with religion, morals or politics.... But in practice he contradicts this by making nearly everything that he writes turn upon some point of morals. And there is a further contradiction in the fact that he is never certain whether he is attacking current morality or defending it. The dialogue of his plays and stories consists almost entirely of eloquent witticisms in which the notions of right and wrong which ruled Victorian society are torn to pieces; but their central theme, curiously enough, often points some quite old-fashioned moral.[30]

The remark is astute. Wilde's rhetorical style—epigrammatic rather than analytic, relying on ironic inversion in place of logical progression, issuing in bold pronouncements instead of careful argumentation—lends itself to a measure of uncertainty about what precisely he means to be saying and often leaves his reasons for saying it utterly mysterious. Besides which, with his love of paradox, he did often seem to affirm what he was also refuting. Sometimes this ambiguity may have been deliberate, and Wilde is known to have disguised his more subversive (and homoerotic) meanings by use of symbolic substitutions, humor, or logical contradiction.[31] On the other hand, it is likely that Wilde sometimes aimed only to provoke, not to establish, or even reveal, his own views. ("I live in terror of not being misunderstood.")[32] And perhaps he saw the tension Orwell describes as part of the driving force of his plots: "it is by a conflict between our artistic sympathies and our moral judgment that the greatest dramatic effects are produced."[33] The antinomian element lay in Wilde's desire that, when such conflicts occur, it is the aesthetic that prevails.

Art for Art's Sake: Two Views

Wilde argued that beauty has a value, not only distinct from, but independent of moral judgments or social concerns. In *Dorian Gray*, for example, he wrote: "There is no such thing as a moral or an immoral book.

Books are well written, or badly written. That is all."[34] But of course that is not quite all. Morality is not so forgiving, or so flexible. It insists on its own supremacy; it positions itself as the value by which all other values are measured.[35] One cannot love beauty more than goodness without coming, at some point, to praise evil. If the good and the beautiful are not everywhere the same, when they diverge, beauty is sin.[36] By insisting that the spheres were separate, Wilde in fact suggested that "Aesthetics is higher than ethics. They belong to a more spiritual sphere. To discover the beauty of a thing is the finest point to which one can arrive."[37]

Aesthetics and morality are not simply different sets of norms or systems of value. Nor are they only competing forms of thought or modes of life. They are all of those things, but they are also something more. The aesthetic and the moral are fundamentally different standpoints from which life is approached. Everything else—values, judgments, thought, and action—depends on the distance between them.[38] "Love art for its own sake," Wilde said, blasphemously, "and then all things that you need will be added to you."[39] He explained: "For the good we get from art is not what we learn from it; it is what we become through it."[40] Wilde wrote in response to—and against—the standards of his time, presenting beauty as a challenge to the stifling Victorian moralism, and seeking to free art from the limits of propriety.

Looking back on this period half a century later, Orwell recognized the necessity of this aesthetic rebellion. As he wrote in "The Frontiers of Art and Propaganda":

> To the mid-Victorian English writer, a book was partly something that brought him money and partly a vehicle for preaching sermons.... But in the later part of the century contact with Europe was re-established through Matthew Arnold, [Walter] Pater, Oscar Wilde and various others, and the respect for form and technique in literature came back. It is from then that the notion of "art for art's sake," really dates.

He notes, however, that while it may have been a necessary corrective, it was also, like so many radical gestures, contingent on the stability of society overall: "the reason why it could flourish so long, and be so much taken for granted, was that the whole period between 1890 and 1930 was one of exceptional comfort and security."[41] The effect of the Great War, oddly absent in this account, Orwell considered at length elsewhere. In his essay on Henry Miller, "Inside the Whale," he recalls:

> Owing probably to the ease and security of life in England, which even the war hardly disturbed, many people whose ideas were formed in the 'eighties or earlier had carried them quite unmodified into the nineteen-twenties.... What was left of the war generation had crept out of the massacre to find their elders still bellowing the slogans of 1914, and a slightly younger generation of boys were writhing under dirty-minded celibate schoolmasters.

The result was a mood in poetry—"Blasphemous, antinomian, 'cynical'"—typified by A.E. Housman: "he stood for a kind of bitter, defiant paganism, a conviction that life is short and the gods are against you, which exactly fitted the prevailing mood of the young."[42] By the middle of the 1920s, another group of writers had emerged—Joyce, Eliot, Lawrence, Forster, Woolf. Literature became, again, largely self-referential, with a renewed emphasis on experimentation and technique and "no attention to the urgent problems of the moment, above all no politics in the narrower sense." Critically, too,

> Art-for-art's-saking extended practically to a worship of the meaningless. Literature was supposed to consist solely in the manipulation of words. To judge a book by its subject-matter was the unforgivable sin, and even to be aware of its subject-matter was looked on as a lapse of taste.[43]

In the 1930s all of that was to abruptly change. The prevailing sense of stability was swept away by the economic depression and Hitler's rise to power.[44] As the thirties progressed, the world seemed a great deal less comfortable and secure, and cultural attitudes adjusted in response. "In a world in which Fascism and Socialism were fighting one another, any thinking person had to take sides, and his feelings had to find their way not only into his writing but into his judgments on literature." That fact "destroyed the illusion of pure aestheticism."[45] As a result, "the tragic sense of life" faded as a major theme, replaced by the "serious purpose" of Auden and Spender.[46] Aesthetic criticism, which ruled in the era spanning Pater to Eliot, was replaced by political criticism:

> As early as 1934 or 1935 it was considered eccentric in literary circles not to be more or less "left," and in another year or two there had grown up a left-wing orthodoxy that made a certain set of opinions absolutely *de rigueur* on certain subjects. The idea had begun to gain ground (*vide* Edward Upward and others) that a writer must either be actively "left" or write badly.[47]

Orwell consistently rejected that notion but never retreated to a position of pure aestheticism.[48] His conclusion is thus characteristically ambivalent, or perhaps simply balanced: "Aesthetic scrupulousness is not enough, but political rectitude is not enough either."[49] Art may not exist entirely for its own sake, but neither can it be understood solely as a political instrument. "All art is propaganda," Orwell argued, but "not all propaganda is art."[50] It follows that no art can be *only* propaganda and remain art. And as much as politics may conflict with aesthetics, still more may it clash with the most elementary demands of morality: "Political language—and with variations this is true of all political parties, from Conservatives to Anarchists—is designed to make lies sound truthful and murder respectable."[51] But whether a poem, painting, or essay promotes virtue or vice in its audience, whether its social effect is progressive or reactionary, nevertheless, it is still true that good art is better than bad.

The Art of Murder

Wilde declared that morality had simply nothing to do with art and concluded that an artist must be above moral claims—not only in his work, but perhaps also in his life. Orwell accepts the distinction between ethics and aesthetics but argues in the opposite direction. He reasons that, if aesthetics and ethics are distinct, then the beauty of art can do nothing to excuse the behavior of its creator: "since ... aesthetic integrity and common decency are two separate things, then at least let us keep them separate and not excuse [Ezra] Pound's political career on the ground that he is a good writer."[52] Likewise, in his essay on the surrealist Salvador Dalí, Orwell writes: "One ought to be able to hold in one's head simultaneously the two facts that Dali is a good draughtsman and a disgusting human being. The one does not invalidate or, in a sense, affect the other."[53] Orwell recognizes that, because "the artist is an altogether exceptional person, he must be allowed a certain amount of irresponsibility."[54] Yet he does not exempt artists from moral demands: "one has the right to expect ordinary decency even of a poet."[55]

He offers murder as a universal limit, a place where morality does definitely constrain aesthetics. He takes the point to be obvious, requiring no argument: No one "should be allowed to commit murder," he writes, "nor would anyone make such a claim for the artist, however gifted."[56] However, the absolute prohibition invites transgression. The aestheticization of violence, and murder in particular, has long been a feature of our literature. But of course, that is *fictitious* murder. There is a smaller tradition that views and evaluates (and sometimes, justifies) *real* murders by the same aesthetic criteria. Wilde (predictably) and Orwell (surprisingly) are both part of that tradition.[57]

Wilde's essay "Pen, Pencil and Poison" is a brief profile of and a sustained meditation on Thomas Griffiths Wainewright, whom Wilde calls,

> not merely a poet and a painter, an art-critic, an antiquarian, and a writer of prose, an amateur of beautiful things and a dilettante of things delightful, but also a forger of no mean or ordinary capabilities, and as a subtle and secret poisoner almost without rival in this or any age.[58]

After a short account of the facts of Wainewright's life, the bulk of the essay concerns his work, especially his criticism. Less than a page is devoted to explaining the murders for which he is infamous, and just slightly more to the legal aftermath. It is only at the end that Wilde comes to the real subject of his essay, the relationship between art and crime. He notes that some people, reflecting on Wainewright's crimes, conclude that his sensitive nature was a ruse and his work therefore empty. Wilde counters: "The fact of a man being a poisoner is nothing against his prose.... There is no essential incongruity between crime and culture." Yet Wilde's argument also goes further: "His crimes seem to have had an important effect upon his art.... They gave a strong personality to his style." He concludes: "One can fancy an intense personality being created out of sin."[59]

Wilde's defense of Wainewright separates his art from his crime, and then reunites them—placing the priority on the aesthetic, and so, in the process, reversing the final judgment. It is a mistake, Wilde argues, to judge a work of art according to the character of the artist, to condemn a poem for the poet's misdeeds. However, he also suggests that the art may sometimes, for material or psychological reasons, *depend* on the crime, and a great personality may discover its perfection in sin. Wainewright is an artist, not only in his work, but in his life; and it follows that, approached aesthetically, both the man and his crimes may be admired, and even praised.

We can see in this essay something of Wilde's philosophical strategy. He divides aesthetics from morality, adopts the aesthetic viewpoint, then declares morality irrelevant. But of course it is only irrelevant *from the perspective of aesthetics*. From the moral point of view, the aesthetics of a crime are irrelevant as well: a stylish murder is as bad as a vulgar one. Wilde could only reply that, "No crime is vulgar, but all vulgarity is crime."[60] It fell to Orwell, instead, to argue that a vulgar murder *is* worse than a stylish one—and not only aesthetically, but in moral terms.

In his essay "Decline of the English Murder," Orwell compares famous crimes of the period 1850–1925 with more recent killings that had captivated the public. He observes that "from a *News of the World* reader's point of view, the 'perfect' murder" in the early period would involve "a little man of the professional class ... living an intensely re-spectable life somewhere in the suburbs" until he begins "cherishing a guilty passion for his secretary or the wife of a rival professional man," producing "long and terrible wrestles with his conscience" until at last he resolves to kill the inconvenient spouse. "In the last analysis he should commit murder because this seems to him less disgraceful, and less dam-aging to his career, than being detected in adultery." The murder itself should be meticulously planned and carefully executed so as to avoid detection. "The means chosen, of course, should be poison." Inevitably, the murder succeeds and the murderer fails, though he should only be betrayed by "some tiny, unforeseeable detail." Under such circumstanc-es, "a crime can have dramatic and even tragic qualities which make it memorable and excite pity for both victim and murderer."[61]

Orwell contrasts this traditional narrative with the "Cleft Chin" murders of 1944. In that case, an Army deserter picked up a teenage girl in a tea shop and the two of them spent a week together, stealing cars for joy rides, robbing and killing random strangers, and betting on dog races. Orwell laments, "There is no depth of feeling in it."[62] And, interestingly, he thought that the whole grisly affair lacked aes-thetic force precisely because it lacked moral weight, though that may also, he thought, help to explain the attention it received:

> This murder probably captured the headlines because it provided distraction amid the doodlebugs [V-1 rock-ets] and the anxieties of the Battle of France.... [And] it is difficult not to feel that this clamour to hang an eighteen-year-old girl was due partly to the brutalising effects of the war. Indeed, the whole meaningless sto-ry, with its atmosphere of dance-halls, movie palaces, cheap perfume, false names and stolen cars, belongs essentially to the war period.[63]

He concludes:

> it is difficult to believe that this case will be so long remembered as the old domestic poisoning dramas,

product of a stable society where the all-prevailing hypocrisy did at least ensure that crimes as serious as murder should have strong emotions behind them.[64]

Likewise, in his novel *Coming Up for Air*, Orwell's narrator George Bowling reads of a murder then in the headlines. "It's queer," he thinks. "All this cutting people up and leaving bits of them about the countryside. Not a patch on the old domestic poisoning dramas." Bowling, too, considers that the aesthetic value depends in part on the moral atmosphere, "the truth being, I suppose, that you can't do a good murder unless you believe you're going to roast in hell for it."[65] The morality of the audience, he thought, also had a great deal to do with their interest in the crime. He recalled his mother, reading the newspaper. "Murders had a terrible fascination for her, because as she often said, she just didn't know how people could *be* so wicked."[66] Such an attitude may be self-serving and hypocritical, but it is at least preferable to a prurient obsession with cruelty for its own sake.

For Orwell, the wickedness of a murder *is* related to its aesthetic aspect; and public taste in such matters is largely determined by the moral outlook of the time. The decline of the English murder was related, in a fairly straightforward way, to a simultaneous decline in English morals; and the public's morbid attraction, coming to settle on the cruelty of both crime and punishment, reflected a decline in English taste as well. Which is the cause, and which the result, or whether they share a common cause—such as "the brutalising effects of the war"—is not the issue. The important thing, for Orwell, is that morality and aesthetics, while distinct, are not entirely separable; and that, while moralists and aesthetes may battle over the supremacy of one value or the irrelevance of the other, in fact, from the perspective of human life, *neither* morality nor aesthetics are ever entirely remote.

Orwell's view—which at first seems so at odds with *fin de siècle* aestheticism—was equally out of favor with mid-century cultural politics. The political did not replace the aesthetic in his hierarchy of values, just as the aesthetic had not replaced the moral. Aesthetic, moral, and political considerations each retain their own weight. They have their own kind of reality, which makes the conflicts between them real as well. "The proof of this is the extreme difficulty of seeing any literary merit in a book that seriously damages your deepest beliefs."[67] On the other hand, Orwell later notes that one's moral or political commitments do not always prevail: "the opposite process can also happen: enjoyment can overwhelm disapproval, even though one clearly recognises that one is enjoying something inimical."[68]

Wilde argues that one's moral disapproval is irrelevant to art, that it represents an impertinence and a kind of category mistake. In the hierarchy of values, Wilde held that the aesthetic was always the highest—a fact that may not only dethrone morality, but banish it. For Orwell, the two sets of values rest, so to speak, on the same plane. He does not wish to see either triumph over the other, but finds meaning in each, and sometimes even in the conflict between them.

The Vulgar Standard of Goodness and the Highest of All Duties

The contradiction, both real and apparent, between Wilde's perspective and Orwell's comes down to a difference in emphasis at the level of meta-ethics.

Wilde used the fashionable aestheticism of his time to launch an attack on morality. As he wrote in "The Critic as Artist": "To be good, according to the vulgar standard of goodness, is obviously quite easy. It merely requires a certain amount of sordid terror, a certain lack of imaginative thought, and a certain low passion for middle-class respectability."[69] It is important that Wilde does not typically argue that the Victorians were *wrong* in their moral judgments, but that they were *too moral* in their judgments.

And yet, while renouncing all morality, Wilde also deduced from aestheticism a system of ethics that prized freedom over obedience, and individual refinement over social restraint.[70] As Lord Henry Wotton put it in *Dorian Gray*: "The aim of Life is self-development. To realise one's nature perfectly—that is what each of us is here for. People are afraid of themselves, nowadays. They have forgotten the highest of all duties, the duty that one owes to one's self..."[71] What this approach points to is a distinction between ethics and morals—also, the difference between individualism and conventionality, freedom and constraint. For, as Lord Henry argues:

To be good is to be in harmony with one's self....
Discord is to be forced to be in harmony with others. One's own life—that is the important thing. As
for the lives of one's neighbors, if one wishes to be a
prig or a Puritan, one can flaunt one's moral views
about them, but they are not one's concern. Besides,
Individualism has really the higher aim. Modern
morality consists in accepting the standard of one's
own age. I consider that for any man of culture to
accept the standard of his age is a form of the grossest
immorality![72]

Wilde uses morality's own language against it, while suggesting a
different kind of *good*, a different set of values, with an entirely different basis: "Even a colour-sense," he writes, "is more important, in
the development of the individual, than a sense of right and wrong."[73]

Oppression and Ugliness

While Wilde's notoriety persists more than a century after his death,
Orwell is renowned for his deep sense of personal integrity, his strong
ethical commitment, and his concern for justice and fair dealing; what
is forgotten is that his outlook, too, was largely shaped by aesthetic
concerns—different aesthetics than Wilde's, but aesthetics nonetheless.[74] In the novel *1984*, the atmosphere of oppression is not merely
a matter of Thought Police and permanent war; it extends, too, into
the feel and aroma of daily life, the dreary, shabby look of things, the
Spartan indifference to comfort, the ugliness:

[Winston Smith] meditated resentfully on the physical
texture of life. Had it always been like this? Had food
always tasted like this? He looked around the canteen.
A low-ceilinged, crowded room, its walls grimy from
the contact of innumerable bodies; battered metal tables and chairs placed so close together that you
sat with elbows touching; bent spoons, dented trays,
coarse white mugs; all surfaces greasy, grime in every

crack; and a sourish composite smell of bad gin and
bad coffee and metallic stew and dirty clothes.[75]

This connection—between the aesthetic, the moral, and the political—comes across as well in a short passage from Orwell's essay, "Will
Freedom Die with Capitalism?" There he characterizes capitalism in
moral terms as "inherently evil," then immediately moves to aesthetic
concerns: "as a result of it human life has deteriorated in certain ways.
The decadence of our language, the hideous vulgarity of our clothes,
the badness of our manners, the disappearance of popular art, are
symptoms of this deterioration."[76] This coarsening, common to both
capitalism and Communism, may be an evil in itself. It is also, certainly, evidence of the evil nature of the social systems that produce it.
More to the point, however, the fact that we *perceive* it as an evil, that
we *feel* it as a decline, helps to show that such conditions are wrong.
Orwell elaborates:

> Always in your stomach and in your skin there was a
> sort of protest, a feeling that you had been cheated of
> something that you had a right to.... Was it not a sign
> that this was *not* the natural order of things, if one's
> heart sickened at the discomfort and dirt and scarcity,
> the interminable winters, the stickiness of one's socks,
> the lifts that never worked, the cold water, the gritty
> soap, the cigarettes that came to pieces, the food with
> its strange evil tastes?[77]

Again, Orwell echoes Wilde. As the latter wrote in *The Soul of
Man Under Socialism*, "Pain is ... a protest. It has reference to wrong,
unhealthy, unjust surroundings.... Pleasure is Nature's test, her sign
of approval."[78]

For both men, aesthetic criteria were political criteria. We revolt
against ugliness just as we revolt against injustice, and pursue beauty
as reliably as we pursue freedom. The beauty of the world and the
pleasures of life become standards by which our political systems may
be judged—not by abstract principles, but "in your stomach and in

your skin"—by the feeling of attraction or the sense of revulsion. Such things are, for most human beings, more present, more immediate, and so much harder to ignore than the doctrines of one's Party, the teachings of one's church, or the whispering of one's conscience, worrying over good and evil or right and wrong.

The Rites of Spring

And so, against the Victory Gin and the Two Minutes Hate—against "the ghastly emptiness of machine civilization"[79] that the heroes of his novels always tried to escape—Orwell offered instead, "the surface of the earth and the process of life."[80] He wrote often of the countryside, and sex, and the coming of spring. Even, or perhaps especially, in the midst of war, he stopped to note the rhythm and beauty of nature coursing all around him. In *Homage to Catalonia*, he wrote, "Spring was really here at last. The blue in the sky was softer, the air grew suddenly balmy. The frogs were mating noisily in the ditches."[81] He returned to this theme, at greater length, in his essay "Some Thoughts on the Common Toad."

> Spring is here, even in London N.1, and they can't stop you enjoying it…. The atom bombs are piling up in the factories, the police are prowling through the cities, the lies are streaming from the loud-speakers, but the earth is still going round the sun, and neither the dictators nor the bureaucrats, deeply as they disapprove of the process, are able to prevent it.[82]

This description of the life process, the bloom of spring, in terms of *the earth going around the sun* appears repeatedly in Orwell's writing. As he reported in "The British Crisis":

> Now and again at intervals of weeks one gets one's head above water for a moment and notices with surprise that the earth is still going around the sun. One day I noticed crocuses in the parks, another day pear blossom, another day hawthorn. One seems to catch vague glimpses of these things through a mist of war news.[83]

Likewise, on March 4, 1941, he wrote in his diary:

> Crocuses out everywhere, a few wall flowers budding,
> snowdrops just at their best. Couple of hares sitting
> about in the winter wheat and gazing at one another.
> Now and again in this war, at intervals of months, you
> get your nose above water for a few moments and not-
> ice that the earth is still going round the sun.[84]

The particular language of these passages is interesting. The reference to the earth circling the sun connects Orwell's love of nature
and the process of life with his commitment to intellectual honesty
and his hostility to absurd dogmas. For it was precisely the fact of the
earth circling the sun that the Catholic Church sought to suppress
in its persecution of Galileo;[85] and the medieval Church is, in *1984*,
named as the forerunner of totalitarianism.[86] Moreover, the metaphor
of getting one's head (or nose) above water seems to point—perhaps
unconsciously—back to the title of his novel *Coming Up for Air*. In
that book, George Bowling, a middle-class salesman, decides to sneak
an unauthorized vacation, return to the village of his boyhood, and
go fishing. On his way, he reflects on "all the people who wouldn't
approve of a trip of this kind and who'd have stopped me if they
could—which, I suppose, would include pretty well everybody."[87] In
"The Common Toad," Orwell reflects, defiantly: "How many times
have I stood watching the toads mating, or a pair of hares having a
boxing match in the young corn, and thought of all the important
persons, who would stop me enjoying this if they could?"[88] Orwell
takes some satisfaction from this small touch of freedom, but Bowling
has a nightmare vision of all those people pursuing him, beginning
with his wife:

> Hilda was in front, of course, with the kids tagging
> after her…. And all the chaps at the office, and all
> the poor down-trodden pen-pushers…. And all the
> soul-savers and Nosey parkers, the people whom
> you've never seen but who rule your destiny all

the same, the Home Secretary, Scotland Yard, the Temperance League, the Bank of England, Lord Beaverbrook, Hitler and Stalin on a tandem bicycle, the bench of Bishops, Mussolini, the Pope—they were all of them after me.[89]

Given this background, it is surely significant that in *1984* Winston and Julia consummate their affair—a "sexcrime," tantamount to treason—in a wooded grove far outside the city.[90] And in *A Clergyman's Daughter*, Dorothy Hare's happiest time is in the countryside, picking hops.[91] Orwell was always something of an amateur naturalist. His nonfiction makes regular mention of the vegetation and animal life that he encounters. And in "Some Thoughts on the Common Toad," he extrapolates from that interest an outlook that is aesthetic, ethical, and political. He aligns, in a few short pages, nature, beauty, sex, freedom, and, in its broadest terms, the enjoyment of life—all on one side—as against war, authority, the capitalist economy, and Marxist dogma on the other.

This schema foreshadows the major themes of *1984*, not only its dystopian vision, but also it's hopeful subtext: Winston, like Orwell, takes it for granted that there is something deep within us, some natural impulse that cannot be permanently silenced, that longs for freedom and rejects oppression. In prison, Winston tells O'Brien, his torturer, "Somehow you will fail. Something will defeat you. Life will defeat you."[92] Elsewhere in the book, this "something," is identified more precisely: "Not merely the love of one person, but the animal instinct, the simple undifferentiated desire: that was the force that would tear the Party to pieces."[93] The Party, as a matter of doctrine, denies any such thing as human nature, though implicitly it acknowledges the potential for rebellion with every repressive measure it adopts.[94] At the end of the novel, Winston is defeated and the Party is victorious: "He loved Big Brother."[95] But then, the Appendix, ostensibly an essay on "The Principles of Newspeak," validates Winston's—and not O'Brien's—predictions. It is written as though the events of the novel occurred in the distant past, suggesting a future in which the Party has fallen.[96]

Part Two:
Ethics—The Problem of Moral Saints

In his essay "Lear, Tolstoy and the Fool," Orwell contrasts Tolstoy (and, in passing, Gandhi) with Shakespeare—as representing morals against aesthetics, and meaning in art versus beauty.[97] He begins by summarizing Tolstoy's polemic against Shakespeare but comes fairly quickly to consider what the critique says about Tolstoy himself. Orwell ends with a reflection on the deeper philosophical questions about art and morality.

Tolstoy opposes Shakespeare, in part, because "Shakespeare taught … that one *may be too good.*"[98] The important difference that Orwell points to is not that between Tolstoy and Shakespeare, nor even between aesthetics and morals—but between human beings and real or aspiring saints; ultimately, "this world against the next."[99] Orwell writes: "The difference between a saint and an ordinary human being is a difference of kind and not of degree. That is, the one is not to be regarded as an imperfect form of the other."[100] Elsewhere, in his "Reflections on Gandhi," Orwell argues that by aiming at perfection, the saint can only move away from sad, flawed humanity: "it is probable that some who achieve or aspire to sainthood have never felt much temptation to be human beings."[101] In fact, Orwell argues, it may well be the desire to separate from humanity that motivates the saint in his perfection. His asceticism is not only a practice of denial, but also an effort to escape—"escape from the pain of living, and above all from love."[102]

Love is a moral danger. Love—not in the abstract but in the immediate sense—makes us partial; it ties us to the drama of this world; it tempts us toward lust and jealousy and anger; and in all these ways it demonstrates that we are incomplete and imperfect. It is for just such reasons, Orwell notes, that Gandhi's asceticism did not end with things like meat and alcohol or even sex: "for the seeker after goodness there must be no close friendships and no exclusive loves whatever." Orwell explains: "If one is to love God, or to love humanity as a whole, one cannot give one's preference to any individual person." And this, he notes "marks the point at which the humanistic and the religious attitudes cease to be reconcilable. To an ordinary human being, love means nothing if it does not mean loving some people more than others."[103]

Likewise, Orwell detects in Tolstoy's "impatience with the Fool" a deeper cause beyond his annoyance with Shakespeare: "what at bottom he probably most dislikes is a sort of exuberance, a tendency to take—not so much a pleasure, as simply an interest in the actual process of life." Tolstoy's "main aim," Orwell tells us, "was to narrow the range of human consciousness. One's interests, one's points of attachment to the physical world and the day-to-day struggle, must be as few and not as many as possible."[104]

As Orwell saw it, sainthood "is perhaps ... noble," but it is also "inhuman." He elaborates in a striking and insightful passage:

> The essence of being human is that one does not seek perfection, that one *is* sometimes willing to commit sins for the sake of loyalty, that one does not push asceticism to the point where it makes friendly intercourse impossible, and that one is prepared in the end to be defeated and broken up by life, which is the inevitable price of fastening one's love upon other individuals.[105]

Shakespeare's tragedies "start out with the humanist assumption that life, although full of sorrow, is worth living, and that man is a noble animal."[106]

As a model for humanity, Orwell offers us, not saints or good Party men,[107] not Tolstoy or Gandhi, not any kind of unitary ideal at all, but a duality:

> If you look into your own mind, which are you, Don Quixote or Sancho Panza? Almost certainly you are both. There is one part of you that wishes to be a hero or a saint, but another part of you is a little fat man who sees very clearly the advantages of staying alive with a whole skin. He is your unofficial self, the voice of the belly protesting against the soul.[108]

Here the body serves as a counterweight to the soul, hedonism as a check on morals, the individual as against society. Orwell's point is not that the soul, morality, and society should be abolished, or that their claims count for nothing, but rather that they cannot be entirely authoritative. "When it comes to the pinch, human beings are heroic," he writes; "it is only that the other element in man, the lazy, cowardly, debt-bilking, adulterer who is inside all of us, can never be suppressed altogether and needs a hearing occasionally."[109] And so he concludes: "On the whole, human beings want to be good, but not too good, and not quite all the time."[110]

Wildean Saints

Wilde, too, was acutely aware of the effect a strict moral code may have on the character of one who adopts it—the risks of morbid detachment, or of self-pity, or worse, of self-righteousness and a heartless, pharisaic severity, "pitiless in … perfection—cold and stern and without mercy."[111] "Philanthropic people lose all sense of humanity," Wilde wrote in *Dorian Gray*. "It is their distinguishing characteristic."[112]

Like Orwell, Wilde believed that an excess of morality may make us *less good*—both in moral terms, and more importantly, in the broader sense of what it means to be a healthy, decent, well-formed, worthwhile human being. But, as a lifelong prospective Catholic, Wilde was more ambiguous in his treatment of the saints.

As he wrote to Rebecca Smith: "There is no doubt something gracious always in the simple record of a blameless life"; however,

> now, new and larger ideals have come to us; to us existence is more many-sided and more varied: we burn with a hundred flames: and culture is a gem that reflects light from a myriad facets, of which religious piety is of course one, but one only, and to me one of the less fine.[113]

Wilde wrote one play, *Salomé*, in which a saint featured prominently, and he began another, the *La Sainte Courtisane*.[114] In both, the saint is presented as an ascetic, and he is set against a woman whose main feature is her sensuality. In each play, these dominant qualities in some sense cancel each other out. In the *La Sainte Courtisane*, the wanton woman is converted: "For I have repented of my sins and I am seeking a cavern in this desert where I too may dwell so that my soul may become worthy to see God." But the saint is also converted: "the scales have fallen from my eyes and I see now clearly what I did not see before. Take me to Alexandria and let me taste of the seven deadly sins."[115] It is a relatively happy ending. In *Salomé*, however, both the sensualist and the ascetic are destroyed by their confrontation. The young princess Salomé finds herself enamored of a prophet being kept as a prisoner in a cistern. She tells him, "Jokanaan, I am amorous of thy body! ... [Of] thy hair ... I am enamored.... It is thy mouth that I desire, Jokanaan." She demands to "touch thy body ... touch thy hair ... kiss thy mouth." The prophet, however, refuses: "Back, daughter of Sodom! Touch me not. Profane not the temple of the Lord God." He advises her instead, "cover thy face with a veil, and scatter ashes upon thine head, and get thee to the desert and seek out the Son of Man."[116] Jokanaan turns away from Salomé and repudiates the temptations of the flesh. He tells her, "I listen but to the voice of the Lord God."[117] Salomé speaks to the prophet of his body, and Jokanaan speaks to the young girl of her soul. Neither is moved by the other, and at the end of the play both are dead.[118]

The prophet Jokanaan's strident moralism, evident in his condemnation of the young princess, stands in sharp contrast to Jesus's compassion and forgiveness, expressed in his treatment of Mary Magdalene.[119] As Wilde recounts in *The Soul of Man Under Socialism*:

> There was a woman who was taken in adultery.... Jesus said that her sins were forgiven her, not because she repented, but because her love was so intense and wonderful. Later on, a short time before his death, as he sat at a feast, the woman came in and poured costly perfumes on his hair. His friends tried to interfere with her, and said that it was an extravagance, and that the money that the perfume cost should have been expended on charitable relief of people in want, or something of that kind. Jesus did not accept that view. He pointed

out that the material needs of Man were great and very permanent, but the spiritual needs of Man were greater still, and in one divine moment, and by selecting its own mode of expression, a personality might make itself perfect. The world worships the woman, even now, as a saint.[120]

Wilde returns to this story in "De Profundis" and concludes that the sinners are as perfect, in their own way, as the saints:

> The world has always loved the Saint as being the nearest possible approach to the perfection of God. Christ, through some divine instinct in him, seems to have always loved the sinner as being the nearest possible approach to the perfection of man.... [H]e regarded both sin and suffering as being in themselves beautiful, holy things, and modes of perfection.[121]

Wilde does not broaden morality by adding some other elements to it; instead, he takes a view of perfection that is far more expansive. This new ideal is not singular or sovereign, as morality is, but individual and autonomous. In fact, it is an ideal *of* individuality and autonomy:

> Individualism does not come to man with any sickly cant about duty ... [or] self-sacrifice.... In fact, it does not come to a man with any claims upon him at all. It comes naturally and inevitably out of man.... And so Individualism exercises no compulsion over man. On the contrary, it says to man that he should suffer no compulsion to be exercised over him.[122]

Aestheticism is not meant to govern us, but to free us. The aesthetic provides a grounding for evaluation, but never a doctrine or a set of commandments.[123] Its commitments are always human; its judgments rely on the values of living human beings, actual human lives—not the word of God, or social utility, or disembodied reason. The aesthetic thus befits our lives in a way that (for example) Jonathan Edwards's sermons, Jeremy Bentham's calculations of utility, or Kant's concept of duty never manage.[124]

What Good Is Morality?

However, Susan Wolf worries, "Perhaps [saints] are unattractive because they make us feel uncomfortable—they highlight our weaknesses, vices, and flaws."[125] In other words, maybe the problem lies not with the saints, or with morality, but with *us*. Maybe we reject sainthood, simply because we are not good enough for it. Indisputably, we are *not* moral people in the way that our theories and our scriptures suggest we should be. But perhaps that is for the best. The "good" people posited by these theories seem inhuman, their lives look empty, and a world inhabited solely by saints would be dystopian.

The important question is, What is morality for?

If morality is to provide an external governor of our actions, then it must be supreme. And, by morality's measure, we are all imperfect, flawed, fallen, etc. We can't judge morality by our corrupt standards. But if its purpose is to improve human life, to strengthen and secure—not diminish—our commitments and relationships, then any ethical standard must be suited to the lives of actual human beings, not the lives of saints.

Wilde's individualism suggests a kind of ethics, but it is an ethic derived from *within* the area of aesthetics. Ethics may restrict the aesthetic, but Wilde's ethics also *rely* on the aesthetic for their own justification. They each have a place in the well-lived life, and personal thriving requires that we not *always* sacrifice our other interests on the altar of goodness. It also, I think, puts the emphasis more on the question of character—what makes for a good human being?—rather than on right action or optimal results. Perfection lies not in what one *does* but in what one *becomes*.[126] Wilde writes of this paradox in *The Soul of Man Under Socialism*:

> A man cannot always be estimated by what he does. He may keep the law and yet be worthless. He may break

the law and yet be fine. He may be bad, without ever doing anything bad. He may commit a sin against society, and yet realise through that sin his true perfection.[127]

Wilde saw the intensification of individuality as the path to self-perfection. But while he celebrated the extraordinary and the unique, he also recognized and respected that sense of human dignity that is universal.[128] Each personality is an expression of this inherent dignity. We best respect that dignity not by suppressing, but by developing, what is unique in each of us. Therefore, Wilde denied that there is anything like a single ideal that all people must approach, or a single standard that applies universally and without exception: "There is no one type for man. There are as many perfections as there are imperfect men."[129]

Wilde denies morality any place in his vision, but he leaves a very large place for sympathy and for love and for conscience. Perhaps that is enough. Justice without decency is only an excuse for cruelty, but decency without justice is still decency. Morality without compassion is only self-righteousness, but sympathy without morality is still humane.

The Gospel According to Wilde

It is, rather surprisingly, Christ whom Wilde presents as an exemplar of post-moral individualism. In Wilde's telling, Jesus stands as a symbolic anti-Puritan, "the most supreme of individualists"[130] and "the true precursor of the romantic movement in life."[131] He does not come to bring us a new law. His Gospel is one of subversion:

> His chief war was against the philistines... their heavy inaccessibility to ideas, their dull respectability, their tedious orthodoxy, their worship of vulgar success, their entire preoccupation with the gross materialist side of life, and their ridiculous estimate of themselves and their importance.... Christ mocked at the "whited sepulchers" of respectability.... He would not hear of life being sacrificed to any system of thought or morals.[132]

Wilde rhetorically invokes the teachings of Jesus in order to launch an attack against his disciples. Drawing selectively from the Gospels, re-imagining their stories in a secular and aestheticist light, Wilde thus undercuts the basis of what are called Christian morals, and offers, in contrast, the purer ideal of Christ's love. As he wrote from Reading Gaol:

> His morality is all sympathy, just what morality should be.... His justice is all poetical justice, exactly what justice should be.... Christ had no patience with the dull lifeless mechanical systems that treat people as if they were things, and so treat everybody alike.... For him there were no laws: there were exceptions merely.[133]

Wilde's Christ represents not orthodoxy, but heresy; not conformity, but individuality; not stereotyped systems, but spontaneous joy; not morals, but beauty; not law, but love. It is not the divinity of Jesus that appeals to Wilde, but the humanity.[134]

The Soul and Its Perfection

The perfection that Christ embodies was distinctly his own, and his lesson to us is not that we should conform to his pattern—"All imitation in morals and in life is wrong"[135]—but rather, that,

> man reaches his perfection, not through what he has, not even through what he does, but entirely through what he is.... And so he who would lead a Christlike life is he who is perfectly and absolutely himself. He may be a great poet, or a great man of science, or a young student at a University, or one who watches sheep upon a moor; or a maker of dramas, like Shakespeare, or a thinker about God, like Spinoza; or a child who plays in a garden, or a fisherman who throws his net into the sea. It does not matter what he is, as long as he realises the perfection of the soul that is within him.[136]

It is worth pausing here to reflect on the title of Wilde's most famous essay, for the "soul" undergoes an interesting transformation in his thought. In his fiction it is sometimes treated as a literal metaphysical entity, a kind of spiritual shadow or ghost. In both *Dorian Gray* and "The Fisherman and his Soul," the protagonists try to rid themselves of their souls, thinking that they will be freed in the process. They succeed to varying degrees, but they suffer for their efforts and are finally destroyed by the results. That represents the reverse of Jokanaan's error, as he tried to live only in soul and deny the body. Wilde warned against the separation in some of his aphorisms, such as: "Those who see any difference between soul and body have neither."[137] And he associated their union with the Hellenic ideal that he sought to recapture through aestheticism, viewing it as a corrective to both religious asceticism and scientific materialism.[138] In "De Profundis" Christ is treated as a secular, rather than magical, figure. ("His miracles seem to me as exquisite as the coming of Spring, and quite as natural.")[139] So, too, in *The Soul of Man Under Socialism*, the soul is not metaphysical or spiritual, but psychological and cultural.[140] Wilde uses *soul* as a synonym for imagination, character, or personality. It can be developed, or neglected; perfected, or marred. But each person must realize it by her own efforts and in her own way.[141]

Part Three: Politics—Utopia and Tragedy

Christ, for Wilde, represented the true artistic life, and the Christian element of Wilde's thought, such as it was, came not as a break from his aestheticism, but as an expression of it.

"[The] Saint and the artistic hedonist certainly meet," Wilde wrote in a letter. "[They] touch in many points." The difference between them is not absolute, and "Right and wrong are not qualities of actions, they are mental attitudes relative to the incompleteness of the ordinary social organism." Therefore, "When one contemplates, all things are good. For myself, I look forward to the time when aesthetics will take the place of ethics, when the sense of beauty will be the dominant law of life." He concludes, ironically, "it will never be so, and so I look forward to it."[142]

Wilde's flare for paradox, his love of impermanence and artifice, his use of contradiction and creative criticism, his emphasis on idealism and imagination, and his disdain for mere facts and common sense—all seem, quite on purpose, to demand the impossible. The fact that his program might be untenable was, from Wilde's perspective, nothing against it.[143] Oscar Wilde was not one to willingly make compromises with reality. But this idealism comes also at a real cost. The effort toward perfect self-realization can only fail. The critical spirit drives us always onward, toward a horizon that continually recedes. "The artist's mission is to live the complete life," Wilde said. One must experience "success, as an episode (which is all it can be)" and "failure, as the real, the final end." Self-realization requires both joy and sorrow:

> Great success, great failure—only so shall the artist see himself as he is, and through himself see others; only so shall he learn (as the artist must learn) the true meaning behind the appearance of things material, of life in general, and—more terrible still—the meaning of his own soul.[144]

Wilde learned "the meaning of his own soul" in prison. In his life and in his work, he had "made art a philosophy, and philosophy an art."[145] He had made a sacrament of pleasure—and for his pleasures, society locked him in a cell. There he "passed through every possible mood of suffering,"[146] only to conclude that "the secret of life is suffering. It is what is hidden behind everything."[147] He resolved then, "to make everything that has happened to me good for me … to absorb into my nature all that has been done to me, to make it part of me, to accept it without complaint, fear, or reluctance."[148] Sorrow, he declared, "is really a revelation…. What one had felt dimly through instinct, about Art, is intellectually and emotionally realised with perfect clearness of vision and absolute intensity of apprehension…. Far off, like a perfect pearl, one can see the city of God."[149] One can see it, but one cannot reach it.

What prison revealed to Wilde had always been present in his work, and Wilde's fate did not come to him entirely as a surprise.[150] As early as 1885, he wrote to his lover, Harry Marillier: "Sometimes I think that the artistic life is a long and lovely suicide, and am not sorry that it is so." The note of tragedy, he follows, at once, with that of Utopia: "There is an unknown land full of strange flowers and subtle perfumes, a land of which it is joy of all joys to dream, and a land where all things are perfect and poisonous."[151]

Tragedy Without Utopia

Orwell's, too, was a philosophy of tragedy. It was tragedy, he argued, that separates Shakespeare from Tolstoy. The saint cannot understand tragedy because he cannot understand what it is to be human, because he cannot accept imperfection, moral luck, or inevitable defeat. Orwell observes,

> It is doubtful whether the sense of tragedy is compatible with belief in God: at any rate, it is not compatible with disbelief in human dignity, and with the kind of "moral demand" which feels cheated when virtue fails to triumph. A tragic situation exists precisely when virtue does *not* triumph but when it is still felt that man is nobler than the forces which destroy him.[152]

Tragedy survives where idealism fails. It exists, in fact, precisely because we are *not* perfect. We are flawed, fallible creatures, but we remain admirable, and sometimes even heroic, all the same—perhaps *more* admirable, even, *because* of our imperfections.[153] But for Orwell, unlike Wilde, the politics of tragedy are not the politics of Utopia. In the end, Orwell's ambitions are more modest. He does not seek perfection—not morally, not politically. It is difficult enough, he suggests, to remain human. It is precisely that sense of humanity that all the saints are trying to escape, and which totalitarianism seeks to stamp out.

In *1984*, Winston Smith reflects on the futility of rebellion: "In this game that we're playing we can't win. Some kinds of failure are better than other kinds, that's all."[154] He concludes that, though it may have no real effect, the inner life of the individual—the very fact that one *has* an inner life, that one remains an individual—still matters: "If you can *feel* that staying human is worth while, even when it can't have any result whatsoever, you've beaten them."[155]

When "there was nothing that a thinking and sensitive person could do, except to remain human, if possible," sometimes "a gesture of helplessness, even frivolity, might be the best way of doing that."[156] Winston Smith's mother represents this view, and becomes for him a model of humanity. He recalls a shameful episode: always hungry and still only a child, he snatched the chocolate ration and ran away. His sister was just a baby, but "conscious of having been robbed of something … set up a feeble wail." His mother, then, "drew her arm round the child and pressed its face against her breast. Something in the gesture told him that his sister was dying. He turned and fled."[157] When he returned, his mother and his sister had vanished. He never saw them again. Looking back as an adult, he considers that his mother,

> had possessed a kind of nobility, a kind of purity, simply because the standards that she obeyed were private ones. Her feelings were her own, and could not be altered from outside. It would not have occurred to her that an action which is ineffectual thereby becomes meaningless. If you loved someone, you loved him, and when you had nothing else to give, you still gave him love. When the last of the chocolate was gone, his mother had clasped the child in her arms. It was no use, it changed nothing, it did not produce more chocolate, it did not avert the child's death, or her own; but it seemed natural to her to do it.[158]

It is with this in mind, that Winston says to Julia,

> When once they get hold of us there will be nothing, literally nothing, that either of us can do for the other. If I confess, they'll shoot you, and if I refuse to confess

they'll shoot you just the same.... The one thing that matters is that we shouldn't betray one another, although even that can't make the slightest difference.... I don't mean confessing. Confession is not betrayal. What you say or do doesn't matter; only feelings matter. If they could stop me loving you—that would be the real betrayal.[159]

What Winston recognizes is that there are certain gestures, emotions, responses, that we do not engage strategically, because of any result they may produce. We do not even adopt them, as it were, for their own sakes, but rather, because they are what make us what we are, and they are part of what tie us together. The inevitability of defeat—ultimately, of death—does not rob such things of their meaning. On the contrary, under some circumstances, it may even be part of what gives them meaning, demonstrating the depth of commitment and loaning an otherwise futile gesture a sense of nobility and grace. The philosopher Alasdair MacIntyre writes:

one central theme of heroic societies is also that death waits for ... [all] alike. Life is fragile, men are vulnerable.... It is defeat and not victory that lies at the end. To understand this is itself a virtue; indeed it is a necessary part of courage.[160]

The significance of a rebellion, its humble dignity, does not depend on its success, just as virtue—in human, not saintly, terms—does not always imply perfection.

What is at stake, Winston realized, was nothing as abstract as an ideal or a principle, whether moral or political. "What mattered were individual relationships, and a completely helpless gesture, an embrace, a tear, a word spoken to a dying man, could have value in itself." It was in this sense that the proles had retained their humanity: "They were not loyal to a party or a country or an idea, they were loyal to one another."[161] Winston wants to regain this sense of humanity, to "relearn [it] by conscious effort" if need be.[162] And so he attaches himself to Julia, knowing it will mean both their deaths. He swears not to betray her, though in the end, of course, he does.

Winston's Dream

Much of this tragedy is foreshadowed early in the book. "Winston was dreaming of his mother," the third chapter begins. More precisely, he was dreaming of his mother and his sister, watching them drown and feeling like "He was out in the light and air while they were being sucked down to death, and they were down there *because* he was up here." In the watching, observing, almost conscious part of his mind, it occurs to him, even while he continues dreaming, that,

> his mother's death ... had been tragic and sorrowful in a way that was no longer possible. Tragedy, he perceived, belonged to the ancient time, to a time when there were still privacy, love, and friendship, and when the members of a family stood by one another without needing to know the reason.... Somehow, he did not remember how, she had sacrificed herself to a conception of loyalty that was private and unalterable. Such things, he saw, could not happen today. Today there were fear, hatred, and pain, but no dignity of emotion or complex sorrow.[163]

The dream shifted, suddenly, and Winston found himself standing in a recurring dream-place that in "his waking thoughts he called ... the Golden Country." It was a "rabbit bitten pasture, with a foot track wandering across it" and "a clear slow-moving stream where dace were swimming in the pools under the willow trees." Julia approached him from across the field and "with what seemed like a single movement she tore off her clothes and flung them disdainfully aside." Winston found himself overwhelmed, not with sexual desire, but with,

> admiration for the gesture with which she had thrown her clothes aside. With its grace and carelessness it

seemed to annihilate a whole culture, a whole system of thought, as though Big Brother and the Party and the Thought Police could all be swept into nothingness by a single splendid movement of the arm. That too was a gesture belonging to the ancient time.[164]

The dream ends as abruptly as it changed form, the telescreen blaring an alarm to wake the office workers for the day. But a last detail slips from his dream into his waking life: "Winston woke up with the word 'Shakespeare' on his lips."[165]

These few paragraphs, spanning not quite two pages, contain many of the themes of Orwell's book, his *oeuvre*, and this essay. Personal loyalty, the guilt of betrayal, the role of tragedy, the free air of the countryside, the liberatory potential of sex, and in the end, even Shakespeare are all present. In the details, too, we find echoes of George Bowling's fishing hole, the dangers of drowning, and a "gesture" that seems so personal and for that very reason is imbued with political meaning. Most of all, though, there is an absorbing sense of loss—a feeling that the world has changed, is changing, and that the results make it a struggle to retain the slightest sense of humanity.

Against Perfection, Against Utopia

Politically, Orwell's anti-perfectionism leads him, logically enough, to an anti-utopianism, just as Wilde's (anti-moral) perfectionism leads him to utopian conclusions.[166]

Orwell wrote against Utopia, not merely because he believed it impossible, and not simply because it might become perverted, but also because he found the very *idea* of perfection repulsive, and even oppressive.[167] In his essay on Jonathan Swift, Orwell worries over "the totalitarian tendency which is implicit in the anarchist or pacifist vision of society." He explains:

> When human beings are governed by "thou shalt not," the individual can practice a certain amount of eccentricity: when they are supposedly governed by "love" or "reason," he is under continuous pressure to make

him behave and think in exactly the same way as everyone else.[168]

The problem, as Orwell saw it, is that Utopias, by definition, are
perfect and that human beings—also by definition—are not. Always
the realist, he concludes that the fault lies with Utopia: that these
dreams of a perfect society are not only impossible, but inhuman and
therefore, by human standards, undesirable.[169] Were they realized, the
practical result could only be a narrowing of the scope of human life.

Hence in the political realm, no less than in the moral, Orwell suggests that the saint and the humanist are aiming at different targets:

> The saint ... is not trying to work an improvement
> in earthly life: he is trying to bring it to an end and
> put something different in its place.... If only, Tolstoy
> says in effect, we would stop breeding, fighting, strug-
> gling and enjoying, if we could get rid not only of our
> sins but of everything else that binds us to the surface
> of the earth—including love, in the ordinary sense of
> caring more for one human being than another—the
> whole painful process would be over and the Kingdom
> of Heaven would arrive.

Orwell contrasts this saintly view with the "humanist attitude ...
that the struggle must continue and that death is the price of life."[170]

In Conclusion

I have argued that Orwell's thought—political, ethical, and aesthetic—at crucial points, coincides with Wilde's. In particular, I suggested that both men confronted the problem of the moral saints, and
where their thought diverged it was because they resolved this problem differently.

Orwell's approach preserved morality but gave up on perfection.
Wilde's sought to keep perfection but do away with morality. Orwell
did not so much solve the dilemma as reconcile himself to it: Morality

remains but so does "the Sancho Panza view of life."[171] The politics that result are anti-utopian. Wilde, on the other hand, addressed the problem largely by changing the subject. He gave up on morality, or at least what was called morality, and derived an ethic from his aestheticist principles. This approach preserved the idea of human perfection, partly by conceiving of it in individual terms. The resulting politics tended toward the anarchistic and the utopian. Both outlooks are, in their own ways, tragic. Orwell's is tragic because perfection proves undesirable; Utopia is not a land fit for human beings to live in. Wilde's is tragic because perfection is unobtainable, and when "Humanity lands" on the shores of Utopia, "it looks out, and seeing a better country, sets sail" once more.[172] In either case, the struggle is heroic, even though (or else because) defeat is certain.

These two outlooks, so closely linked, may be logically incompatible, but there is really no need to choose between them. We can prefer Orwell's formulation of the problem but Wilde's resolution just as we can admire Wilde's idealism but Orwell's pragmatism. Given the course of events since 1900 (the year of Wilde's death), we might feel that history has justified one man's view and not the other's. The fact that I do not need to say which is which proves the point. But we should remember, too, how much of Wilde's outlook there was in Orwell's—even in the nightmare of *1984*. In any event, for the Left, both the Orwellian and the Wildean elements are equally necessary. Neither can be surrendered without a real loss. For Wilde, like the rest of us, inherited a world in many ways already Orwellian; and Orwell, as much as anyone, longed for a more Wildean mode of life—freer and more pleasurable and fundamentally decent.

Chapter Three

On Common Decency

IN HIS SHORT BOOK *THE ENGLISH PEOPLE,* GEORGE ORWELL OBSERVES that his countrymen are "indifferent to fine points of doctrine," and "to twentieth-century political theories they oppose not another theory of their own, but a moral quality which must be vaguely described as decency."[1] The same can be, and likely has been, said of Orwell himself.[2] The idea of decency is fundamental to Orwell's moral view, and he uses the term with a frequency that must strike the reader as deliberate, but may have seemed natural, or even inevitable, to the writer. Orwell never analyzes the concept or even defines the word. Likely he thought that decency—or its absence—must be obvious to any decent person.[3] If so, then the idea would require no explication and need no defense, just as honest people do not need a reason to tell the truth.

Bourgeois Morality

Orwell's notion of decency was, in fact, the essence of the Christian morality, stripped of its superstitious and ascetic qualities.[4] As he wrote in a letter to Humphry House, "the churches no longer have any hold on the working class ... [but] you can always appeal to common decency, which the vast majority of people believe in without the need to tie it up with any transcendental belief."[5] He expanded on this idea in explaining "The Moral Outlook of the English People": "Asked what he meant by 'Christianity,' the average man would define it wholly in ethical terms ... [as] 'unselfishness,' or 'loving your neighbor.'"[6] Hence, the role of the Church and the Bible might be in decline, but

> there is one sense in which the English common people have remained more Christian than the upper classes, and probably than any other European nation. This is in their non-acceptance of the modern cult of power worship.... While almost ignoring the spoken doctrines of the Church, they have held on to the one that the Church never formulated, because taking it for granted: namely, that might is not right.[7]

This fact, Orwell suggests, explains "the gulf between the intelligentsia and the common people," and also why "the Marxist version of Socialism has found its warmest adherents in the middle class" and not the workers themselves: "Its methods, if not its theories, obviously conflict with what is called 'bourgeois morality' (i.e., common decency), and in moral matters it is the proletarians who are bourgeois."[8]

Therefore, while the intellectuals rush to adopt "habits of thought that derive ultimately from Machiavelli,"[9] in doing so they risk overlooking "the special thing that [the English] could contribute" to politics, namely "their habit of *not killing one another.*" Practically speaking, Orwell notes, "England is the only European country where internal politics are conducted in a more or less humane and decent manner"—meaning, "armed men do not prowl the streets and no one is frightened of the secret police."[10]

Liberal Values

Arguing in a different vein, in a 1946 editorial in *Polemic,* Orwell counterposes "common decency" with "totalitarian habits of thought" like cynicism, obscurantism, the worship of success, and intellectual dishonesty.[11] In this short piece, the Machiavellian outlook, shared by authoritarians of both the Left and the Right, is contrasted with "certain moral and intellectual values whose survival is dangerous from the totalitarian point of view. These are what is loosely called the liberal values," including especially "the freedom of thought and speech that has been painfully won during the past four hundred years" and "a conception of right and wrong ..., which has been responsible for all true progress for centuries past, and without which the very continuance of civilised life is by no means certain."[12]

Here Orwell outlines three aspects of decency—moral, intellectual, and political—each of which is attached not to a specific doctrine, but to a broad approach to such questions and, notably, to a sense of historical continuity—which is to say, to a tradition. In *The English People,* that tradition is identified as "Christian," and in *Polemic* as "liberal." Neither serves as a full description and, what is more, there are elements of each (for instance, puritanism and the defense of private property, respectively) which Orwell saw as *conflicting* with decency. I believe that the character of the tradition in which decency is grounded will become clearer in the discussion that follows, as I trace the use of the term in Orwell's novels, his long nonfiction, and in two further essays.

For now, let us note that decency is a virtue—it is an attitude, a disposition, a characteristic—not a theory or a law. It is more fundamental than any specific commandments and as such also more sound. A *theory* of decency must invite disputation, and a *rule* of decency could only lead to casuistry. Virtues may be taught, but more by illustration than exposition. We learn of courage from *High Noon* or *The Hobbit,* not from *The Nicomachean Ethics.* It is therefore fitting that Orwell's discussion of decency centers more on examples than on principles, though it is also typical of his approach that his meaning is better conveyed in the nonfiction than in the novels.

Ambiguous Fictions

The word *decency* appears dozens of times in Orwell's fiction, with different, conflicting, but often related meanings. In the early novels, he sometimes uses the word ironically to refer to what is *worst* in the English character—"A dull, decent people, cherishing and fortifying their dullness behind a quarter of a million bayonets."[13] Prudish, bigoted, narrow-minded, and hypocritical, they scowl, ostentatiously disapproving and secretly terrified of anything even slightly unfamiliar. They pretend to hide their snobbery with the distance of manners, hoping all the while that it will be mistaken for moral superiority.

At times, decency is almost identical with a sort of middle-class respectability, and a peculiarly English sense of propriety. Thus, in *A Clergyman's Daughter* "decently down-trodden villagers still touched their hats to 'parson,'"[14] while a quotation from Shakespeare is enough to send "an electric thrill of horror through fifteen decent Nonconformist homes."[15] ("We're all of decent God-fearing folk," an offended father lectures, "and we try to bring our children up decent and save them from knowing anything about the Facts of Life.")[16] Likewise, in *Burmese Days*, Elizabeth Lackersteen, a young woman fresh from England, identifies decency as a matter of pure conventionality, even to the point of conscious philistinism:

> Real people, she felt, decent people—people who shot grouse, went to Ascot, yachted at Cowes—were not brainy. They didn't go in for this nonsense of writing books and fooling with paintbrushes; and all these Highbrow ideas—Socialism and all that. 'Highbrow' was a bitter word in her vocabulary. And when it happened, as it did once or twice, that she met a veritable artist who was willing to work penniless all his life, rather than sell himself to a bank or an insurance company, she despised him.... That a man should turn deliberately away from all that was good and decent, sacrifice himself for a futility that led nowhere, was shameful, degrading, evil.[17]

Gordon Comstock, the (anti-)hero of *Keep the Aspidistra Flying*, is just such a penniless artist, or tries hard to be—choosing poetry and failure, deliberately outraging middle-class notions of responsibility and success, only at the end to surrender under the pressures of impending fatherhood. Unfortunately, Comstock (the name itself signals puritanism) shares Elizabeth's understanding of decency, though he feels it is something to be rejected and resisted.[18] The two stand as nearly opposite figures, fingers pointed at one another in mutual condemnation. Neither is an attractive character and, from a distance, looking from one to the other, we might be tempted to conclude, in despair, that in their bitterest judgements they are both right.

In *Keep the Aspidistra Flying* the obverse of decency is poverty. The book is full of phrases like "a decent income,"[19] "a decent living,"[20] "decent clothes,"[21] "a fairly decent unfurnished room."[22] Decency is linked inextricably to class, and the middle class in particular. It is this sense of decency that Gordon Comstock is desperate to escape by sinking into squalor. Inevitably, however, he learns that poverty is its own trap and comes to resent that as well. At one point he rants at Ravelston, his friend, editor, and benefactor:

> You don't know what it means to have to crawl along on two quid a week. It isn't a question of hardship—it's nothing so decent as hardship. It's the bloody, sneaking, squalid meanness of it. Living alone for weeks on end because when you've no money you've no friends. Calling yourself a writer and never even producing anything because you're always too washed out to write. It's a sort of filthy sub-world one lives in. A sort of spiritual sewer.[23]

But the novel does also present, with little notice, another, more subversive notion of decency. Under this alternate conception, decency is still inextricably tied to money—some people can afford to be decent and others cannot—but it is equally tied to a sense of discomfort in the face of inequality. Ravelston is decent precisely because he has money but is "acutely ashamed" of it, using "his time and a large part of his income ... editing an unpopular Socialist monthly" and supporting a "tribe of cadgers ranging from poets to pavement-artists." The paradoxical result of these democratic impulses is that Ravelston appears truly aristocratic:

> Ravelston had not merely a charm of manner, but also a kind of fundamental decency, a graceful attitude to life.... Undoubtedly it was bound up with the fact that Ravelston was rich.... But in some ways Ravelston was not even like a moneyed person. The fatty degeneration of the spirit which goes with wealth had missed him, or he had escaped it by a conscious effort. Indeed his whole life was a struggle to escape it.[24]

Ravelston, because of his sympathy with the proletariat, all the more closely resembles a proper gentleman. Comstock, however, by trying to renounce the world of middle-class phoneys (to use a word borrowed from Salinger) and sink into the abyss of honest failure, only manages to outrage his true nature and never becomes a great poet. The difference, Gordon would tell you, is money. Both men are trapped by the money-world. Gordon is ensnared by poverty, and Ravelston by wealth. Gordon's burden is to earn money, and Ravelston's is to give it away. The greater difference, however, is that Ravelston embodies his sense of decency, while Gordon flees his own. Gordon's mistake, which Ravelston's example reveals, is to *identify* decency with money. It is the outlook of the middle-class snob, which Gordon retains intact, though for a while he tries to invert it. If there is a moral to *Aspidistra*, it lies in recognizing this error.

Comstock never comes to see it in these terms, but he does at last realize what there is to admire in the world from which he has exiled himself. Walking along a "typical lower-middle-class street," looking at the houses, wondering about the families living there, it suddenly occurs to him that it is "not, on the whole, the kind of street that he wanted to see blown to hell by bombs." He does not hate these people—the "small clerks, shop-assistants, commercial travellers, insurance touts, tram conductors"—and he even reflects that "It mightn't be a bad thing, if you could manage it, to feel yourself one of them, one of the ruck of men." After all, "they were *alive*" in a way that "the saints and the soul-savers" never were. "They were bound up in the bundle of life." While he had been failing as a poet and collecting grudges, they were "busy being born, being married, begetting, working, dying." Though they may be "puppets dancing when money pulled the strings," he sees that "they had their standards, their inviolable points of honour. They 'kept themselves respectable'—kept the aspidistra flying." Somehow, while remaining the slaves of the money-god, they yet managed to preserve their dignity and avoid corruption: "Our civilization is founded on greed and fear, but in the lives of common men the greed and fear are mysteriously transmuted into something nobler.... they lived by the money-code, sure enough, and yet they contrived to keep their decency."[25]

There is no such inner reconciliation in *Burmese Days*. There, too, competing notions of decency, and the barrier inequality places in the way of friendship, combine to produce the central moral conflict of the novel. Facing a proposal to admit a single "Oriental" to the Kyauktada Club, John Flory finds himself unsettled and irresolute.[26] One possible candidate is his only real friend, Dr. Veraswami, and Flory knows that "in common decency it was his duty to support the doctor."[27] But on the other side there is the force of social expectation: "I should have thought ... you'd have the decency to back me up," one of the other Club members declares indignantly, "when it's a question of keeping those black, stinking swine out of the only place where we can enjoy ourselves."[28] As a dilemma, the crisis is never convincing. It is perfectly apparent what Flory ought to do. The only tragedy is that he fails to do it. Flory is cowardly and vacillates terribly, which ultimately, though in a very circuitous way, leads to his disgrace and then his suicide.

The stakes are no less high for George Bowling in *Coming Up for Air*, though as a character he is among Orwell's most likable and least conflicted. For Bowling the idea of decency is tied up with, not only some minimal level of physical comfort and a religious/moral attitude, but also with *the past*—symbolized, significantly, by his parents. Even as large firms drove their family shop steadily toward bankruptcy,

George's father never gave up the idea that "with thrift, hard work, and fair dealing a man can't go wrong." Likewise, his mother "never lived to know that the life she'd been brought up to, the life of a decent God-fearing shopkeeper's daughter and a decent God-fearing shopkeeper's wife in the reign of good Queen Vic, was finished for ever."[29] As far as they could see,

> The old English order of life couldn't change. For ever and ever decent God-fearing women would cook Yorkshire pudding and apple dumplings on enormous coal ranges, wear woolen underclothes and sleep on feathers, make plum jam in July and pickles in October, and read *Hilda's Home Companion* in the afternoons, with the flies buzzing round, in a sort of cosy little underworld of stewed tea, bad legs, and happy endings.... They thought it was eternity. You couldn't blame them. That was what it felt like.[30]

This memory, nostalgic even for the outdated discomforts, is readily contrasted with "the world we're going down into, the kind of hate-world, slogan-world." That world is characterized by "coloured shirts ... barbed wire ... rubber truncheons ... [and] secret cells where the electric light burns night and day."[31] The "ghastly thing" Bowling concludes "is that nearly all the decent people, the people who *don't* want to go round smashing faces in with spanners" cannot see the danger, because they cannot shake the idea that the world always must be the way that it once was. One suspects, in fact, that they cannot imagine the worst *because* of their very decency.[32]

> They're decent, but their minds have stopped. They can't defend themselves against what's coming to them, because they can't see it, even when it's under their noses. They think that England will never change and that England's the whole world. Can't grasp that it's just a left-over, a tiny corner that the bombs happen to have missed.... all the decent people are paralysed.[33]

As in the other novels, decency in *Coming Up for Air* is caught up with the trappings of middle-class domesticity. Beneath that there is a moral outlook of which the old-fashioned home life is only the outer presentation. As with Orwell's editorial in *Polemic*, decency remains tied to a traditional English way of life, contrasted with and imperiled by totalitarianism. It is likewise no doubt significant that the word only appears once in *1984*—"a decent dark suit"—and even then, it occurs as a detail in a memory from Winston Smith's childhood.[34] Decency, it seems, is one of those concepts the Party must abolish.

Paris, London, Wigan, Barcelona

A different understanding of decency arises in Orwell's long nonfiction, in his journalistic and autobiographical books. In the fiction, decency remains little more than an impression, or an impulse. It is primarily an individual attribute, albeit one intimately attached to class status. In the nonfiction, it is described more in terms of specific social practices, which our institutional arrangements may either support or stifle.

In Orwell's first book, *Down and Out in Paris and London*, the word *decency* is used with its full range of meaning, and it does not yet seem to have acquired for Orwell a special moral sense. It chiefly describes a middle-class respectability, with its connotations of cleanliness and propriety. Its opposite, *indecency*, is a synonym for obscenity, especially as it relates to sexual matters.[35] However, as in *Keep the Aspidistra Flying*, decency is also somewhat subversively associated with social equality: Valenti, a waiter, "was a decent sort, and treated me almost as an equal when we were alone."[36] And the sidewalk artist, Bozo, "considered himself in a class above the ordinary run of beggars, who, he said, were an abject lot, without even the decency to be ungrateful." In contrast to his peers, Bozo "had neither fear, nor regret, nor shame, nor self-pity" and thus declared himself "the enemy of society" and rejected the virtues conventionally prescribed for a person of his station. He refused to be humble, grateful, faithful, thrifty, sober, or honest.[37] This rebellious dignity—and the maintenance of self-respect even in degrading circumstances—must have impressed Orwell greatly. Bozo succeeded where Gordon Comstock failed.

The moral sense of decency emerges more clearly, albeit still only as a kind of secondary matter, in *The Road to Wigan Pier*. There the word applies, first of all, to *houses*, calling forth some combination of cleanliness, soundness, and adequate space. But the two meanings are related, as the moral is itself entwined with an image of domesticity: "In a working-class home," Orwell writes, "you breathe a warm, decent, deeply human atmosphere."[38] It must have seemed perfectly obvious to him that decent people live in decent houses. At the same time, and equally obvious, it is wicked and obscene to smash whole families together into a couple of damp rooms and then blame them for the resulting squalor: "their circumstances do not encourage self-respect," he writes. "[With] six children in a three-roomed house it is quite impossible to keep anything decent."[39] And, he adds, "A fifty yards' walk to the lavatory or the dust-bin is not exactly an inducement to be clean."[40] On the other hand, "Give people a decent house and they will soon learn to keep it decent. Moreover, with a smart-looking house to live up to they improve in self-respect and cleanliness, and their children start life with better chances."[41]

Decency, in *Wigan Pier* most clearly, has both moral and material aspects, and it is not always possible to separate one from the other. For Orwell, the trappings of middle-class respectability—the tidy homes, the well-made clothes, even the sense of staid propriety—are all markers of a certain type of self-regard, and more to the point, possession of them will encourage the practices necessary to maintain that attitude. To treat other people decently is simply a matter of extending them the same consideration. In the exercise of these twin virtues, neither material comfort nor bourgeois manners are strictly necessary, and Orwell saw, especially early on, that they can even be hindrances. Still, he was honest enough to recognize that extreme deprivation, especially prolonged and pointless deprivation, will in most cases have a demoralizing effect on those who suffer it.[42]

The alternative, as he learned in revolutionary Spain, is a "community where no one was on the make, where there was a shortage of everything but no privilege and no boot-licking."[43] He recalls the sense of austerity that accompanied revolution:

> The town had a gaunt untidy look, roads and build-
> ings were in poor repair, the streets at night were dimly
> lit for fear of air-raids, the shops were mostly shabby
> and half-empty. Meat was scarce and milk practically
> unobtainable, there was a shortage of coal, sugar, and
> petrol, and a really serious shortage of bread.[44]

Despite these deficiencies, however, "the people were contented and hopeful." Surely it helped that, though no one could rise very high, there was a level below which it was impossible to fall: "There was no unemployment, and the price of living was still extremely low; you saw very few conspicuously destitute people, and no beggars except the gipsies." The moral atmosphere, as well as the economic conditions, had changed. "Above all, there was a belief in the revolution and the future, a feeling of having suddenly emerged into an era of equality and freedom. Human beings were trying to behave as human beings and not as cogs in the capitalist machine."[45] As a result, "Many of the normal motives of civilized life—snobbishness, money-grubbing, fear of the boss, etc.—had simply ceased to exist."[46]

Orwell credited the "innate decency [of the Spaniards] and their ever-present Anarchist tinge"[47] for making "even the opening stages of Socialism tolerable." It was impossible, he thought "to be thrown as I was among the Spanish working class … and not be struck by their essential decency; above all, their straightforwardness and generosity." This generosity operated at two levels: first, in "the ordinary sense of the word"—for example: "If you ask [a Spaniard] for a cigarette he will force the whole packet upon you." In the midst of such overall scarcity, that can hardly be thought a trivial thing. But more important, Orwell said, "there is generosity in a deeper sense, a real largeness of spirit, which I have met with again and again in the most unpromising circumstances."[48]

One story, from the darkest days when revolution had collapsed into counter-revolution, may serve to illustrate what he meant. The POUM (Workers' Party of Marxist Unification), with which Orwell had fought, was being suppressed by the government and denounced by the Communists as traitors. Though Orwell himself was living a semi-underground existence—sleeping in burned-out buildings and dodging the secret police—he nevertheless embarked on an effort to get his commander, George Kopp, released from prison. Of course it was pointless. But while there was hope at all, Orwell saw that he had to take the chance. He went, then, to the War Department and made his appeal.

He recalled: "Slightly to my surprise I was granted a hearing.... [A] little slip of an officer in a smart uniform, with large and squinting eyes, came out to interview me in the ante-room." Orwell insisted on Kopp's innocence, that he was still under orders, and that his return to command was urgently needed.

"Yes," the officer agreed, "it sounded as though there might have been a mistake. Clearly the matter should be looked into.... This Major Kopp—what force was he serving in?"

Orwell answered with great trepidation, but seeing that the truth could not be avoided, he admitted that they served with the POUM.

The junior officer retreated into the colonel's office, and Orwell waited, expecting to be arrested. In the end, however, his interviewer did everything he could to help. He escorted Orwell to the police station, and then secured documentation of Kopp's orders and promised that "the proper inquiries would be made." Orwell saw that it was at most "a tiny victory," but there was nothing else he could do. Probably there was nothing anyone could do.

However, "then there happened a strange and moving thing. The little officer hesitated a moment, then stepped across, and shook hands with me." It was a small thing, merely a gesture, but under the circumstances not an insignificant one. It was a mark of respect, perhaps of gratitude, and it demonstrated that at least something remained of the feelings of comradeship that were so prominent just a short time before. It meant that something of the ideals of the revolution remained—even here, in the police precinct, surrounded by a "filthy gang of tale-bearers and *agents provocateurs*."[49] It was a generous move, certainly, but it was more than that. Extending his hand, the junior officer undoubtedly also put himself at some risk; in that sense, it was also an act of solidarity.

Of course the gesture was futile. It could change nothing. Just as Orwell's attempt to free Kopp was futile. Just as the whole revolution was futile. And yet the simple handshake—in part because it was all that could be offered under the circumstances, and it was given freely—moved Orwell profoundly. It is symbolically tied to another handshake, from his first days in Spain. In the opening scene of *Homage to Catalonia*, Orwell described an encounter with an Italian militiaman, who "stepped across the room and gripped my hand very hard." It touched something deep within him. "It was as though his spirit and mine had momentarily succeeded in bridging the gulf of language and tradition and meeting in utter intimacy." Though they saw each other only the once, Orwell felt a lasting connection, a bond central to the ideals that drew them both to a foreign land where they meant to fight and willingly risk their lives. The militiaman, his gesture, and the moment of connection, came to symbolize "the special atmosphere of that time."[50]

Orwell was later to reflect,

> When I remember ... his shabby uniform and fierce, pathetic, innocent face, the complex side-issues of the war seem to fade away and I see clearly that there was at any rate no doubt as to who was in the right.... [The] central issue of the war was the attempt of people like this to win the decent life which they knew to be their birthright.... The question is very simple. Shall people like that Italian soldier be allowed to live the decent, fully human life which is now technically achievable, or shan't they?[51]

With absolutely no way of realizing it, in offering his hand, the officer of the Popular Army echoed, at the end of Orwell's war, this other handshake from the beginning. It was a sad echo, emptied of the hope and the sense of purpose. Yet it showed, even in impossible conditions, that some decent impulse survived.[52]

A General Description

It is by this point possible to assemble a general picture of what Orwell meant by *decency*, in the specifically moral sense.

The moral meaning was, for Orwell, primary—the intellectual and political aspects being expressions of the moral. Decency was more a matter of approach than content, and was therefore not inherently connected to any specific political program or body of ideas.[53] For an individual, *decency* suggests, at a minimum, intellectual honesty, a generous spirit, and a desire for equality—all of these in the deep, and not the trivial, sense. The word implies a healthy measure of self-respect, especially in times of adversity, and, what is more, a tendency to treat others with the same regard.

Decency is, in all these particulars, very nearly the opposite of totalitarianism, whether marching in its fascist or its Communist uniform. As Orwell saw it, totalitarianism requires systematic dishonesty (even to the point of self-deception), cruelty, and a hunger for power; it demands a cowardly self-abasement, even among those it enlists in its corps of bullies, Blackshirts or commissars.[54]

Orwell could see that, in the time that he was writing, the world was moving in the direction of totalitarianism, even within the liberal democracies. His hope for changing that direction, and his manner in expressing that desire, must have appeared—at least to those who pride themselves on being modern and sophisticated—not only unfashionable but absolutely backward.[55] That judgement was of course exacerbated by Orwell's tendency to over-identify decency with the trappings of English middle-class conventionality and to exaggerate its purely traditional aspects. And Orwell himself knew that this idea of decency was always in danger of lapsing into a code of status-obsessed and narrow-minded conformity.[56] However, he also saw that the real reserve of common decency was the common people—not the pathetic middle-class snobs, soul-saving preachers, temperance crusaders, doctrinaire socialists, or cloistered intellectuals.[57] Decency appears in Orwell's work as an ideal at once deeply traditional and potentially revolutionary. This paradox is characteristic of his political values, and it is reflected in his depiction of two men who, while in some respects very different, both serve as exemplars of these virtues. The first, and fairly obvious, is Charles Dickens; the second, more surprising, is Charlie Chaplin.

Two Giant-Killers

Dickens, Orwell writes, "has been popular chiefly because he was able to express in a comic, simplified, and therefore memorable form the native decency of the common man."[58] Chaplin, likewise, "stand[s] for a sort of concentrated essence of the common man, for the ineradicable belief in decency that exists in the hearts of ordinary people, at any rate in the West."[59]

The two men spoke, Orwell saw, as part of the same tradition. "A good-tempered antinomianism rather of Dickens's type is one of the marks of Western popular culture," he wrote, pointing to examples as varied as "the history of working-class Socialism," anti-imperialist protests, "the impulse that makes a jury award excessive damages when a rich man's car runs over a poor man," and "dream-figures like Mickey Mouse and Popeye the Sailor (both of them variants on Jack the Giant-Killer)."[60] Of this final archetype he was later to add another example: "One of the basic folk-tales of the English-speaking peoples is Jack the Giant-Killer—the little man against the big man. Mickey Mouse, Popeye the Sailor, and Charlie Chaplin are all essentially the same figure."[61] The thing that connects them "is the feeling that one is always on the side of the underdog, on the side of the weak against the strong."[62] Therefore, as Orwell put it elsewhere: "Chaplin's appeal lies in his power to reassert the fact ... that *vox populi is vox Dei* and giants are vermin."[63] Orwell elaborates in an appreciative review of *The Great Dictator:*

> We live in a period in which democracy is almost everywhere in retreat, supermen in control of three-quarters of the world, liberty explained away by sleek professors, Jew-baiting defended by pacifists. And yet everywhere, under the surface, the common man sticks obstinately to the beliefs that he derives from the Christian culture.... Any intellectual can make you a splendid "case" for smashing the German Trade Unions and torturing the Jews. But the common man, who has no intellect, only instinct and tradition, knows that "it isn't right."[64]

The undefined, non-theoretical character of this moral sense is not always the disadvantage it is thought to be. It is the very thing that makes decency adaptable, that allows it to appeal to large numbers of people from various ranks of society across long stretches of time. Dickens, too, Orwell observes, "without the slightest understanding of Socialism etc, would have seen at a glance that there is something wrong with a regime that needs a pyramid of corpses every few years."[65] Yet Dickens never moves much beyond this most basic level. "The truth is that Dickens's criticism of society is almost exclusively moral," not political: "It would be difficult to point anywhere in his books to a passage suggesting that the economic system is wrong *as a system.*" Instead, "His whole 'message' is one that at first glance looks like an enormous platitude: If men would behave decently the world would be decent."[66] As a result, "he has no constructive suggestions, not even a clear grasp of the nature of the society he is attacking, only an emotional perception that something is wrong."[67] Nevertheless, the emotional, moral response, however indistinct, is also the more durable one: "The vagueness of his discontent is the mark of its permanence." And Dickens's message—"Behave decently"—though undeniably simple, "is not necessarily so shallow as it sounds." It only sounds banal, it only seems obvious, because it is so familiar. That is, Dickens's radicalism is defined by a return to foundational principles. "Roughly speaking," Orwell remarks, "his morality is the Christian morality.... [It is a] quasi-instinctive siding with the oppressed against the oppressors. As a matter of course he is on the side of the underdog, always and everywhere."[68] Thus, "the strongest single impression one carries away from his books is that of a hatred of tyranny."[69]

Charlie Chaplin, likewise, returns to the basic moral sense, and even explicitly to the Gospels, though he was able to more fully elaborate the political implications. In the climactic scene of *The Great Dictator*, Chaplin, playing a slapstick Jewish barber mistaken for a fascist *Führer*, takes the platform before a Nuremberg-style rally. Then, in Orwell's description, "Instead of making the speech that is expected of him, Charlie makes a powerful fighting speech in favor of democracy, tolerance, and common decency." Orwell is impressed, without equivocation: "It is really a tremendous speech, a sort of version of

Lincoln's Gettysburg address done into Hollywood English, one of the strongest pieces of propaganda I have heard for a long time."[70] Decades later, the speech remains quite moving, and it is worth quoting at length:

> I'm sorry, [Chaplin begins,] but I don't want to be an emperor.... I don't want to rule or conquer anyone. I should like to help everyone if possible—Jew, Gentile, black men, white.... We all want to help one another. Human beings are like that. We want to live by each others' happiness, not by each other's misery. We don't want to hate and despise one another....
>
> In the seventeenth chapter of St. Luke, it's written, "the kingdom of God is within man," not one man nor a group of men, but in all men! In you! ... You, the people, have the power to make this life free and beautiful, to make this life a wonderful adventure....
>
> Let us fight for a new world, a decent world that will give men a chance to work, that will give youth a future and old age a security.... Let us fight to free the world! To do away with national barriers! To do away with greed, with hate and intolerance! Let us fight for a world of reason, a world where science and progress will lead to all men's happiness. Soldiers, in the name of democracy, let us all unite![71]

The scene, as Orwell notes, is a total break from the rest of the film. It seems that Chaplin forgets his role and speaks at last in his own voice.

Chaplin's speech touches on many of the themes of our discussion here, and neatly reflects what I take to be Orwell's own moral view. The fact that this summation does not come from Orwell himself, and not from any theologian or social theorist, but from a popular motion picture only serves to underscore the point about how *common* "common decency" really is. Equally notable, and for similar reasons, are the tone and rhetorical strategy of the address. Chaplin does not argue, he does not harangue, he does not scold. What he does instead is to *appeal.* He appeals directly, to you, as an individual, and to us, as a society, and to something good and basic that he assumes, with a touching sincerity, must exist within each of us.

In its simplicity, in its plain manner and direct form, it is unlike anything else in the movie.[72] "So completely is the thread broken," Orwell observes, "that after that the story can go no further, and the film simply fades out."[73] Nothing can follow the crescendo, and so nothing does. The plot cannot proceed. There can be no word in reply.

Chapter Four

"Between the Bullet and the Lie"
Ethics in Warfare[1]

WRITING IN HIS PERSONAL DIARY, ORWELL RECORDED AN AMUSING episode concerning "a mouse which had slipped down into the sink and could not get up the sides." In an effort to aid in its escape, he and his wife, Eileen, "went to great pains to make a sort of staircase of boxes of soap flakes etc, by which it could climb out." Predictably, however, "it was so terrified that it fled under the lead strip at the ends of the sink and would not move, even when left alone for half an hour or so." At last, more direct methods were employed: "In the end E gently took it out with her fingers and let it go."[2]

What is interesting about this oddly tender story is the context. The date is June 30, 1940. England is at war. Orwell has just been rejected for military service, owing to his poor health, and he begins this entry discussing the "confused state" of the Land Defense Volunteers and other, less formal, preparations for guerrilla warfare in the event of a Nazi invasion. ("Already people are spontaneously forming local defense squads, and hand-grenades are probably being manufactured by amateurs.")[3]

The paragraph concerning the mouse begins by addressing a totally different subject, the death of Marshall Italo Balbo, the head of the Italian Air Force. Orwell reports himself as being "thoroughly pleased" with the news, and "E also delighted." Even some friends who were "all but pure pacifists" he judged "were not ill-pleased."[4] This joy over the death of a human being stands in marked contrast with the ridiculous concern for a kitchen mouse. Orwell ends the passage: "This sort of thing does not matter ... but when I remember how the *Thetis* disaster"—in which a British submarine was lost, and all the crew with it—"upset me, actually to the point of interfering with my appetite, I do think it a dreadful effect of war that one is actually pleased to hear of an enemy submarine going to the bottom."[5]

In Orwell's writing during this period, the "brutalising effects of the war" were a constant worry.[6] Of course, Orwell was no pacifist. He had gone to Spain to fight "against Fascism" and "*for* ... Common decency," and that impulse carried over to his views about World War II.[7] But he also saw how difficult it could be to sustain the sense of decency while also doing the fighting. What troubled him about English attitudes toward the war was how ready people were to surrender their moral sense to nationalism, cruelty, and a longing for vengeance.

Two Minutes Hate

It was not long after the incident with the mouse that Orwell noted a shift in public opinion, especially about the issue of aerial bombing. "Two years ago," he wrote in his diary, "we would all have been aghast at the idea of killing civilians." Of course, that was when the Nazis were doing it and the bombs were falling on London. Orwell predicted at the time that the English conscience might not be so scrupulous were German cities being destroyed: "I remember saying to someone during the blitz … 'In a year's time you'll see headlines in the *Daily Express*: "Successful Raid on Berlin Orphanage. Babies Set on Fire."'"[8]

The remark—so sharp, so cynical and, sadly, astute—finds a fuller illustration in the first pages of *1984*. There, in *his* diary, Winston Smith writes:

> Last night to the flicks. All war films. One very good one of a ship full of refugees being bombed somewhere in the Mediterranean…. then you saw a lifeboat full of children with a helicopter hovering over it. there was a middleaged woman might have been a jewess sitting up in the bow with a little boy about three years old in her arms. little boy screaming with fright and hiding his head between her breasts as if he was trying to burrow right into her and the woman putting her arms around him and comforting him although she was blue with fright herself. all the time covering him up as much as possible as if she thought her arms could keep the bullets off him. then the helicopter planted a 20 kilo bomb in among them terrific flash and the boat went all to matchwood. then there was a wonderful shot of a child's arm going up up up right up into the air … and there was a lot of applause from the party seats.[9]

One person objected to the spectacle: "a woman down in the prole part of the house suddenly started kicking up a fuss and shouting they didn't oughter of showed it not in front of the kids they didnt it aint right not in front of kids it aint."[10] The police came and took the woman away, which one can only imagine would occasion further applause. Even Winston disdained her "typical prole reaction."[11] And, yes, there is something absurd about decrying the image rather than the act. For this woman seems to accept, without protest and perhaps without reflection, that ships full of refugees will be sunk and children murdered in their mothers' arms. What she cannot accept, it seems, is the *sight* of it—especially "in front of kids."

On its face, this woman's reaction—wanting to protect *her* children from the knowledge of what their country is doing to *other* children—must seem the most craven hypocrisy. But perhaps not all hypocrisy is the same. Sometimes, as Orwell suggests elsewhere, hypocrisy serves as a way of keeping morality alive.[12] And isn't she also right to protest, if not the display, precisely, then the obscene cheering, the celebration of atrocity?

Orwell responded to a different sort of criticism—and, we might say, a different kind of hypocrisy—in his *Tribune* column "As I Please." There, he told of a letter he had received "Apropos of saturation bombing": The correspondent "recognized ... that 'the Hun had got to be beaten' ... [but] objected to the barbarous methods that we are now using."[13]

Orwell's reply is almost perversely contrarian: "Now, it seems to me," he writes, "that you do less harm by dropping bombs on people than by calling them 'Huns.'" He goes on to argue that, though violence is obviously terrible, "I cannot feel that mere killing is all-important." What is worse—in fact, "truly evil"—is "to act in such a way that peaceful life becomes impossible." That is not simply a matter of fighting, but of hating the enemy and leading others to hate him:

> War damages the fabric of civilisation, not by the destruction it causes ... not even by the slaughter of human beings, but by stimulating hatred and dishonesty. By shooting at your enemy you are not in the deepest sense wronging him. But by hating him, by inventing lies about him and bringing children up to believe them, by clamouring for unjust peace terms which make further wars inevitable, you are striking not at one perishable generation, but at humanity itself.[14]

In *1984*, that sort of hatred was one of the few strong emotions permitted the citizens of Oceania, and as such it had been ritualized. Shortly before noon, the workers in Winston Smith's office would pull their chairs from their cubicles and assemble them before a tele-screen. It would then broadcast images of marching Eurasian troops, overlaid with Emmanuel Goldstein's heretical ranting. The effect is "a painful mixture of emotions"—anxiety, loathing, fear, contempt, and rage. The small crowd soon becomes frenzied, "leaping up and down in their places and shouting at the tops of their voices in an effort to drown the maddening bleating voice that came from the screen."[15] They shout, they stomp, they throw things at the image of Goldstein's face. Even Winston Smith, who is so unhappy and who hates the Party and the world it has created, nevertheless finds himself shouting along.

> The horrible thing about the Two Minutes Hate [he later reflected] was not that one was obliged to act a part, but that it was impossible to avoid joining in. Within thirty seconds any pretense was always unnec-essary. A hideous ecstasy of fear and vindictiveness, a desire to kill, to torture, to smash faces in with a sledge hammer, seemed to flow through the whole group of people like an electric current, turning one even against one's will into a grimacing, screaming lunatic. And yet the rage that one felt was an abstract, undirect-ed emotion which could be switched from one object to another like the flame of a blowlamp.[16]

The uses of such hatred are multiple. It helps to sustain the war hysteria, and serves as a consolation for all those other emotions that must remain rigorously suppressed, all those desires that are endlessly frustrated—the personal attachments, the animal lusts, blackmarket chocolate, fresh razor blades, the temptations of thoughtcrime, own-life.[17] For a good Party member, none of these are attainable, and even the desire for them, the pain of their absence, the desperation and bitterness that inevitably result, must themselves be suppressed. What the Party offers instead is "a boot stamping on a human face—forever": a social system driven by cruelty—cruelty directed outward, against the enemy of the moment; cruelty directed inward, against spies and saboteurs and thoughtcriminals; cruelty directed downward, against lower Party members and proles, subordinates and unpersons; and cruelty against oneself in the form of rigid discipline and the pride of sacrifice.[18] The fact that this hatred is vague and abstract is crucial, not merely because today's ally might be tomorrow's adversary, and today's orthodoxy tomorrow's heresy, but paradoxically, because depersonalizing the enemy, robbing him of any human features or distinctive characteristics allows us to hate him with so much more force. He ceases, in one sense, even to be real to us, to have any existence except as an object of our hatred. And we, by the same process, cease to exist except as vessels for that hatred.

A War Prayer

Orwell believed that it was possible to fight, and to win, without hatred, without stirring up war hysteria, without depicting the enemy as a monster or reducing him to an abstraction.

Again, the discussion centers on his understanding of hypocrisy: "I am not shocked," he writes, "by the Church condoning war," or by "bishops blessing the colours of the regiments." People outraged by such displays have fallen prey to "the sentimental idea that fighting is incompatible with loving your enemies." Instead, Orwell argues, "you can only love your enemies if you are willing to kill them in certain circumstances."[19] That is: there are times—and the Second World War, for Orwell, was surely one of them—when the only way to preserve the idea of a shared humanity is to wage war against certain other human beings. Sometimes, and war is only the clearest example, our noblest ends can only be advanced by the most ignoble of means.

Recognizing the necessity may trap one in a contradiction, but it is not of itself hypocritical. What *is* hypocritical, however, is the refusal to admit the contradiction. "What is disgusting ...," Orwell writes, "is the absence of any kind of self-criticism." He notes how pious and superior—and thus, how hollow—the moralizing of the clergy comes to sound: "God is asked 'to turn the hearts of our enemies, and to help us to forgive them; to give them repentance for their misdoings, and a readiness to make amends.' Nothing about our enemies forgiving *us*."[20]

In contrast, he suggests, "the Christian attitude would be that we are no better than our enemies, we are all miserable sinners, but that it so happens that it would be better if our cause prevailed."[21]

The difference is subtle, but important. In the first case, "Apparently God is expected to help us on the ground that we are *better* than the Germans."[22] Likewise, we do not pray for forgiveness, presumably because we do not need it; instead we pray that we might offer forgiveness, which quietly implies that we have a right to judge and punish our enemies if we so choose. In fact, as Orwell stated repeatedly elsewhere, such verdicts generally represent "punishment of the guilty by the guilty."[23] Orwell's proposed alternative recognizes the general corruption of warfare, that all are guilty and everyone is in need of forgiveness, but it still holds that our cause is better than the enemy's (that is, England's is better than the Nazis'). And, we might add, it is better in part *because* it would allow for mutual forgiveness and reconciliation. It would not make peaceful life impossible. Framed this way, the peace that Orwell is pursuing—along with others, including some who are actually fighting—looks very different from that which the bishop proposes. By "peace," here, we must also mean victory. And if the victory is different, so too, is the war.

Why We Fight

One fights a war to win it, or one ought not fight at all. But what counts as winning is not always obvious. "I don't think any defeat or victory in the narrow military sense matters," Orwell wrote privately, "so much as demonstrating that we are on the side of the weak against the strong."[24] Put differently, one might say that in the struggle for common decency and against fascism, military success would count for nothing if, in the process, we surrender our decency and become fascists.

Consider one relatively minor controversy in the prosecution of the war: The British had bound the hands of soldiers captured during a raid on Dieppe. The Germans retaliated by chaining British POWs, leading the British to chain German POWs in return. On October 11, 1942, Orwell's diary comments: "The authorities in Canada have now chained up a number of German prisoners equal to the number of British prisoners chained up in Germany. What the devil are we coming to?"[25]

Noting that this move "aroused extraordinarily little protest," Orwell then wrote a letter to *The Times* (which they declined to print). In it, he argued against these reprisals, first because it showed an attempt to "descend … to the level of our enemies," and second, because such an attempt would surely fail: "in the matter of ruthlessness we are unlikely to compete successfully" against the Nazis. The likely result, he predicted, would be worse and worse atrocities on each side until inevitably "we shall become disgusted with the process first." The English, then, would "have acted both barbarously and weakly," compromising an important principle without gaining any tactical advantage. Orwell suggested, instead, that the British government should publicly *refuse* to retaliate, issuing a statement: "You are Nazis, we are civilized men. This latest act of yours simply demonstrates the difference."[26]

Later he employed a similar logic in a column considering the execution of collaborators. There, too, Orwell noted that, "this whole business of taking vengeance on traitors and captured enemies raises questions which are strategic as well as moral." On the strategic end, he worried that

> if we shoot too many of the small rats now we may have no stomach for dealing with the big ones when the time comes.… [It] could well happen that all the truly guilty people will escape in the end, simply because public opinion has been sickened beforehand by hypocritical trials and cold-blooded executions.[27]

Notice that both arguments present the moral limits as a given. In Machiavellian terms, that approach may seem naive, but it is only realistic. If there *are* certain limits beyond which you will not go, your strategy ought to recognize that fact and not depend on an escalation beyond those limits. But Orwell also loops the strategic concerns back into his ethics. The English cannot match the Nazis' cruelty—in part because they *shouldn't*. If our aims include common decency, our strategy may well be undermined by bloodlust or hatred. Therefore, Orwell reasoned: "Whether we do or don't shoot the Fascists and quislings who happen to fall into our hands is probably not very important in itself. What is important is that revenge and 'punishment' should have no part in our policy or even in our day-dreams." That is because in England, unlike Oceania, hatred is not a practical basis for policy: "Results are what matter," Orwell reminds us, "and one of the results we want from this war is to be quite sure that Germany will not make war again." Reaching that goal will rely upon a clear strategy and the proper means: "Whether this [aim] is best achieved by ruthlessness or generosity I am not certain: but I am quite certain that either of these will be more difficult if we allow ourselves to be influenced by hatred."[28]

Revenge Is Sour

Soon after the war, Orwell wrote a short essay, titled "Revenge Is Sour." In it, he related an incident he observed during the Allied occupation, in which a young Jewish soldier, an Austrian serving in the American army, kicked a captured German officer. By the officer's history—early membership in the Nazi party, high rank in the SS, commanding position at a concentration camp—"he represented everything that we had been fighting against during the past five years." And yet, as he stood before them—"scrubby, unfed, unshaven," a prisoner of war herded with others in an airplane hanger, sleeping on the concrete floor, and "only doubtfully sane"—the effect was ridiculous and deflating. "So this Nazi torturer of one's imagination," Orwell reflected, "the monstrous figure against whom one had struggled for so many years, dwindled to this pitiful wretch, whose obvious need was not for punishment, but for some kind of psychological treatment."[29]

Orwell is careful to say that he does not blame the young soldier.[30] What struck him instead was the futility of the gesture, even emotionally. It seemed pointless and empty, perhaps to the soldier himself:

"He wasn't really enjoying it," Orwell realized. "[He] was merely—like a man in a brothel, or a boy smoking his first cigar, or a tourist traipsing round a picture gallery—*telling* himself that he was enjoying it, and behaving as he had planned to behave in the days when he was helpless."[31] Orwell concluded, then, that "the whole idea of revenge and punishment is a childish day-dream. Properly speaking, there is no such thing as revenge. Revenge is an act which you want to commit when you are powerless and because you are powerless: as soon as the sense of impotence is removed, the desire evaporates also."[32]

Or rather—it *ought* to evaporate. The urge for vengeance is ill-suited to the circumstances in which such vengeance finally becomes possible. And yet, too often, there is a lingering sadism, a desire *not* to put the past behind us, an absolute refusal of reconciliation, and a demand that our enemies, now vanquished, suffer the same pains and degradations that they had previously inflicted upon us. The political uses of these spiteful impulses are of course clear—the vindication of national "honor," the seamless transition from defensive to aggressive warfare, scapegoating as a means of covering mistakes and dodging accountability, the inciting of witch hunts and pogroms, and the stoking of paranoia as a means of maintaining control. Of course, petty reprisals may also be called justice, by the schoolyard standard of justice, but they bring with them the unpleasant consequence that oppression continues, though the victims and executioners have for the moment switched places. It also means that we, understandably or not, come to resemble exactly the thing that we have fought against.

For instance: "I have before me an exceptionally disgusting photograph," Orwell wrote in the *Tribune*. It shows "two partially undressed women, with shaven heads and with swastikas painted on their faces, being led through the streets of Paris amid grinning onlookers." The photograph had been widely published, as had many others like it, seemingly with approval. Orwell, however, was unnerved by the familiar feeling it evoked.

As soon as I saw this *Star* photograph, I thought, "Where have I seen something like this before?" Then

I remembered. Just about ten years ago, when the Nazi regime was beginning to get into its stride, very similar pictures of humiliated Jews being led through the streets of German cities were exhibited in the British press—but with this difference, that on that occasion we were not expected to approve.

In connection with this observation, Orwell goes on to quote Nietzsche: "He who fights too long against dragons becomes a dragon himself." He clarifies: "'Too long,' in this context, should perhaps be taken as meaning 'after the dragon is beaten.'"[33]

The Nietzsche reference may be unexpected, but it is also entirely appropriate. It was Nietzsche, after all, that most incisive critic of *ressentiment*, who warned us that vengeance is a kind of poison, and advised, "Mistrust all in whom the impulse to punish is powerful."[34] Instead Nietzsche wished "that man be delivered from revenge, that is for me the bridge to the highest hope, and a rainbow after long storms."[35]

Broader Morals

As Orwell struggled in his writing with the question of violence, two major observations came to light. The first is that *how* one fights ought to follow in some fashion from *why* one fights. Or, put differently: that your tactics ought to reflect your aims and not those of your enemies. The second, related point is that while a certain amount of ruthlessness is undoubtedly necessary to achieve victory, the violence and even cruelty of warfare ought not to be motivated by hatred, sadism, vengeance, or—what comes to the same thing, only dressed up for chapel—a desire to punish. Together they point to a broader moral, or perhaps even a broader morality, which demands that we recognize the humanity of our enemies, even as we fight against them. In fact, Orwell suggests, the Left fights—at the time, against fascism—because we *do* recognize such humanity, and it is that recognition which separates our cause from theirs.

Orwell tried to adapt himself to violence by separating it from hatred and hysteria, by refusing to be poisoned by resentment, by pursuing reconciliation rather than revenge, and by remaining clear-eyed and pragmatic while admitting that there are limits to what one is willing to do, and then refusing to transgress those limits. He understood, as too few of us do, that we cannot pursue an ideal of shared humanity while also treating our enemies as monsters. By doing so, we defeat our own purposes and become monsters ourselves. We must, instead, make our fighting an expression of our ideals. That means, among other things, refusing to dehumanize our enemies or to celebrate cruelty, avoiding deliberate atrocities, resolving to greet victory with magnanimity.

Know You Are Lying[36]

Evil means may sometimes be necessary in defense of the good; but the good requires that we never forget that such means remain evil. In this, Orwell's attitude toward violence finds an analogy in his attitude toward lying. He held a great reverence for the truth, almost as a moral principle. Yet he saw that sometimes, in evil circumstances, the only option was to lie. That may be bad, certainly, even if it was the least bad alternative. What truly frightened him however was the idea, which was increasingly gaining ground, that when lies are backed by political power they therefore become the truth.

In his "Notes on Nationalism," Orwell reflected on the mind-set that made possible this sort of deception—and often, simultaneously, self-deception:

> The primary aim of propaganda is, of course, to influence contemporary opinion, but those who rewrite history do probably believe with part of their minds that they are actually thrusting facts into the past. When one considers the elaborate forgeries that have been committed in order to show that Trotsky did not play a valuable part in the Russian civil war, it is difficult to feel that the people responsible are merely lying. More probably they feel that their own version *was* what happened in the sight

of God, and that one is justified in rearranging the records accordingly.[37]

In *1984*, of course, this belief in the mutability of facts is the essence of the totalitarian outlook: "Who controls the past controls the future; who controls the present controls the past."[38]

Orwell worked for the BBC Eastern Service from 1941 to 1943—"two wasted years"—producing cultural programming and writing commentary on the progress of the war.[39] The situation was deeply ironic. As he wrote to his superiors, responding to an Intelligence Officer's suggestion that they capitalize on his notoriety: "If I broadcast as George Orwell I am as it were selling my literary reputation, which so far as India is concerned probably arises chiefly from books of anti-imperialist tendency, some of which have been banned in India." In other words, this reputation, based partly on his books being suppressed as subversive to English rule, became an asset in the propaganda effort to promote loyalty to the Empire. Therefore, Orwell reasoned, to preserve his credibility "as an independent and more or less 'agin the government' commentator," he would have to be allowed "reasonable freedom of speech"—though he also offered to "avoid mention of subjects on which I could not conscientiously agree with current Government policy."[40] Such silence was not only prudent, it was directly enforced: Orwell's commentary was subject to a triple censorship. Before broadcast, his scripts had to be cleared by the Ministry of Information both to avoid breaches of security and to ensure congruence with official policy. Then, during the broadcast itself, an Anglican clergyman listened from the control booth, ready to kill the mic should the discussion start to stray.[41]

Though he could not say everything he wanted, Orwell at least avoided saying things he *didn't* want to say. "On no occasion," he wrote in his resignation letter, "have I been compelled to say on the air anything that I would not have said as a private individual."[42] But that is not to suggest that he always told the truth. As he recorded in his diary: "one rapidly becomes propaganda-minded and develops a cunning one did not previously have." For example: "I am regularly alleging in all my newsletters that the Japanese are plotting to attack

Russia" even though "I don't believe this to be so." Under the circumstances, Orwell thought, perfect honesty was not merely a luxury, but an impossibility. He reasoned, in the same diary entry: "All propaganda is lies, even when one is telling the truth. I don't think this matters so long as one knows what one is doing, and why."[43] Therefore, at the BBC, Orwell's standard became not public truthfulness but a kind of private clarity. One could utter falsehoods, as long as one did so resolutely, with clear purpose and without self-deception. The point was not so much to speak the truth, but to preserve one's own outlook, the sense that there *is* a truth independent of any doctrine, or any party's line. One could become a liar and yet retain a sense of integrity.

That struggle for mental freedom, the notion that one might find refuge in his own private thoughts, became the basis for the central conflict of *1984*. And Orwell's refusal to *believe* the lies, even those of his own side, constantly created friction with doctrinaires of all kinds, from Stalinists to anarchist-pacifists. As he wrote in an exchange with Alex Comfort:

> All propaganda's lying, yours or mine;
> It's lying even when its facts are true ...
> But there are truths that smaller lies can serve,
> And dirtier lies that scruples can gild over ...
> It's mean enough when other men are dying,
> But when you lie, it's much to know you're lying.[44]

The important thing, then, is that the *idea* of truth be preserved, even as one sins against it, just as the crucial issue is whether the ideals of peace and brotherhood—or, simply, common decency—survive in the midst of bloody warfare. It is these values which are at stake—more so than victory in some particular battle, or the deaths of some individual people, or the specific number of lies appearing below the headline.[45]

The Saner Self

Orwell was willing to own the lies that he told, to take responsibility for them, and not to defer to his instructions or to blame his superiors.

He told his lies, not because he was ordered to, but because in his personal judgment it was the best thing to do.

It is a crucial difference—that between honesty and integrity. The first may be required by one's ethics, but the latter is ethics' very foundation. By and large, that sense of integrity is identical with remaining an individual, a distinct human being connected to but distinguishable from others, with one's own judgments, tastes, inclinations, and interests. That sense of individuality, of *ownlife* in the Newspeak jargon of *1984*, was, Orwell saw, central to the very notion of freedom. And it was precisely that sort of freedom that totalitarianism threatened.

Orwell's conclusion, then, is in some sense, to separate belief from action—to "recognise that a willingness to *do* certain distasteful but necessary things does not carry with it any obligation to swallow the beliefs that usually go with them"—and thereby to hold steady the difference between principle and necessity.[46] In the course of a conflict, you might have to commit any number of vicious and regrettable acts, but you do not have to indulge in hatred or self-deception. Instead, you must "keep part of yourself inviolate." This "saner self ... stands aside, records the things that are done and admits their necessity, but refuses to be deceived as to their true nature."[47] It views clearly what you do, and resists all false consolations. The troubled conscience is one sign that the values you defend, but cannot embody, are still alive within you.

Therefore: lie, when you must, but do not become tempted to believe your own lies. Fight, and even kill, if you have to—but do so without giving in to hatred, or vengeance, or cruelty. Understand that, however noble our ends, the means available will often be unworthy of them. And never deceive yourself, that because some action is *necessary*, it is also for that reason *good*. Good ends may require terrible means—no less terrible for the ends that they serve.

Part Two
Orwellian Reflections

Chapter Five

"A Place Worth Living In"
Notes on Patriotism and Nationalism

Part One: Patriotic at Heart

England's Dreaming
GEORGE ORWELL'S FIRST PUBLISHED WORK WAS A PATRIOTIC POEM reminiscent of Kipling, "Awake! Young Men of England." Writing under his given name, Eric Blair, he urges,

> Oh! think of the War Lord's mailed fist,
> That is striking at England today:
> And think of the lives that our soldiers
> Are fearlessly throwing away.[1]

It was 1914, the Great War had just begun, and Eric Blair was at the time eleven years old.

A quarter-century later, returning from Spain, Orwell again invoked the theme of quiet England, roused late from a peaceful slumber, with danger already at the door. *Homage to Catalonia* closes with an image of the tranquil country:

> Down here it was still the England I had known in my childhood: the railway-cuttings smothered in wild flowers, the deep meadows where the great shining horses browse and meditate, the slow-moving streams bordered by willows, the green bosoms of the elms, the larkspurs in the cottage gardens; and then the huge peaceful wilderness of outer London, the barges on the miry river, the familiar streets, the posters telling of cricket matches and Royal weddings, the men in bowler hats, the pigeons in Trafalgar Square, the red buses, the blue policemen— all sleeping the deep, deep sleep of England, from which I sometimes fear that we shall never wake till we are jerked out of it by the roar of bombs.[2]

This passage—lyrical and a touch sentimental, so different from the preceding account of revolution and betrayal—would have been more at home in Orwell's following book, *Coming Up for Air*. There, the protagonist, George Bowling, sees the signs of war everywhere, knows that it can only be a disaster, and yet feels powerless to stop it. Bowling, too, compares London to a wilderness—"a great wilderness with no wild beasts." He elaborates, with a tone of admiration and amazement: "No guns firing, nobody chucking pineapples, nobody beating anybody else up with a rubber truncheon. If you come to think of it, in the whole of England at this moment there probably isn't a single bedroom window from which anyone's firing a machine-gun." But then he asks, can it possibly last? "How about five years from now? Or two years? Or one year?"[3]

Orwell himself was at this time somewhat desperate to avert a war with Germany, fearing that no matter who won militarily, politically the result would be the introduction of fascism in England. He also felt—and this gave his writing on the subject a hopeless, sinking quality—that the war was bound to come, not because it was inevitable but, more maddening still, because it was what the rulers wanted and the common people could not grasp the real danger.[4]

Of course the war did come, the English people were shaken awake by the sound of bombs—and so, to his surprise, was Orwell. By 1940, he would recall,

> For several years the coming war was a nightmare to me, and at times I even made speeches and wrote pamphlets against it. But the night before the Russo-German pact was announced I dreamed that the war had started. It was one of those dreams which, whatever Freudian inner meaning they may have, do sometimes reveal to you the real state of your feelings. It taught me two things, first, that I should be simply relieved when the long-dreaded war started, secondly, that I was patriotic at heart, would not sabotage or act against my own side, would support the war, would fight if possible.[5]

The sequence here is interesting: The war had long been a metaphorical nightmare; then it became a literal nightmare; and at last Orwell woke to find that the nightmare had become reality. The literal dream made him less afraid of the actual event and caused him to reverse his previous opposition. Whereas weeks earlier he had been writing anti-war pamphlets and conspiring to resist militarization,[6] all at once he was now clamoring for the government to make some use of him in the war effort.[7] It did do so, eventually—first, as a noncommissioned officer in the Home Guard,[8] and then, in a propaganda capacity for the BBC's India division.[9]

The reversal is startling, if only because it is rare to hear an intellectual admit, so suddenly, so decisively, and so totally, that he had been wrong. It is somewhat less surprising if we remember that Orwell's opposition to the war was really only an interlude amidst a series of more important transitions—from service in the Indian Imperial Police to the anti-imperialism of *Burmese Days*; then, in Spain, from anti-fascist Republicanism to revolutionary Socialism.

It is less shocking still if we recognize that beneath these other changes, there remained a set of basic continuities. In fact, the particular form that his jingoism took—the view that "We cannot win the war without introducing Socialism, nor establish Socialism without winning the war"[10]—was a direct adaptation of the POUM's line in Spain, even using the same words: "The war and the revolution are inseparable."[11]

More important, however, was the fact that—for the war, or against—Orwell's political thought was animated by the same set of concerns: "common decency," a desire for liberty and equality, and a love for England. It is the third of these that sounds incongruous—indeed, a bit scandalous—to those on the Left. But for Orwell, the three were inextricably connected. He loved England, and part of what he loved was the country's liberal traditions and the moral outlook of its people. He likewise loved liberty, equality, and decency—and, unlike most of the rest of us, he had enough self-awareness to realize that he loved them in large part because he had been raised in a tradition that taught him that such things are important, and in a country where these values are upheld in principle even as they are thwarted in practice.[12]

Orwell, therefore, was a patriot and a revolutionary. And unlike many of his defenders, and a greater number of his critics, he did not view this as a contradiction, or even as a paradox. He was a patriot for *the same reasons* as he was a revolutionary, and what is more, his revolutionary politics were an extension of his patriotism.

The war and the revolution, in his estimation, were interdependent but not indistinct. One was a struggle for survival, the other for the soul of the nation. They would be won or lost together, but that does not mean they were of equal import: "Compared with the task of bringing the real England to the surface, even the winning of the war, necessary though it is, is secondary."[13] The revolution gave the war meaning, while the war only made revolution possible.

England, His England

Orwell wrote extensively of England—its people and their character, customs, and culture.[14] He wrote of the culture both high and low—*King Lear* and Charles Reade,[15] detective novels and cartoon postcards[16]—but more importantly he wrote of the culture as it is lived, the world of pubs and parks and "a nice cup of tea."[17] He wrote of England both fondly and critically, with a gift for understanding it from the inside while also seeing how it appears from without. (In one passage, he imagines a foreigner visiting London for the first time: "Almost certainly he would find the salient characteristics of the English people to be artistic insensibility, gentleness, respect for legality, suspicion of foreigners, sentimentality about animals, hypocrisy, exaggerated class distinctions, and an obsession with sport.")[18] Orwell wrote of both the best and worst of his country, often in span of a few lines. In *The English People*, he admires his compatriots for their "extremely considerate" manners on one page and scorns their "xenophobia" on the next.[19] A single paragraph from his preface to *Animal Farm* praises England as "a country in which people have lived together for several hundred years without knowing civil war, in which the laws are relatively just and official news and statistics can almost invariably be believed, and … in which to hold and to voice minority views does not involve any mortal danger," and he laments that "England is not completely democratic," that it "is also a capitalist country with great class privileges and … great differences in wealth."[20]

The Lion and the Unicorn and *Coming Up for Air* likewise blend the paean and the rebuke. The censure generally owes its force to the tenderness of the tribute. Orwell often tries to segregate the good qualities and the bad by point of time. The best are nostalgically assigned to the past (especially the period before 1914); the worst are menacingly projected into the future. The effect is to place the present in crisis, to make it—*now*—the crucial moment in which we are in danger of losing all that we value and condemning ourselves to a kind of eternal nightmare. This schema reaches its fullest expression, of course, in *1984*, though it is also central to *Coming Up for Air*. The orientation is reversed, in some respects, in *The Lion and the Unicorn*. There, Orwell assigns the worst abuses to the past, and sees the present as an opportunity to build a better future on the foundation of society's existing virtues. By far Orwell's most optimistic work, *The*

Lion and the Unicorn cheers for the social leveling imposed by the war and both urges and predicts that it may be the beginning of "the English Revolution."[21] What is common to each of these books is the underlying motive, and the treatment of both the patriotic urge and the dissenting urge as essentially the same.

Mere Revolution

"Nations do not escape from their past merely by making a revolution."[22] Revolution, Orwell thought, was neither a break with the past, nor a return to a better era, but a way of "bringing the real England to the surface" and developing its better qualities: "By revolution we become more ourselves, not less.... Nothing ever stands still. We must add to our heritage or lose it, we must grow greater or grow less, we must go forward or backward."[23] Revolution would not destroy the country, but save it—change it, and yet miraculously preserve it.

He explained:

> An English Socialist government will transform the nation from top to bottom, but it will still bear all over it the unmistakeable marks of our own civilisation.... [Its approach] will not be doctrinaire, nor even logical.... It will leave anachronisms and loose ends everywhere.... It will show a power of assimilating the past which will shock foreign observers and sometimes make them doubt whether any revolution has happened.

By way of examples, he suggests that a revolution "will abolish the House of Lords, but quite probably will not abolish the Monarchy." It will retain "the judge in his ridiculous horsehair wig and the lion and the unicorn on the soldier's cap-buttons." And it "will disestablish the Church, but not persecute religion," and will instead "retain a vague reverence for the Christian moral code" and even "from time to time ... refer to England as 'a Christian country.'" Rather than "disintegrating the Empire," it will transform it "into a federation of

Socialist states, freed not so much from the British flag as from the money-lender, the dividend-drawer and the wooden-headed British official." Most of all, the revolution will preserve the sense of democratic pluralism, the freedom of speech and even of political opposition, and "will never lose touch with the tradition of compromise and the belief in a law that is above the State." Despite its irregularities, or because of them, "it will have done the essential thing. It will have nationalised industry, scaled down incomes, set up a classless educational system. Its real nature will be apparent from the hatred which the surviving rich men of the world will feel for it."[24]

Orwell was wrong, we know now, about the changes in store for England.[25] Nevertheless, whether we understand it as prescription or prediction, this account does offer a valuable insight. For I think it is probably right that lasting change will be uneven in its pace, inconsistent in its application, and ultimately illogical in terms of what it spares or abolishes.[26] There are numerous reasons for this likelihood, among them the limits of human planning, the practical necessity of compromise, a respect for diversity and local autonomy, and the tendency of people to cling to their customs. But what must also be counted among those reasons is the fact that any genuine revolution—I am excluding here elite coups and invasions by foreign "liberators"—can only develop within the society it seeks to overturn. Inevitably, something of the culture of the old system, if nothing else the elements that nurtured and nursed the growing revolt, will necessarily leave an imprint and be carried forward into the new society. Revolution is a continuation of tradition as much as an attack upon it.

That is bad news for a Left preoccupied with its own sense of exceptionalism and prone to choosing symbolic battles over structural changes. Any revolution worth the name must be the work of many millions of people. For that very reason it will fail to please the more orthodox revolutionaries who specialize in finding fault and who view any idea with genuinely broad appeal as ideologically suspect. Much as the Left may disapprove, it is quite probable that Americans will give up on capitalism long before they stop playing "The Star-Spangled Banner" at baseball games. And if the people in this country ever again overthrow the government, it is a safe bet that they will view it as a struggle for democracy—though by "democracy" they may mean something radically different from our current system of unresponsive representation legitimized by occasional ballot-casting.

In practical terms, the lesson may be: Love what is best about your country, confront what is worst. That means, of course, not being blind to its faults but equally not being blind to its virtues. Both mistakes, though in different ways, have less to do with the positive ideal of patriotism than with Orwell's conception of nationalism. "Nationalism is not to be confused with patriotism," he wrote.

> By "patriotism" I mean devotion to a particular place and a particular way of life, which one believes to be the best in the world but has no wish to force upon other people. Patriotism is of its nature defensive, both militarily and culturally. Nationalism, on the other hand, is inseparable from the desire for power. The abiding purpose of every nationalist is to secure more power and more prestige, *not* for himself but for the nation or other unit in which he has chosen to sink his own individuality.[27]

In common parlance, *patriotism* and *nationalism* are treated as near-synonyms, the latter being simply a concentrated and programmatic version of the former. Orwell used the terms more precisely, though also idiosyncratically, and argued that they in fact refer to very different things. Importantly, neither is quite properly an idea. One is an emotion; the other, a worldview. Both involve questions of loyalty and values, but the specific values and the kinds of loyalty diverge sharply. Patriotism, Orwell suggested, is at least potentially admirable, while nationalism—or what he meant by "nationalism" (really a kind of *ur*- or *uber*-nationalism) is inherently pernicious.

Part Two:
Nationalism—Power Hunger and Self-Deception

Diagnosis

Orwell begins his essay "Notes on Nationalism" by admitting that *nationalism* is not really the right word, but something of an approximate term for what he means to be discussing. He explains:

> By "nationalism" I mean first of all the habit of assuming that human beings can be classified like insects and that whole blocks of millions or tens of millions of people can be confidently labelled "good" or "bad." But secondly—and this is much more important—I mean the habit of identifying oneself with a single nation or other unit, placing it beyond good and evil and recognising no other duty than that of advancing its interests.[28]

Elsewhere he describes nationalism more simply as "the lunatic modern habit of identifying oneself with large power units and seeing everything in terms of competitive prestige."[29]

Writing immediately following the Second World War and just at the beginning of the period of decolonization, Orwell surely selected *nationalism*—as opposed to *chauvinism* or *fanaticism*—for sound but historically specific reasons. Today he may have chosen *fundamentalism*, though it is equally far from his specific meaning. He later produced a whole vocabulary to describe this process of thought: *blackwhite, crimestop, doublethink, goodthink*.[30] The important thing is the *kind* of attachment the nationalist forms, not the particular object of that attachment: "the emotion I am speaking about does not always attach itself to what is called a nation.... It can attach itself to a church or a class, or it may work in a merely negative sense, *against* something or other and without the need for any positive object of loyalty."[31]

Within this framework, Orwell lists three "principal characteristics of nationalist thought":

1- "*Obsession.* As nearly as possible, no nationalist ever thinks, talks or writes about anything except the superiority of his own power unit." His special mission is to prove that his chosen nation is in all respects better than its rivals. Therefore, even to the outer limits of plausibility, any question may be traced back to this central issue. No detail is indifferent, no fact is neutral.

2- "*Instability.*" The content of the nationalist's belief, and even the object of his devotion, is liable to change as circumstances do. "What remains constant in the nationalist is his own state of mind"—the relentless, reductive, uncompromising fervor. The point is to keep oneself always in a frenzied state concerning vicarious contests of honor, whether indulging in spasms of rage over perceived insults or in sadistic ecstasies celebrating some new triumph. It is the single-minded intensity that matters, not the ostensible cause.

3- "*Indifference to Reality.*" Nationalists achieve by instinct the kind of doublethink that the denizens of Airstrip One cultivated by conscious effort: "Nationalism is power hunger tempered by self-deception. Every nationalist is capable of the most flagrant dishonesty, but he is also—since he is conscious of serving something bigger than himself—unshakably certain of being in the right."[32] His fundamental belief, he feels sure, *must* be true; therefore, the facts will have to be made to fit it.

Orwell classifies the prominent types of nationalism as "Positive Nationalism" (which is *for* one's own country; *e.g.*, Celtic Nationalism or Zionism), "Negative Nationalism" (which is *against* some other group; for example, Antisemitism or Trotskyism in its purely anti-Soviet version), and "Transferred Nationalism" (identification with a race, class, or country—in Orwell's day, usually the USSR—other than one's own).[33] Naturally, it is possible to hold any of these beliefs and *not* succumb to "nationalism" in the Orwellian sense. The problem is not inherent to any specific body of thought, just as no particular theory will guarantee an immunity. The issue is less the philosophical content and more the subjective manner by which the individual relates to it. The nationalist holds his special doctrine not only as the unassailable truth, but also as an absolute standard by which the truth may be judged. Its scope is not limited to moral or political matters, and *all* questions, whether of fact or value, may be answered in advance by referring to the nationalist's creed—or, more precisely, to the "competitive prestige" of the "power unit" to which he has committed himself.

The Continuing Appeal

The dominant ideologies may have changed since Orwell's day but the broad pattern of thought his essay describes is still apparent. "Nationalism" (in the Orwellian sense) was almost the official theology of George W. Bush's presidency,[34] and continues to be practiced in even more vulgar form by Donald Trump.[35] It announces itself less bombastically on the other side of the aisle, but it is undoubtedly there: for example, large numbers of progressive Democrats supported Barack Obama's continuation of war-on-terror atrocities, including the operation of an extra-legal prison camp at Guantanamo Bay (53% of "self-identified liberal Democrats" approve) and using drones to assassinate suspected terrorists (77%).[36] When those poll results were released in 2012, Glenn Greenwald rightly chastised the so-called progressives for their "repulsive liberal hypocrisy" and "oozing, limitless intellectual dishonesty," but he also pointed to a problem much deeper than mere opportunism. He reminded his liberal readers that they had applauded, just a few years before, when he had compared the "Bush-supporting Right" with an "authoritarian cult" because "its adherents had no real, fixed political beliefs; instead, I argued, their only animating 'principle' was loyalty to their leader, and they would support anything he did no matter how at odds it was with their prior ostensible beliefs." One election later, Greenwald continued, it was

> Remarkable to see these authoritarian follower traits manifest so vibrantly in the very same political movement—sophisticated, independent-minded, reality-based progressives—that believes it is above that, and that only primitive conservatives are plagued by such follower-mindlessness.[37]

It is more distressing still to find among the radical Left the same sort of intellectual blindness and groupthink (though typically without the leader worship). It remains tediously at the heart of any socialist sect that imagines itself emerging from obscurity as our Bolshevik saviors. It is likewise endemic to what is generally understood (though never by its adherents) as "identity politics," whether in its racial, ethnic, feminist, or queer guise. And it is equally evident in the inverted snobbery of those class reductionists who believe that simply to call something "working class" is necessarily to praise it, and to label it "bourgeois" is enough to condemn it, no matter what "it" is—an accent, an idea, an organization, an individual, a style of dress, a choice of beer. People who engage in such thinking are often notably puritan in their outlook, expressing so forcefully their disgust for "privilege" that they sometimes seem instead to praise privation as virtuous in itself.

Nationalism is there, too, almost consciously so, in "ally politics" and the older "anti-imperialism" from which it is derived.[38] In each instance members of some oppressor group try to expunge their personal guilt by transferring loyalty to their perceived victims—not a bad impulse in itself, except when it means surrendering one's own judgment, not only on some particular point of strategy or tactics, but also on questions of fact, on the goals of liberation, or on basic matters of right and wrong.[39] Owing to this demand for unquestioning, unwavering faith, from the outside transferred nationalism often looks creepy and cultish.[40]

Purely negative nationalisms also abound—anti-civ (that is, anti-civilization, or what used to be called *primitivist*), anti-fascist, and post-left individualist politics often succumb to this malady. The adherents of such views typically come across as nurturing an unhealthy obsession with the object of their scorn, often losing all sense of proportion as a result. In their more extreme forms some versions of negative nationalism bend toward a generalizable misanthropy. A friend once told me of mischievously starting a chant at an Earth First! rendezvous and then feeling dismayed at how eagerly it was taken up: "Four legs good; two legs bad!"[41]

As Orwell noted, there is a lot of overlap between the various tendencies. A purely negative anti-Zionism easily bleeds into a transferred loyalty to anyone who happens to be fighting Israel, which can (and has) in turn produced support for Islamists and anti-Semites.[42]

It also remains common for individuals or groups to move between different kinds of nationalism, sometimes swinging from one extremist position to a contrary one, often without any intervening step: Orwell's example was the "bigoted Communist who changes in a space of weeks, or even days, into an equally bigoted Trotskyist."[43] The modern equivalent would be the Maoist who converts to nihilism, or the single-minded activist who simply swaps one reductive monocausal theory for another, ceasing to believe (for example) that "it's all about class" and deciding instead that "it's all about race." Sometimes these are purely personal vacillations, sometimes they affect entire movements. The faddishness of radical politics does at least seem to promise that no particular kind of foolishness will survive for very long, but the problem remains even if, from time to time, sensible positions do come to the fore. As Orwell commented, in his original preface to *Animal Farm*: "To exchange one orthodoxy for another is not necessarily an advance. The enemy is the gramophone mind, whether or not one agrees with the record that is being played at the moment."[44]

I am not talking about people who, whatever their own views, are willing to pragmatically involve themselves with some movement that they see making headway so long as they broadly agree with its aims. Nor am I discussing those people who opportunistically *pretend* to adopt or abandon principles when they think that they may gain a following by doing so. Nor do I mean people, individuals or groups, who run up against the limits, contradictions, or failings of one line of thought and boldly alter their course, who simply change their minds after encountering new arguments or fuller evidence, or who adhere to the same basic principles, but over time arrive at new conclusions.

I mean instead those people who are vocal, insistent, dogmatic, and even somewhat fanatical about their positions, with minds that seem completely closed to any alternative, yet who suddenly turn around and—despite the change, if it is even acknowledged—hold their new opinions with exactly the same vehemence and certainty. Usually such people have an unerring knack for always being part of a fashionable avant-garde, continuously pursuing the new and therefore shedding ideas the moment they become dated. Sometimes they are attracted to extremism *per se* and therefore may be drawn as easily to the far Right as to the far Left. What is important is that they move from one extreme to another and do not, for example, endure a period of quietism or moderation. For the point, as Orwell noted, is that they can preserve the same sort of fundamentalist outlook, despite the change in doctrine.

The Structure of "Nationalist" Thought

The instability of nationalist thinking—the potential for shifting allegiances, the tendency for principles to become their opposites, the total disregard for consistency paired with a perversely rigid concern with doctrine—means that all judgments are based on an implicit acceptance of double standards. "Actions are held to be good or bad," Orwell remarked, "not on their own merits but according to who does them, and there is almost no kind of outrage … which does not change its moral colour when it is committed by 'our' side."[45]

Of course, the easiest way to justify an atrocity is never to hear of it. When a journalist for the *Tribune* reported on conditions in Europe under Soviet occupation, the paper received letters that "violently accused him of untruthfulness" and also "seemed to imply that the facts he brought forward ought not to be published even if true." What happens to the people of Austria, apparently, is less important than whether the reports show the Red Army in a favorable light. Orwell summarized the position: "100,000 rape cases in Vienna are not a good advertisement for the Soviet regime: therefore, even if they have happened, don't mention them." He explains the reasoning that justifies such a conclusion: "if one divides the world into A and B and assumes that A represents progress and B reaction, it is just arguable that no fact detrimental to A ought to be revealed." Such an argument, Orwell says, is always "dishonest, in the sense that people only use it when it suits them." It represents a kind of special pleading to exempt one's own party from criticism, or even scrutiny. "Beneath this argument there always lies the intention to do propaganda for some single sectional interest, and to browbeat critics into silence by telling them that they are 'objectively' reactionary."[46] Such thinking can be pushed to absurd lengths:

"To criticize the Soviet Union helps Hitler: therefore 'Trotskyism is Fascism.'"[47]

One thing that may have changed since Orwell's time—or perhaps he misconstrued it—is that today's nationalisms, though undoubtedly power-hungry (especially in small things) are not triumphalist. On the Left in particular, it is unusual for the members of a group to celebrate their power or proclaim their imminent ascendancy. They insist instead on their *powerlessness* and base their claims of legitimacy on their status as an oppressed group. This shift is certainly tied to the end of grand narratives suggesting the inevitable victory the international proletariat, the Great Nation, the master race, or some other specially chosen historical subject. When various kinds of determinism were more in vogue, it was much more tempting to declare the inevitable victory of one's own side. Such an outlook allowed one to treat even minor successes as crucial markers in the direction of history, while dismissing important failings as temporary setbacks (if, indeed, they were acknowledged at all). Since the fall of the Soviet Union, such world-historical fairy tales seem to carry much less weight, at least on the Left, which has not altered the line of reasoning so much as simply reversed its direction. Where once success was seen as its own justification, increasingly defeat is. In any case, Orwell seems to have, without overestimating the bullying impulse, underestimated the power of *ressentiment*, even in its transposed, guilt-ridden, masochistic form.[48]

Fading Out

The dangers of nationalist thinking extend far beyond any particular error and even beyond the movements that become infected with it. For once nationalism spreads past a certain point, it will tend to degrade the overall quality of political debate and therefore of political thought—and, because no fact or idea is irrelevant to nationalist ambitions, ultimately *all* thought.

In what is likely the most despondent passage in his diary, Orwell wrote:

> We are all drowning in filth. When I talk to anyone or
> read the writings of anyone who has any axe to grind,

I feel that intellectual honesty and balanced judgment have simply disappeared from the face of the earth. Everyone's thought is forensic, everyone is simply putting [forward] a "case" with deliberate suppression of his opponent's point of view, and, what is more, with complete insensitiveness to any sufferings except those of himself and his friends.... One notices this in the case of people one disagrees with, such as Fascists or pacifists, but in fact everyone is the same, at least everyone who has definite opinions. Everyone is dishonest, and everyone is utterly heartless toward people who are outside the immediate range of his own interests and sympathies. What is most striking of all is the way sympathy can be turned on or off like a tap according to political expediency.... I am not thinking of lying for political ends, but of actual changes in subjective feeling. But is there no one who has both firm opinions and a balanced outlook? Actually there are plenty, but they are powerless. All power is in the hands of paranoiacs.[49]

Political discussion, in such a setting, cannot constitute an attempt to get at the truth or to achieve some degree of mutual understanding or to persuade others of one's own view, or even simply to make oneself understood. It is instead a kind of game in which both the victory and the stakes are largely imaginary. Orwell analyzed the nationalist's motives: "What he wants is to *feel* that his own unit is getting the better of some other unit, and he can more easily do this by scoring off an adversary than by examining the facts to see whether they support him." Since both sides are, as a rule, equally "uninterested in what happens in the real world," the outcome of such disputes "is always entirely inconclusive," and "each contestant invariably believes himself to have won the victory."[50]

In this sort of competition it is nearly inevitable that fantasies come to stand in for facts, fallacies overtake arguments, and character assassination becomes a favored tactic on all sides. A fog of uncertainty soon settles over every account, "which makes it harder and harder to discover what is actually happening," and therefore "makes it easier to cling to lunatic beliefs. Since nothing is ever quite proved or disproved, the most unmistakable fact can be impudently denied."[51] But no matter. Uncertainty quickly curdles into indifference. Facts are selected or suppressed in order to make a case; if need be, the necessary facts are simply invented or, contrariwise, erased.

What worried Orwell most was that individual people—perhaps even millions of them—might come to draw their sense of integrity from the willing submission to shifting dogmas, rather than respect for the truth or the demands of one's own conscience. They might then cease to recognize that such things as fabricating evidence and slandering your opponents were despicable—or even simply dishonest. He found the thought "frightening ... because it often gives me the feeling that the very concept of objective truth is fading out of the world."[52]

In *1984*, he presses the tendency to its logical conclusion. O'Brien, the Inner Party official, the teacher-torturer, lectures poor Winston Smith in his cell within the Ministry of Love:

> We, the Party, control all records, and we control all memories.... we control the past.... You believe that reality is something objective, external, existing in its own right.... But I tell you, Winston, that reality is not external. Reality exists in the human mind, and nowhere else. Not in the individual mind, which can make mistakes, and in any case soon perishes; only in the mind of the Party, which is collective and immortal. Whatever the Party holds to be truth *is* truth. It is impossible to see reality except by looking through the eyes of the Party.[53]

In the end, Winston is broken. He becomes converted to the Party's view. He had once written that "Freedom is the freedom to say that two plus two make four."[54] But at last he learns that "Sometimes they are five. Sometimes they are three. Sometimes they are all of them at once."[55] His loyalty to the Party is ensured by—more, it is *identical with*—the surrender of his own judgment.

Remedy

As with his prescriptions for improving poor writing, Orwell's strategy for addressing the fallacies of nationalism is to teach us to recognize them, and then to appeal to our own good sense.[56] The first step, he suggests, may lie in recognizing our own imperfection, fallibility, and bias. He writes:

> As for the nationalistic loves and hatreds that I have spoken of, they are part of the make-up of most of us, whether we like it or not. Whether it is possible to get rid of them I do not know, but I do believe that it is possible to struggle against them, and that this is essentially a *moral* effort. It is a question first of all of discovering what one really is, what one's own feelings really are, and then of making allowance for the inevitable bias.... The emotional urges which are inescapable, and are perhaps even necessary to political action, should be able to exist side by side with an acceptance of reality.[57]

One may not be able to avoid bias, but one need not adopt bias as a principle. One can, if nothing else, refuse to surrender one's own individual judgment. That will be partly a question of character: the ability to distinguish between what you wish and what you know, "the power of facing unpleasant facts,"[58] the will to live without comforting lies. Perhaps what is needed most of all is a continued belief in the existence of an objective truth while maintaining a severe, demanding skepticism concerning all claims to know what it is.

That is of course but a partial solution. It may help to keep an individual mind sane and honest, but it does little to change the overall atmosphere. Orwell realized as much and yet toward the end of his life that question of individual thought became his central concern. Faced with the continued threat of totalitarianism, Orwell came to view the struggle for freedom as occurring not solely between classes or nations but first and perhaps most importantly within "the few cubic centimetres inside your skull."[59]

The Opposite of Nationalism

Sustaining that mental fight may require that one find a positive alternative to nationalist thinking. Yet Orwell never specifically attempted to outline such an alternative. If "nationalism" is not the right word—and Orwell admitted that it is not—he might also have struggled to try to name its opposite. Likely, however, the contrary view seemed to him too obvious to require a detailed description.

The opposite of "nationalism," in Orwell's peculiar sense, will not necessarily be "internationalism" or "anti-nationalism." Adherents to those perspectives are every bit as susceptible as their enemies to the malady that Orwell describes. The fact is that any ideology, political tendency, or group loyalty may suffer from, or produce, the same sorts of distortions in thought. Conversely, and more optimistically, though I have chided various factions across the political spectrum for displaying these tendencies, such faults are only *inherent* to the most authoritarian of personality cults. It is even in principle possible for some actual nationalists to resist the fallacies of "nationalism" in Orwell's sense.

The challenge for the Left is to oppose and dismantle inequality in all its forms without sheltering ourselves psychologically in a dualistic fantasy world, without resorting to essentialism and prejudicial classifications, without blinding ourselves to facts simply because they pose problems for our cherished convictions. If nationalism is characterized by self-deception and power worship, its opposite would be intellectual honesty and human sympathy. The opposite of nationalism, in Orwell's terms, is decency.

Postscript: Toward European Unity

In the summer of 2016, as I was writing this chapter, the citizens of the United Kingdom unexpectedly voted to leave the European Union. The vote was widely recognized as a victory for the right wing and it was immediately followed by an ugly wave of hate crimes.[60]

In the background were broader European tensions concerning the largest influx of refugees since the Second World War. The crisis is primarily driven by the civil war in Syria, where more than 250,000 people have been killed, 7.6 million internally displaced, and the Islamic State (ISIS) has imposed a form of theocratic rule involving the reintroduction of slavery, the conscription of child soldiers, and capital punishment for adultery, homosexuality, and blasphemy. Over four million people have fled, but most European countries have tightened their borders and accepted relatively small numbers of refugees.[61] Both the war and the rise of ISIS are among the many unintended consequences of the 2003 American invasion of Iraq,[62] an act of aggression rationalized by accusations—against all evidence—that Saddam Hussein's government was manufacturing biological, chemical, and even nuclear weapons, and had been involved in planning the terrorist attacks of September 11, 2001.[63] Those attacks, in fact, were the work of al Qaeda, a fundamentalist group devoted to forcing the US out of the Middle East and destroying the state of Israel.[64] Viewing this series of disasters, one is tempted to conclude that the problem is nationalism *all the way down*.

Given these events, it is worth making one additional point about Orwell's conception of patriotism, and the ways in which it differs from nationalism. Patriotism is an emotion, a feeling of love or belonging connected to a specific patch of earth, group of people, and way of life. Nationalism includes a similar emotional component, but it is perverted by a combination of self-deception and power worship, such that the nationalist views his own chosen group as in every way superior to all others and he allows that outlook to dictate his beliefs on questions of both value and fact. Orwell argued (perceptively, I think) that not only does patriotism not necessarily produce a nationalist outlook, but also that in many ways the two contradict one another. The sort of delusions in which nationalists indulge are in fact obstacles to loving one's country.

The love of one's own country, religion, or ethnic group—that feeling of belonging to a particular culture in a unique and even involuntary way—does not imply hostility to any other country, religion, or ethnicity. It is well to remember that, as much as he wrote about and identified with the English and their Englishness, many of Orwell's formative experiences were among foreigners—in Burma, Paris, Spain, and Marrakech—and he wrote about them with great sympathy, if not always with admiration.[65] Orwell was likewise concerned by the increasing difficulty of international travel as borders were lined with "barbed wire, machine-guns and prowling sentries, frequently wearing gas masks."[66] He expressed his frustrations with the ill-informed opposition to immigration, both from businessmen and from trade unions.[67] And he even worried about such relatively trivial matters as the tendency of "international sporting contests [to] lead to orgies of hatred."[68]

Toward the end of *The Lion and the Unicorn*, he quotes a few lines from Shakespeare:

> Come the four corners of the world in arms
> And we shall shock them: naught shall make us rue
> If England to herself be true.

He then comments: "It is right enough, if you interpret it rightly.... England has got to be true to herself." However: "She is not true to herself while the refugees who have sought our shores are penned up in concentration camps."[69]

Orwell both opposed the Empire and was wary of England becoming a satellite state like Airstrip One, but he was not for all that an isolationist. What he wished to see come after the Empire was not a progressive disintegration into smaller and smaller nation-states, mutually suspicious and potentially hostile, but a continued confederation on a new basis of mutual benefit and equality—that is to say, of justice. Likewise, his hope for Europe following the defeat of the Nazis was not a return to the *status quo ante*, and still less a division between American and Soviet blocs, but "the federation of the western European states, transformed into Socialist republics without colonial dependencies," which he conceived of as a "Socialist United States of Europe."[70]

"The first step toward a European Socialist federation," he argued, would have to be the end of imperialism, and in particular the end of British rule in India. The second step would be the forming of new relations between the European powers and their former colonies: "the position of the indigenous peoples of those countries must be changed out of recognition," and their

countries "must cease to be colonies or semi-colonies and become autonomous republics on a complete equality with the
European peoples." This realignment, he readily admitted, would
require "a vast change of outlook" among the Europeans, alongside "a bitter, complex struggle," and ultimately, probably, "bloodshed"—yet it seemed to him both necessary and right.[71]

Orwell loved England but not in the nationalist sense of wanting her advantage over others. He did not see a contradiction, or
even a tension, between patriotism and a much broader humanism.
Patriotism was, if anything, a smaller exercise of the same impulse—a
recognition of commonality that need not be constricting but might
instead, aided by values like equality and justice, prove expansive.
Something of what I am trying to get at comes across in the poem he
wrote about meeting an Italian militiaman when he arrived in Spain.
Despite barriers of language and culture, they could immediately recognize in one another a common humanity, shared hopes, a sense of
purpose, and from all that, solidarity:

> Good luck go with you, Italian soldier!
> But luck is not for the brave;
> What would the world give back to you?
> Always less than you gave....
>
> But the thing that I saw in your face
> No power can disinherit:
> No bomb that ever burst
> Shatters the crystal spirit.[72]

The theme of those lines is not that far removed from the sentiment
that produced the hand-on-heart patriotism of "Awake, Young Men of
England." There remains, for instance, something of the boyish sense
of duty, but the character of that duty has changed. The horizons have
grown broader, the vision more encompassing, the hopes much greater,
and the resolve deeper—even with the knowledge of defeat.

Orwell ends his essay "Patriots and Revolutionaries" by describing a
poor neighborhood in London that had been decorated by the residents

to celebrate the Silver Jubilee. Walking down a poverty-blighted street strewn for the moment with the Union Jacks, Orwell recalls, "I saw chalked across the asphalt two slogans: 'Poor, but loyal' and 'Landlords, keep away.'"[73] He pondered what the juxtaposition might imply, concluding, "They were patriotic, but they were not Conservative." The anonymous scriveners saw themselves as a part of the country, even if that country kept them half-starved and trapped in a slum; but they would not, for all that, pretend that inequality was anything other than inequality, or that injustice was anything but injustice. Their loyalty might extend to the king, who served as a symbol of the nation, but not to the landlord, who more than symbolized the class system. "And did they not show a sounder instinct," Orwell wondered, "than those who tell us that patriotism is something disgraceful and national liberty a matter of indifference?" In fact, he asked, "was it not the same impulse that moved the Paris workers in 1793, the Communards in 1871, the Madrid trade unionists in 1936—the impulse to defend one's country, and to make it a place worth living in?"[74]

Chapter Six

"Strict Discipline Combined with Social Equality"

The Question of Revolutionary Leadership[1]

IN HIS ESSAY, "LOOKING BACK ON THE SPANISH WAR," GEORGE Orwell relates a brief but illuminating anecdote about life in a revolutionary army: "I was a 'cabo,' or corporal, in command of twelve men," he begins.

One day a man suddenly refused to go to a certain post, which he said quite truly was exposed to enemy fire.... I seized hold of him and began to drag him towards his post.... Instantly I was surrounded by a ring of shouting men: "Fascist! Fascist! Let that man go! This isn't a bourgeois army. Fascist!" etc., etc.[2]

Elsewhere he concludes the story:

After this, for some weeks or months ... this kind of argument recurred over and over again, i.e. indiscipline, arguments as to what was justifiable and what was "revolutionary," but in general a consensus of opinion that one must have strict discipline combined with social equality.[3]

War and Revolution[4]

The situation was typical of the militia system in Spain, at least from what Orwell saw of it, and it was a peculiarity of the type of war in which he was fighting. As he later recalled:

There was occurring a revolution of ideas that was perhaps more important than the short-lived economic changes. For several months large blocks of people believed that all men are equal and were able to act on their belief. The result was a feeling of liberation and hope that is difficult to conceive in our money-tainted atmosphere.[5]

Orwell traveled to Spain as a journalist but "joined the militia almost immediately, because at that time and in that atmosphere it seemed the only conceivable thing to do."[6] The situation in Spain was complex, urgent, and full of possibilities. The Spanish Left had been making gains for years, both electorally and through trade unions (especially the anarchist CNT). After the 1936 election, when a "Popular Front" coalition of Communists, socialists, unionists, and liberals took control of the government, the country was polarized—workers and peasants on one side; the army, the Church, landowners, Royalists, and the fascist Falange on the other. It wasn't long before the Right launched a coup, led by General Francisco Franco. With the army pitted against the government it fell to the people to defend themselves—and they did. Unions and political parties organized militias, and soon the fascist advance was halted. Spain was divided.

There were wars within wars and revolutions within revolutions. With government control almost absent outside of Madrid, the population quickly pushed beyond the reforms of the Popular Front. Workers took over factories. Peasants collectivized land. Anarchists burned churches. Women took an active role—sometimes fighting in the militias, more commonly working in the factories. In many places, money itself was abolished. By attacking when they did, the fascists paralyzed the government and made possible exactly the revolution they had sought to prevent.

Republican Spain appealed for help, but the western democracies declared themselves neutral. Britain, France, and the United States did worse than stand idly by: they actively prevented munitions and even humanitarian supplies from reaching the Republic. They froze the Spanish government's funds, but they allowed trading to continue with the Nationalist side. Among governments, only the Soviet Union sent substantial aid.[7] Still, one cannot say that the Republic was abandoned. While their governments stood aside, tens of thousands of people sympathetic to the Republican cause enlisted in International Brigades, traveled to Spain, and fought. Most, but not all, were Communists. Hundreds of them died there.

Owing to his association with the Independent Labour Party, Orwell ended up joining the militia of a Trotskyist organization, the Workers' Party of Marxist Unification, or POUM.[8] With them he spent some months on the Aragon front until he was wounded by sniper fire. Ultimately, as the Communist Party gained control in the Republican territory, their rivals—including the POUM—were suppressed, and Orwell had to flee. Then, in 1939, the Republic fell and

Franco declared victory. Spain remained a dictatorship for more than three decades.

An Untrained Mob

Both the revolutionary aims of the war and the haste with which the Loyalists assembled themselves were evident in the armed forces, such as they were. At the beginning, the militias were made up entirely of volunteers, with little knowledge of firearms and no experience in combat. The division to which Orwell was assigned, for example, he described as "an untrained mob composed mostly of boys in their teens."[9] And their commanders were hardly more seasoned: "Men, who in private life were factory workmen, or lawyers, or orange growers, found themselves within a few weeks officers, commanding large bodies of men." Nearly everyone on the Republican side was forced "to learn the art of war virtually by practice."[10]

"How on earth could the war be won by an army of this type?" he wondered.[11] The very organization of the militia seemed to encourage insubordination: "There were officers and N.C.O.s, but there was no military rank in the ordinary sense; no titles, no badges, no heel-clicking and saluting."[12] And in general "a man could choose which section he should belong to and ... could also change to another bandera if he wanted to,"[13] and could resign without penalty at any time when he was due leave.[14] But, "considering the circumstances," Orwell admits, "they were better troops than one had any right to expect." Furthermore:

> it is a tribute to the strength of "revolutionary" discipline that the militias stayed in the field at all. For until about June, 1937, there was nothing to keep them there, except class loyalty.... A conscript army in the same circumstances—with its battle-police removed—would have melted away.[15]

Whatever their shortcomings, this rabble—with their ill-fitting uniforms, ancient rifles, and their refusal to salute—held the line against the fascist advance while a regular army assembled and trained at the rear. Were it not for the militia volunteers, Franco would have marched across Spain practically unopposed, and the Republic would have fallen almost without a fight.[16]

A Popular Army, or the People Armed?

After about a year, the volunteer militias were either disbanded or absorbed into the Communist-controlled Popular Army, "modeled as far as possible on an ordinary bourgeois army, with a privileged officer-caste, immense differences of pay, etc etc." This consolidation was explained at the time as a matter of military necessity, but it ultimately proved to be a kind of counter-revolution. As Orwell saw it,

> the undoubted purpose of the change was to strike a
> blow at equalitarianism. In every department the same
> policy has been followed, with the result that only a
> year after the outbreak of war and revolution you get
> what is in effect an ordinary bourgeois State, with, in
> addition, a reign of terror to preserve the *status quo*.[17]

Whether the process of army-building is inherently counter-revolutionary, I am not sure, but there is a good case to be made. At the very least, it seems to be the logical consequence of putting the priority on the military aspects of the conflict rather than on the political dimension. The theory was that the war had to be won before the revolution could proceed, but in fact, militarization only insured that the revolution was over before the war was. Where untrained and ill-equipped workers had fought the fascists to a stalemate while simultaneously reorganizing society, the new army, with its formal discipline and Soviet guns, abandoned the revolution and decisively lost the war.

Orwell was later convinced that the only way to win would have been to let the revolution proceed.[18] He saw that the workers had fought, often against great odds, because they had seen the gains they had made and felt instinctively that they were worth defending. "For the Spanish militias, while they lasted, were a sort of microcosm of a classless society."[19] As he explained in *Homage to Catalonia*: "The essential point of the [militia] system was social equality between officers and men. Everyone from general to private drew the same pay, ate the same food, wore the same clothes, and mingled on terms of complete equality."[20] By embodying the ideas of the revolution, making its aims something more than trite slogans or distant goals, the militia system put the whole relationship of rank, and the process of discipline, on an entirely new basis:

> In a workers' army discipline is theoretically voluntary. It is based on class-loyalty, whereas the discipline of a bourgeois conscript army is based ultimately on fear.... When a man refused to obey an order you did not immediately get him punished; you first appealed to him in the name of comradeship.[21]

This arrangement may sound idealistic, but Orwell argued, "In practice the democratic 'revolutionary' type of discipline is more reliable than might be expected." And moreover, "The discipline of even the worst drafts of militia visibly improved as time went on." His own experience in command gave him the opportunity to witness this change:

> In January the job of keeping a dozen raw recruits up to the mark almost turned my hair grey. In May for a short while I was acting-lieutenant in command of about thirty men, English and Spanish. We had all been under fire for months, and I never had the slightest difficulty in getting an order obeyed or in getting men to volunteer for a dangerous job.[22]

This "gradual improvement in discipline," he thought, "was brought about almost entirely by 'diffusion of revolutionary consciousness.'" But this consciousness was not a matter of learning to think in Marxist slogans, or unquestioning adherence to the prevailing doctrine.[23]

Instead it was developed through "endless arguments and explanations as to *why* such and such a thing was necessary."[24] Revolutionary discipline, in other words, was founded on principles exactly opposite those of normal military discipline.

Because the fighters understood what was at stake, and because they could see the ideals they fought for being realized, both in the larger society and in the militia itself, they were willing to accept discipline and follow orders. They would endure hardship and expose themselves to danger in part because the goal was a worthy one, but as importantly, because they could see that the risks and the sacrifices were shared, if not precisely equally, then at least among equals. Orwell would later reflect:

> Almost certainly the main reason why the Spanish Republic could keep up the fight for two and a half years against impossible odds was that there were no gross contrasts of wealth. The people suffered horribly, but they all suffered alike. When the private soldier had not a cigarette, the general had not one either.[25]

Three Lessons

One should always be careful when drawing lessons from extraordinary circumstances. And it is important that we not romanticize the facts of revolutionary warfare:

> The essential horror of army life ... is barely affected by the nature of the war you happen to be fighting in.... Bullets hurt, corpses stink, men under fire are often so frightened that they wet their trousers.... A louse is a louse and a bomb is a bomb, even though the cause you are fighting for happens to be just.[26]

However, Orwell's view of the Spanish militias seems to me to present several considerations that will be important to any organization trying to achieve both internal democracy and revolutionary discipline.

First, it is striking that what initially may appear to be the organizational weaknesses of the militia system—the challenging of authority, the refusal of automatic obedience, "the fact that you often had to argue for five minutes before you could get an order obeyed"[27]—turned out, in fact, to be its real virtues. For these were deep expressions of the values for which the soldiers were fighting. They were the features that distinguished their army from the enemy's. And so they were precisely the means by which loyalty was cemented and discipline ensured. Orwell described "those enormous arguments" as the "means [by] which discipline is gradually hammered out in revolutionary armies."[28]

Second, the move toward military discipline and centralized authority was *not* a temporary expedient necessitated by the war. It signaled, instead, the political defeat of the revolution and may have accelerated the military defeat as well. By separating the aims of the war from the goals of the revolution, the Communist government greatly damaged public morale, undercut the basis for international working-class solidarity, divided the left-wing forces against one another, and eliminated any possibility of a revolt occurring behind Franco's lines.[29] "They made a militarised conscript army possible, but they also made it necessary."[30] This fact suggests, at the least, that we should be wary of sacrificing the democratic aspects of our organizations in the name of security, or to achieve some immediate tactical advantage. Military victory cannot be bought at the expense of political defeat.

And finally, there is the insight that "orders had to be obeyed, but … when you gave an order you gave it as comrade to comrade and not as superior to inferior."[31] There is a quality to the relationship between comrades, as opposed to that between superior and subordinate, that changes what it means to issue, or receive, instructions. In such circumstances it matters very much whether we act from a sense of trust or out of fear; whether the order can be challenged and rationally defended; whether the context is one of mutual respect and shared sacrifice, or contrariwise, whether we are treated as instruments rather than as an individuals. A great deal depends on the difference between a comrade and an apparatchik.

The militia system managed to combine a respect for authority with a resistance to authoritarianism. The militia (as Orwell quickly learned) did not tolerate the bullying of troops by their commanders. It attached neither material incentives nor social privileges to promotion through the ranks. Though it depended on a combination of personal loyalty and political commitment to ensure discipline, it did nothing to discourage questioning orders or voicing dissenting opinions.[32] In all these respects, the militia differed from a regular army—whether that army was controlled by fascists, Communists, or simply a bourgeois officer class—and further, the militia system worked as well as it did precisely because of those differences.

Two Cases from My Own Experience

In my political work, which has been chiefly anarchist—or, at least, anarchistic—more is accomplished through persuasion than ever attempted by command. Yet I have also, at times, been in the position of issuing instructions or receiving them.

For example, as a member of Rose City Copwatch, I was occasionally chosen by my peers to lead a copwatch team, a job that largely consisted of making tactical decisions about where to position our observers, how to coordinate our movements, and the like. Performing that role at an anti-police demonstration—one of a series characterized by escalating clashes between cops and anarchists—I once sent people I love rushing toward the spot where riot police were moving in against the black bloc.[33] Violence seemed inevitable, and I sent my team straight into the fray.

On the other hand, in a different context, I once received a cryptic phone call summoning me to a meeting. Not knowing with whom I was meeting or why—only that the call came from a trusted source, and he said it was urgent—I canceled my plans and headed across town. When I arrived I was given a quick synopsis of the situation and asked to serve as a sentry. I spent that night, alert but bored, with a small group watching over the home of a man who had been threatened by a gang of white supremacists—likely the same group who had recently shot and crippled a local anti-racist skinhead.

Such instances are not typical of my experience, but it was precisely the day-to-day familiarity—the discussion, the cooperation, the concern, even the arguments—that made it possible to act under those heightened circumstances. No one could have *made* me lose a night's sleep to protect an aging peacenik, and no one had to. And I was aware, even as I gave my instructions to the copwatch team, that there was nothing I could do to force them to obey. Had they refused, I could only give up my position.

As it happened, they did not refuse; they did not even hesitate. They hurried, instead, toward the conflict, toward the danger. And while I am sure that my judgment was sound—that any other copwatcher, in fact, would have made the same decision, and that I would have followed just as readily—had any of my team been hurt, I know I would have been responsible, and I would have blamed myself deeply. I knew it even as I gave the instructions. That responsibility was, in a sense, implied by the very act.

My authority depended entirely on their trust in me. And that trust—not only in my intent, but in my tactical sense and my judgment—was precisely the reason they selected me for the job. Their trust in *me* was largely forged in the process of working together, of planning and debating, and navigating disagreements. More importantly, though, their trust in *the position* depended on the organization's egalitarian, democratic culture. The "Decision-Maker on Patrol" (DMOP) was elected at the beginning of each shift specifically to make tactical decisions according to our training, established guidelines, and copwatching policy. It was expected that, time permitting, after every police encounter the entire group would debrief, discussing how we did and how we could perform better. Questions or concerns about the DMOP's decisions would be raised then and, if the group wished, the position could be rotated at that point as well.

More broadly, though, authority could be delegated this way for particular types of tasks precisely because in the normal course of events everyone's voice counted, everyone had a say. We could entrust a single person to make tactical decisions *because* we were used to making decisions together. Our decision-making process, to which we were obsessively devoted, emphasized deliberation and encouraged patient discussion. As our facilitation guidelines outlined:

> In general, debate should be treated as a valued part of the decision-making process, not as an obstacle or a distraction between the proposal and the vote. Thinking and discussing together allows us to improve our understanding, correct for individual biases, and refine our ideas. Disagreements will inevitably occur, and should be seen as a valuable aspect of the democratic process. Our willingness to respectfully consider diverse opinions, to both offer and accept criticism, will be a mark of our commitment to democracy.[34]

Not only had the political and strategic decisions been made collectively and in advance, but also the organization's democratic structure—and as important, its democratic culture—worked to ensure that the authority bestowed in one area not expand or become generalized.

Of course, not everything is guard duty or copwatching, and we can find less dramatic examples of the type of leadership I'm discussing in the regular events of our daily lives. Usually they go unremarked on or even unnoticed. I'm talking about things as simple as deferring to the expertise, experience, or technical proficiency of our colleagues. And sometimes authority is just a matter of appointing someone to coordinate some area of activity and then letting them coordinate it. In that sense, it can be a trivial accompaniment to any division of labor—delegating routine executive or administrative decisions to the people doing the work. That limited notion of authority is not at odds with autonomy; it can actually be an expression of collective self-management.

Leadership as Privilege

One problem that persists, even within radically democratic organizations, is the tendency to select leaders from among those groups already privileged in the larger society.[35] The method of selection is almost a matter of indifference if the *same people* tend to gain power.[36] Orwell reported:

> In the POUM militia there was a slight but perceptible tendency for people of bourgeois origins to be chosen as officers. Given the existing class-structure of society I regard this as inevitable. Middle-class and upper-class people have usually more self-confidence in unfamiliar circumstances, and in countries where conscription is not in force they usually have more military tradition than the working class.[37]

Leadership, of course, comes in many varieties and each type suggests something of the virtues required of those who exercise it. Characteristics laudable in a teacher, an advisor, or a moderator will not always be the same as those required in an editor or a militia captain.[38] Those who would serve in a position of command need to have not only a grasp of strategy and the ability to make themselves understood, but also a sort of personal bearing that communicates, silently and effectively, that their instructions are to be followed. This personal quality is sometimes described as charisma, but that is not quite right: effective leaders may be personally disliked and yet retain their sense of authority and respect.[39] What the position requires, as Orwell suggests, is a kind of confidence—a decisiveness, a willingness to commit and take responsibility, and perhaps above all, an assumption that what one says *matters* and the expectation that it will be taken seriously. In the society we live in—stratified by race, class, gender, nationality, and so on—some people are trained to give orders almost from birth, and others are drilled in taking them. The means of instilling these lessons can be as subtle as the rules of etiquette or as blunt as a policeman's club. As Orwell observed:

> A person of bourgeois origin goes through life with some expectation of getting what he wants, within reasonable limits. Hence the fact that in times of stress "educated" people tend to come to the front; they

are no more gifted than the others and their "education" is generally quite useless in itself, but they are accustomed to a certain amount of deference and consequently have the cheek necessary to a commander. That they *will* come to the front seems to be taken for granted, always and everywhere.[40]

Now, these habits of entitlement and deference, ingrained as they are into each of us, do not go away just because we become ideologically committed to equality. And what poses greater difficulties, the difference is not merely one of outlook or perception; it is likely also to correspond to real differences in experience, and in the particular social skills needed to make one's voice heard and to achieve compliance. These personal characteristics and interpersonal skills are even more important where coercive measures are unavailable or impractical—in other words, in an egalitarian organization rather than a rigid hierarchy, in a revolutionary militia rather than a traditional army.[41]

There is no perfect answer for this problem. The ultimate solution naturally lies with changing society, so that inequalities based on race, gender, and so on disappear and cultural expectations about what leaders are *like* grow broader. In the short term, it may be that the best we can do will be to help encourage the qualities of leadership in *all* the members of our organizations, and take practical steps to help develop them. I believe that democratic practices, almost by definition, do much to assist that process. But it is important that we all become more accustomed—simultaneously—to collective decision making, *and* to the exercise of responsible leadership when the duty falls to us, *and* to taking orders and following instructions as one aspect of our commitment to democracy. Strict discipline and social equality are not, in this sense, in opposition; the exercise of each relies on the other.

Limiting Leadership

The important thing to note about such exercises in leadership is just how *limited* they are. Authority in these cases is contextual, it is contingent, and it is restricted to a fairly narrow sphere of competence. We must always be alert to keep it inside those bounds. We must guard against the danger of authority reaching beyond its justifications, or leadership ossifying into a permanent hierarchy. (Orwell was later to state that the "moral" of *Animal Farm* is "that revolutions only effect a radical improvement when the masses are alert and know how to chuck out their leaders as soon as the latter have done their job.")[42] Of course structural checks, such as rotating roles and making leaders subject to immediate recall, go some distance toward preserving the democratic character of the relationship. But the *culture* of our organizations is at least as important. Those who are in positions of responsibility, and those they direct, should always keep in mind exactly *why* they are in that position, what its purpose is, and what its limits are. Leaders cannot be allowed to insulate themselves from criticism, or to suppress disagreements; their position must always depend on the approval of their comrades, especially those they lead. They must not be above debate; instead, their position ought to *invite* debate. Likewise, no one should be allowed to use his position to accrue personal privileges or advance a private agenda. In a healthily functioning group, the surest way to lose leadership would be to abuse it.

It may be helpful in closing to recall this remark, from the anarchist Mikhail Bakunin:

> Hostile as I am to the authoritarian conception of discipline, I nevertheless recognize that a certain kind of discipline, not authoritarian but voluntary and intelligently understood, is, and will ever be, necessary whenever a greater number of individuals undertake any kind of collective work or action. Under these circumstances, discipline is simply the voluntary and considered coordination of all individual efforts for a common purpose.
>
> At the moment of revolution, in the midst of the struggle, there is a natural division of functions according to the aptitude of each, assessed and judged by the collective whole: Some direct and others carry

out orders. But no function remains fixed and it will not remain permanently and irrevocably attached to any one person. Hierarchical order and promotion do not exist, so that the executive of yesterday can become the subordinate of tomorrow. No one rises above the others, and if he does rise, it is only to fall back again a moment later, like the waves of the sea forever returning to the salutary level of equality.[43]

There are times in all of our lives, even as we fight for our freedom, when we have to do things that we would rather not do, when we must act with imperfect information and even against our own inclinations, when we must serve as one part of a larger unit, and do so reliably if only because others rely on us. There are times when we must give things up, even things that are very dear, and we may not always know whether what we gain has been worth the price. And sometimes, what may be harder still, we may have to ask similar sacrifices of others.

Chapter Seven

"Meanwhile, What About Socialism?"
Why the Left Fails

"Meanwhile," Orwell begins the eleventh chapter of *The Road to Wigan Pier*, "what about Socialism?"[1]

The question comes after more than a hundred pages detailing the conditions of English miners and after a fifty-page autobiographical interlude meditating on the differences between the lower and the middle classes (from the perspective of the latter). The fact that Socialism makes its appearance abruptly, and in a question, is significant. Socialism is not a logical consequence of what has come before; it is not a foregone conclusion. It is one possibility among many, and, while Orwell considers it the best system available, he does not take that judgment for granted. Though he feels that the essence of Socialism—"the idea that we must all co-operate and see to it that everyone does his fair share of work and gets his fair share of the provisions"—is "elementary common sense," he nevertheless recognizes that "Socialism is *not* establishing itself," that "Socialists almost everywhere are in retreat," and "[the] average thinking person ... is actively hostile to Socialism." Orwell then, contemplates the reasons for this state of affairs, looking at the question from the perspective of "the ordinary objector to Socialism," and taking seriously "the kind of thing ... [such a person] always starts by saying when you tax him on the subject."[2]

First Impressions

Of the problems Orwell identifies, the first—and perhaps the hardest to correct—is the character of the Socialists themselves: "As with the Christian religion, the worst advertisement for Socialism is its adherents."[3]

In *Coming Up for Air*, Orwell did his best to picture what the Left must look like to an unusually observant but otherwise typical member of the sinking middle classes. George Bowling, a middle-aged insurance salesman, visits a meeting of the Left Book Club. The evening's lecture is titled "The Menace of Fascism," and the presenter is introduced as a "'well-known anti-Fascist,' very much as you might call somebody 'the well-known pianist.'"[4] The talk itself is a bore—"Democracy, Fascism, Democracy"—and Bowling barely bothers to listen. "But somehow it interested me to watch him. A rather mean little man, with a white face and a bald head, standing on a platform, shooting out slogans. What's he doing? Quite deliberately, and quite openly, he's stirring up hatred. Doing his damnedest to make you hate certain foreigners called Fascists."[5] Bowling closes his eyes for a moment and, blocking out the words, concentrates simply on the man's voice, on its pitch and timbre. He tries to put himself in the mind of a person who would speak in such a way.

For about a second I was inside him.... I saw the vision
that he was seeing.... What he's *saying* is merely that
Hitler's after us and we must all get together and have a
good hate. Doesn't go into details. Leaves it all respectable. But what he's *seeing* is something quite different.
It's a picture of himself smashing people's faces in with
a spanner.... Smash! Right in the middle! The bones
cave in like an eggshell and what was a face a minute
ago is just a great big blob of strawberry jam. Smash!
There goes another! ... And it's all O.K. because the
smashed faces belong to Fascists. You could hear all
that in the tone of his voice.[6]

Not so much listening to the speaker as observing him, Bowling re-
alizes something else as well: "He *means* it. Not faking at all.... Every
slogan's gospel truth to him. If you cut him open all you'd find inside would be Democracy-Fascism-Democracy.... Perhaps even his
dreams are slogans."[7]

Looking around at the audience hardly improves Bowling's mood.
There is the event organizer ("a mild-looking chap, with a pink, baby's bottom kind of face," which gives the impression "that he's probably a virgin"); a row of women, most of whom sit passively "like
lumps of pudding"; two old men, lifelong members of the Labour
Party, confused after years of agitation and blacklisting to find themselves suddenly outflanked and irrelevant; the full membership of
the local Communist Party ("All three of them very young"); and
finally, a single Trotskyist ("even younger ... very thin, very dark,
nervous-looking"). Of these last four, Bowling remarks, "You knew
they'd be on their feet the moment question-time started." He recognizes, however, that the eager activists are the exception and, in fact,
"only about half a dozen" among the audience "had really grasped
what the lecturer was talking about."[8] The effect, more than anything else, is one of mild disappointment. "We're the West Bletchley
revolutionaries," Bowling reflects with a certain self-conscious irony.
"Doesn't look hopeful on first sight."[9]

Unsatisfactory Types

Orwell, owing both to his circumstances and to his disposition, was harsher when speaking in his own voice, announcing that Socialism "appeals chiefly to unsatisfactory or even inhuman types." The most common of these, as outlined in *The Road to Wigan Pier*, are two: "On the one hand, you have the warm-hearted unthinking Socialist, the typical working-class Socialist, who only wants to abolish poverty and does not always grasp what this implies."[10] Such naive and well-meaning people are always the soul and the strength of the movement. They do genuinely want a world of freedom and equality—though their idea of it may not extend much beyond "better wages and shorter hours and nobody bossing you about."[11] They are the people you can count on to show up to your early-morning picket, without worrying about them second-guessing your tactics, denouncing your demands as reformist, or scrutinizing your handbills for minor deviations from their own preferred line. In fact, Orwell claims, "The working-class Socialist, like the working-class Catholic, is weak on doctrine and can hardly open his mouth without uttering a heresy, but he has the heart of the matter in him."[12] Of course their influence is nil.

Prominent positions—ideological, cultural, or institutional—seem always to go to the *other* type: "the intellectual, book-trained Socialist," invariably "from the middle class." This second group includes an array of smaller sub-types, such as:

> the foaming denouncers of the bourgeoisie, and the more-water-in-your-beer reformers of whom [George Bernard] Shaw is the prototype, and the astute young social-literary climbers who are Communists now, as they will be Fascists five years hence ... and all that dreary tribe of high-minded women and sandal-wearers and bearded fruit-juice drinkers who come flocking towards the smell of "progress" like blue-bottles to a dead cat.[13]

Somehow these are the people who inevitably set the tone of meetings, who write the columns in newsletters, who fuel sectarian rifts and petty controversies, and who reliably manage to find fault with any idea not originating from their own special clique.

In a movement so crowded with eccentrics and crackpots, it is only natural that "the ordinary decent person, who is in sympathy with the *essential* aims of Socialism, is given the impression that there is no room for his kind."[14]

The Broad Left

Orwell ties this rather unappealing picture to something called "Socialism" (with a capital *S*). But it is important to remember that his concept of "Socialism" was extremely broad: "Socialism means justice and common decency."[15] Moreover, Orwell's complaints apply equally well across the Left, from tepid liberals to insurrectionary anarchists to cultish Maoists, and likewise also to movements that are clearly progressive, but not chiefly concerned with the economic system (*e.g.*, feminism, pacifism, environmentalism, animal rights, and so on). Admittedly, the sketch he offers us is a caricature, and so the worst qualities are exaggerated. And many of the details—especially sneering references to vegetarians and feminists—date rather badly, since the ideas he was so quick to dismiss have since gained a wider, and practically mainstream, acceptance. Still, the fact that the image he presents remains immediately recognizable most of a century later may tell us something about the weaknesses of our movements.

In the Left today, we find on the one hand the figure of the "serious" activist, for whom "organizing" and "actions" are as much ends as means. His evenings are filled with meetings, his vocabulary cluttered with acronyms and jargon, and he looks forward to the next "demo" the way other people look forward to a long weekend. One can never quite tell what inspires such tireless commitment, since he seems to *have* no other interests outside of his chosen cause. Then there is his opposite number: the scenester, the hipster, the *poseur*—a type common to every counterculture, whose views on politics are exactly on par with his taste in clothing and just as liable to change. What must strike any outside observer is the multiple points at which these two contrasting types actually connect—their moralism and obsessive purity, their rigid and doctrinaire thinking, the strict adherence to articles of faith even in the face of overriding evidence, the constant tone of outrage that they attach to every possible subject, the bitter sectarian squabbling, the self-righteousness and self-importance.

Beyond these two main types, there are also those for whom the movement represents a fad or an amusement; those who treat politics as an affordable alternative to therapy; those who see it as a way to make friends or get laid; those who pursue it as a career, either among the underpaid and ineffectual staff of a progressive nonprofit, or else in the suffocating cocoon of academia; and the status-seekers who want chiefly to put themselves on display and be admired.

Playing With Fire

It goes without saying that if a movement allows such submerged motives and blatant dysfunction to predominate, it will only ever succeed, even in trivial matters, by accident. That may be just as well, however, since the objectives such people declare, often as not, seem undesirable on their face. Writing in the thirties, Orwell was suspicious of the Left's love for industrialization, regulation, and the sort of soft Utopia in which all the difficulty, and with it all the meaning, has been drained from human life. (That worry supplies the substance of the twelfth chapter of *Wigan Pier*.) His concerns reflected the dominance of Marxism at the time. Today we have almost the opposite problem, as radical politics becomes little more than a hoarding of rejections—a movement of many Nos and zero Yeses, which defines itself always *against* some preferably indistinct adversary but proposes no positive ideal toward which to move.[16] At the extremes, such thinking tips over into "anti-civ" (that is, anticivilization) apocalypse fantasies or a confused nihilism whose moralistic hectoring is ill-concealed by its anti-moral rhetoric. Closer to the center, we find those insurrectionists who insist on militancy as a kind of first principle but refuse to formulate any specific goals for which they are fighting.

We have thus become locked in a vicious cycle of purism and defeat, convinced that since no victory is ever total, no victory is ever real—which, as Orwell pointed out, amounts to saying that "half a loaf is the same as no bread."[17] If there's no chance for victory, then there is no need for strategy, no room for compromise, no point in hard work and sacrifice. Actions may yet be taken—but only the purest actions, and only as a kind of self-expression. Since it can have no real effect, the important thing is the act itself—its symbolic value, its emotive quality. Orwell felt that such complacency, in addition to being sickening, was in fact also dangerous. He thus upbraided Auden for using the phrase "necessary murder" in the poem "Spain," declaring: "It could only be written by a person to whom murder is at most a *word*," the sort of person who "is always somewhere else when the trigger is pulled." The problem was not unique to Auden; he was simply a prominent example of a common fault—advocacy divorced from any realistic notion of the implications. Violence, Orwell thought, is easier to romanticize when one enjoys, in daily life, the expectation of a certain amount of peace and security. As a result, "So much of left-wing thought is a kind of playing with fire by people who don't even know that fire is hot."[18]

A great many Leftists seem to have little notion, or even concern, as to what practical outcomes might follow were their proposals put into effect. The primitivist's destruction of civilization, the Leninist's proletarian dictatorship, the pacifist's disavowal of all violence, the anarchist's refusal of all coercion, the separatist's ethnic state—all of these, aside from obvious questions about whether they would be workable, inevitably entail some consequences that would be not only undesirable but unacceptable. Adherents of such "smelly little orthodoxies"[19] usually respond either by retreating to an idealized version of the post-revolutionary paradise, in which all inherent difficulties have been resolved by some combination of magical thinking and good intentions, or else they celebrate the inevitable human suffering as evidence of their own hard realism and revolutionary virtue.

At the same time, there is the utter failure to think seriously about what it would take to actually bring about any sort of radical change, a failing facilitated by what Orwell described as our "utter ignorance of the way things actually happen."[20] Leftists are often astonishingly ignorant about the institutions they oppose and seek to overthrow—whether private companies, national governments, the local police, the courts, or the media—and so they frequently read complicated and conspiratorial motives into mere bureaucratic routine, assign absurd importance to trivial details and expend enormous effort pressuring the wrong targets and forwarding irrelevant demands. They are likewise quick to talk in vague and idealized terms of general strikes, insurrections, ruptures, and revolutions, of workers taking over factories, or communities controlling institutions like hospitals and schools—all without any concrete idea of how to organize on the scale required or any notion of the way large institutions operate internally.

All of that is understandable given the complexity of modern society. What is less understandable, and certainly less forgivable, is the refusal to learn from our mistakes or even to develop a healthy curiosity about the source of our failures. So much political thought takes the form of a Just-So story in which things always happen by a predictable moral formula: downtrodden masses, wicked oppressors, heroic revolt, brutal repression, cynical betrayals—a cycle repeated endlessly until the inevitable, yet always deferred, final victory and the arrival of Utopia. Questions of fact become confused with questions of principle, and ideological certitude is substituted for empirical enquiry. Our thinking becomes circular, our movements insular.

Static Extremism

Such practices make sense if we simply want to clamor for change, but remain indifferent as to whether it actually arrives. Looking back on the wasted opportunities of the thirties, Orwell wrote:

> All through the between-war years no Socialist programme that was both revolutionary and workable ever appeared; basically, no doubt, because no one genuinely wanted any major change to happen. The Labour leaders wanted to go on and on, drawing their salaries and periodically swapping jobs with the

Conservatives. The Communists wanted to go on and on, suffering a comfortable martyrdom, meeting with endless defeats and afterwards putting the blame on other people. The left-wing intelligentsia wanted to go on and on, sniggering at the [Colonel] Blimps, sapping away at middle-class morale, but still keeping their favoured positions as hangers-on of the dividend-drawers. Labour Party politics had become a variant of Conservatism, "revolutionary" politics had become a game of make-believe.[21]

Again, simply altering the proper nouns, the situation is only too familiar.

The temptation is clear: there is a freedom in knowing that nothing one advocates will ever come to pass, but it is the freedom of irresponsibility. By insisting on only the most radical position, one can, in a single stroke, free oneself from responsibility for the world as it is and from any responsibility to alter it. One can also, therefore, free oneself from the burden of figuring out how to achieve one's aims, of questioning and challenging our own best theories, of concern for the truth. All that is required, instead, is an obsessive focus on the incidentals—the right idiom, the right diet, the right books, the right sexuality, the right friends—in an awkward combination of Puritanism and status-seeking.[22] Most of all, one must maintain a hypocritical concern with *other people's* choices and be always willing to castigate them, in public if possible, for falling short of standards that must be at once exacting and undefined. For those who take this route, "the whole Socialist movement is no more than a kind of exciting heresy-hunt."[23] Rather than seeming destructive, distracting, or simply unfortunate, by this way of thinking the endless drama of disputes, denunciations, call-outs, confessions, expulsions, purges, and splits is largely *the point* of politics. The tendency, then, is not to build a movement, but to winnow it, and to encourage in its remaining loyalists a mindset characterized not by feelings of solidarity and shared hopes for a better future, but by mutual suspicion and competitive fault-finding.[24]

Identity and Solidarity

At the center of this outlook, the thing that makes it an ideology rather than simply a neurosis, is an expansive, impervious, and unyielding concept of "privilege."

What was once a theory of social stratification has become instead a measure of individual authenticity and personal worth.[25] Privilege—whether attached to race, class, gender, age, physical ability, mental health, nationality, education, linguistic fluency, housing, body type, or whatnot[26]—exists in an inverse proportion to left-wing credibility. The logical outcome is not only an identity politics, but also an identity epistemology: all claims are to be evaluated not by weighing the available evidence or the reasons proffered, but simply according to the status of those making the case. All arguments, then, become arguments from authority; all disagreements are only ever power struggles; and the only critique that matters is the *ad hominem* attack. Even to come from a reasonably comfortable background is enough to permanently cast suspicion on your political commitments and disqualify your opinions on a whole range of subjects. Oppression, on the other hand, makes a person infallible—at least until his ideas are challenged by someone *more* oppressed.

The reasons for this outlook are generally a confused mix combining a vanguardist quest for "the revolutionary subject," a philanthropic (and often paternalistic) urge to help "the most oppressed," personal guilt and a desire to overcome feelings of complicity in grave injustices, and a psychological need to feel oneself a part of something large and important while also surrendering personal responsibility. The resulting approach, as one of the contributors to the collection *Taking Sides* concludes, "doesn't move us in a liberatory direction—only toward increased self-righteousness and plays for power."[27]

The problem is not with the concept of "privilege" as such and not even with the recognition that people who enjoy such privileges will have to make real sacrifices in the struggle for equality. The problem instead is with the Left's tendency to convert sociological analyses into moral categories, to flatten complexity and multiplicity into simplistic dualisms, to devolve political struggle to the level of individual virtue, and in the process to turn good ideas into their approximate opposites.[28] By stressing the differences dividing groups rather than the commonalities connecting them, such thinking discounts the possibilities of solidarity, putting in its place the more tentative, and less mutual, concern for being a good "ally."[29] The tendency is to invert hierarchies rather than dismantle them, which can quickly devolve toward the position that "some … are more equal than others."[30] One result is a perverse competition that has commonly been derided as the "Oppression Olympics."[31] Another is the branding as enemies of people we ought to be recruiting.[32]

In the worst case, these practices may encourage members of privileged groups to respond in kind, adopting a reactionary identity politics of their own and fighting to preserve their favored position. When the Left pushes away whole groups of people, there is always the danger that where we push them will be to the Right. Taking himself as a sample case, Orwell writes:

> Once again, here am I, with my middle-class origins and my income of about three pounds a week from all sources. For what I am worth it would be better to get me in on the Socialist side than to turn me into a Fascist. But if you are constantly bullying me about my "bourgeois ideology," if you give me to understand that in some subtle way I am an inferior person because I have never worked with my hands, you will only succeed in antagonising me. For you are telling me either that I am inherently useless or that I ought to alter myself in some way that is beyond my power. I cannot proletarianise my accent or certain of my tastes and beliefs, and I would not if I could.

The choice, as he describes it, is simple:

> Economically, I am in the same boat with the miner, the navvy and the farm-hand; remind me of that and I will fight at their side. But culturally I am different from the miner, the navvy and the farm-hand; lay the emphasis on that and you may arm me against them.[33]

This note of caution is not meant to suggest that injustices within the movement should go unchallenged. People with various kinds of privilege, if they are to be a useful part of a movement for equality, will necessarily need to learn to work with others as equals. That may be unfamiliar and even uncomfortable for them. "There is, after all, a real difference of manners and traditions between a bank clerk and a dock labourer, and the bank clerk's feeling of superiority is very deeply rooted." Sooner or later, "he will have to get rid of it"[34]—a process likely to involve a fairly intense period of self-examination, the challenging of assumptions, the broadening of sympathies, confronting subtle and even unconscious prejudices, and learning to recognize when a sense of entitlement or a tendency toward self-assertion might impose on, insult, or actually harm somebody else. It may even, ultimately, entail accepting material sacrifices, just as the end of imperialism may produce "at least a temporary drop in the English standard of life."[35]

That is all as it must be. But these sorts of changes in personal outlook are much likelier to be successful, or even earnestly attempted, *in the course of struggle*, rather than as a *prerequisite*. If, as Orwell suggests, "the sinking middle class" clings to their sense of rank "under the impression that it keeps them afloat," then "it is not good policy to *start* by telling then to throw away the life-belt."[36] However, "when Socialism is a living issue, a thing that large numbers of Englishmen genuinely care about, the class-difficulty may solve itself more rapidly than now seems thinkable." That is, "when the widely separate classes who, necessarily, should form any real Socialist party have fought side by side, they may feel differently about one another. And then perhaps this misery of class-prejudice will fade away."[37] Recalling his days as a tramp, Orwell wrote, "I have often been struck by how easy it is to get people to take you for granted if you and they are really in the same boat, and how difficult otherwise."[38]

The Left's approach of late has generally not been to engage with people on the basis of our shared hopes or common needs but instead to stress the differences between the righteous, enlightened few and the dull, ignorant, backward many—in other words, between *us* and *everyone else*. Such distinction ought not be a source of pride. The fact that a radical is always a rather exceptional sort of person—even amid growing inequality, prolonged economic crises, environmental catastrophes, international warfare, and widespread disillusionment with electoral politics—can only speak to the failures of the Left overall.

The wound is not only self-inflicted, it is partly deliberate. Too often "radical" is understood as a synonym for "marginal," and so our goals, our demands, our propaganda, our ways of organizing—in short, all of our efforts—are designed *not* to appeal to the millions of people who ought, whether from personal conscience or naked self-interest, to be on our side. We instead adopt practices that seem, and often in fact are, directed toward provoking, offending, chastising, and ultimately excluding those very same people. The failure of a movement to grow, by this way of thinking, is evidence of its radical virtue.[39]

Back to Basics

Orwell offers Socialism as the remedy to capitalism, but given this sorry report, one must wonder what will remedy Socialism. He thus begins the thirteenth chapter of *Wigan Pier*, again, with a question: "And finally, is there anything one can do about it?"[40]

The fantasy, of course, is that "the sandals ... could be put in a pile and burnt, and every vegetarian, teetotaler and creeping Jesus sent home to Welwyn Garden City to do his yoga exercises quietly! But that, I am afraid, is not going to happen."[41] However, "if the movement were invaded by better brains and more common decency, [then] the objectionable types would cease to dominate it." For the time being, there is no choice but to "set one's teeth and ignore them; they will loom much smaller when the movement has been humanised."[42]

To humanize the movement—to attract sufficient numbers that the crackpot theories and the petty dramas will be drowned in a sea of activity—"All that is needed is to hammer two facts home into the public consciousness. One, that the interests of all exploited people are the same; the other, that Socialism is compatible with common decency."[43] Whatever our differences, Orwell argues, "The only thing *for* which we can combine is the underlying ideal of Socialism: justice and liberty." But, then, he admits:

> it is hardly strong enough to call this ideal "underlying." It is almost completely forgotten. It has been buried beneath layer after layer of doctrinaire priggishness, party squabbles and half-baked "progressivism" until it is like a diamond hidden under a mountain of dung. The job of the Socialist is to get it out again.[44]

This task of digging the gem out of the dung heap and returning to essentials has nothing at all to do with ideological purity, political orthodoxy, or the "dialectic of the dialectic and what Trotsky said in 1917."[45] That, in fact, is the *opposite* of what Orwell had in mind. What he meant was something broader, something more vague but nevertheless more real, almost a feeling rather than an idea—like the stir of emotion drawn forth by the theme from *Star Wars*, the *Marseillaise*, Chaplin's address at the end of *The Great Dictator*, or Springsteen's tribute to Steinbeck's Tom Joad. What Orwell sought was the "original, half-forgotten objective of human brotherhood"[46]—an ideal that our slogans still sometimes invoke, yet cover like a shroud.

Chapter Eight

"Political Writing Is Bad Writing"

Anarchism and the English Language[1]

IN HIS CLASSIC ESSAY, "POLITICS AND THE ENGLISH LANGUAGE," Orwell makes the case that "the English language ... becomes ugly and inaccurate because our thoughts are foolish, but the slovenliness of our language makes it easier for us to have foolish thoughts."[2]

The vices Orwell catalogued—vague phrases, dying metaphors, jargon, and general pseudoscientific pretentiousness—all help to sustain our boring prose. But worse, they also produce a stagnant and stifling mental atmosphere in which *thought* is commonly replaced with the automatic recitation of certain prescribed words or phrases "tacked together," as Orwell memorably put it, "like the sections of a prefabricated hen-house."[3]

The effect on readers is certainly bad enough, but the implications for writers are more serious still. Sometimes, of course, vague and shoddy prose—and the readiness with which such is accepted—makes it possible for a writer to deliberately pass off one thing as another, or to hide bad reasoning in a rhetorical fog. More often, however, a well-meaning writer just accepts the standard currently in use and out of witless habit uses language that alters, obscures, or nullifies his own meaning. In such cases, the writer, too, is the victim: he means to say one thing and says another; or, he means to say something but says nothing instead.

This dynamic poses special problems for anarchism, as a mode of thought that shuns orthodoxy on principle and should be above defrauding an audience in the fashion typical of politicians and their parties. Anarchists face the further problem that, through clumsiness and inattention, our ideas become unintelligible. This destruction of meaning occurs at many levels simultaneously: It is impossible to convince people of an idea if one cannot explain it; it is equally impossible to explain an idea if you do not understand it yourself; and it is impossible to adequately understand an idea if its only means of expression frustrate any efforts to define or analyze it. Through this process political theories are transformed into something like the Latin mass: we in the congregation may not understand the priest's ritual mumblings, but we believe that the words will save us.

Consider, for example, a sentence like "To be allies, cis men need to check their privilege."

Such a sentence is, by contemporary anarchist standards, utterly unremarkable and may even be regarded as a truism. And it contains several features that make it representative of the type of writing I am discussing. The first thing one ought to notice is the unattractive and the peculiarly *un*-persuasive quality of the language. Simply reading the words, it is very difficult to accept that only a single century separates this writing from the prose of Edward Carpenter or Peter Kropotkin.

Even apart from its plain ugliness, the writing is indecipherable to the uninitiated. It is dense with vague jargon terms and offers neither a single original turn of phrase, nor an image of any kind. Of its brief ten words, one—*cis*, an abbreviation of *cisgender*—only exists in certain marginal academic departments and in a very narrow sliver of the political spectrum. Three others—*allies*, *check*, and *privilege*—are everyday English words that here take on specialized meanings. And one of these is so ambiguous as to render the sentence practically meaningless: Does *check* mean to examine, or to verify? Does it mean to physically block (as in hockey), or threaten (as in chess), or to decline a bet (as in poker)? Does one check one's privilege the way one checks one's coat at the theater, to be retrieved again after the show? Like a lot of moralistic language, this phrase manages to be prescriptive without actually being instructive: it offers us a command, but it lacks the necessary specificity to actually tell anyone what they should do in any real-world circumstance.

I'm not complaining here that the language is difficult—on the whole it is not—but that it is unsalvageably vague. It is, or should be, a problem if your idiom makes it impossible for other people to grasp your ideas; but how much worse is it if your language helps you to hide your meaning even from yourself? To a very large degree, the language here is standing in for thought. People who write this sort of thing may have some general idea of what they are trying to say—but they needn't have. They've absorbed the correct words, the way a child memorizes the Pledge of Allegiance, without much concern as to whether the words correspond to anything in particular, either in the real world or even in one's imagination.

My above example is drawn from queer politics, but one could easily multiply the cases if one so chose. All branches of anarchism—primitivists, syndicalists, insurrectionists, CrimethInc—are similarly guilty, though the required code words and the preferred rhythm of the language may vary somewhat from clique to clique. You need only pick up any issue of any anarchist publication—no matter what faction it represents—to find at least one example of similar writing.

Many of the words that occur most commonly in anarchist writing are used, I suspect, with no precise meaning in mind—or at times, with a meaning quite different from the typical usage. *Accountability, community, solidarity,* and *freedom* are used, in the overwhelming number of cases, simply as markers to signify things we like or favor. When we read, for instance, that "organizers should be accountable to the community," we are left to wonder who this relationship is supposed to involve and are much less certain about what it is supposed to look like. When we read that some group wants to "hold sex offenders accountable," it is a fair and obvious question to ask what they propose to actually *do*. Do they want them to make a public statement of apology? Do they plan to beat them up? Or do they mean, by circular logic, that they will hold them accountable by calling for them to be held accountable? It is striking how seldom such questions are ever answered—but it is more striking still how seldom they are actually *asked*. In both cases, the key word—*accountability*—has been invoked, and that is thought somehow to be sufficient.

Too often, the point of writing this way is not so much to communicate a specific idea to some real or potential readership. The words serve instead to indicate a kind of group loyalty, an ideological border between our side and the other side: we believe *this*, and they don't. Or rather: we talk in *this* way and say *this* sort of thing; *they* talk in some other way, and say some other sort of thing.

Adopting the proper style allows one to demonstrate how radical one is. And it is a symptom of one's writing being shaped by concerns, often suppressed concerns, about orthodoxy. It becomes important, not only to think the right thoughts but also—sometimes even more so—to use the right words, as though one needs to punch in the correct code but doesn't need to remember why that particular series of letters was selected in the first place.

Underneath this practice of mental mimicry is the sense that words are imbued with a kind of mystical essence—some being good, others bad—irrespective of context or the use to which they are being put. The policing of language naturally follows, usually in the form of self-censorship but sometimes under public pressure. (I was once chastised for using the word *riot*; the more vague *uprising* or *rebellion* being preferable.) Once euphemism begins to creep in, it is a short distance to travel between political politeness and pure dishonesty.

At the same time, and following from the same impulse, much of our rhetoric takes on a ridiculously inflated quality. Protests become uprisings, on the one hand, while a drunken fight is described as *acting out* (unless, for other reasons, we label it *abuse*). In either case, the tendency is to write according to what *should have happened* under the terms of one's own favorite theory, rather than struggling to discover and describe events as they actually occurred.

The tendency toward rhetorical inflation is driven, I believe, by a desire to make ourselves seem bigger, better, or more important than we are—even if the only people we fool are ourselves. *Actions* sound tougher than *protests* or *rallies*, even if all we do at these actions is walk about with signs. And it is rather embarrassing in a political context to say "me and my friends," so instead we say *community* when we really mean scene, and *scene* when we really mean clique. But, isn't there the nagging suspicion that something has gone awry when we begin using the word *community* in a way that excludes our neighbors, the mail carrier, and members of our immediate family?

Once this pattern sets in, all sense of proportion washes out of our language. Descriptions of events shrink or swell, not according to any observable feature of anything that has happened but according to an *a priori* formula. One need only glance at the statements issued by competing sides in some recent anarchist controversy—the latest instantiation of the perennial debates over violence and nonviolence, or militant action versus base-building, will do—to recognize that the two sides do not just disagree about this or that specific incident, but where questions of fact arise each side takes an attitude of almost perfect indifference.

The linguistic drift is dangerous because it makes honest discussion impossible. And, maybe more worrisome, people are surprisingly willing to fall for their own propagandistic tricks. A political movement cannot expect to succeed, or even survive, if it cannot face reality. Moreover, if its members in very large numbers do lose touch with the world beyond their own manifestos, the movement probably will not even *deserve* to survive.

Anarchists, of course, are not the only people to write as though the words don't matter. Much current writing is straightforward nonsense—not only political writing, but also advertising copy, academic prose, legal decisions, religious sermons, and love songs. But aside from the slipshod quality of contemporary English, and beyond even the special vices of political propaganda, anarchism has acquired several faults that are more or less distinctive.

For instance, we seem to have acquired the dubious habit of adopting an everyday word, narrowing its meaning, and turning it into a kind of jargon. The above-mentioned *allies, privilege, accountability,* and *actions* are all examples—as are *process* (as a verb), *facilitate, recuperate, lifestyle* (as an adjective), *bottom-line* (verb), *safe space, spoke* (noun), *care* (noun), and *harm.*

Similarly, we sometimes take words that are necessarily relative and use them as though they were absolute. *Accessible* (or *inaccessible*) and *alternative* are the chief examples. Nothing just is accessible. It must be accessible *to someone.* Likewise, something can only be an alternative *to something else.* Saying that it's an alternative to the mainstream is just question-begging.

More embarrassing still, many of our jargon terms are not even our own, but have been appropriated, or misappropriated, from other traditions—Marxist, Foucauldian, post-modern, feminist, or Queer Theory. There's nothing wrong with that on its own, and I personally admire a willingness to take good ideas regardless of the source. But we've started writing like undergraduates imitating their professors. We say *hegemony* when we really just mean influence, and *contradiction* when we're talking about conflict, *performativity* instead of behavior, and so on. The results of this imitative habit are sometimes pretty odd: because of Foucault, it is now common in political writing to refer to *people* as *bodies.* Thanks to Hardt and Negri, we talk about Empire rather than imperialism. And, in a related development, we commonly talk about Capital rather than capitalism, and do so in a way that makes it sound like an ill-tempered deity rather than an economic system.

We too frequently present simple ideas with complex language because we think it makes us look smarter, edgier, or more radical. We pepper our language with technical terms just to show that we've done our homework. There seems to be an agreement on the Left that it is better to write in the style of badly translated Hegel than to write like John Steinbeck. It is even easier, provided you don't care to be understood.

The problem of course is not with the words themselves. The problem isn't even with abstraction. Any effort to apply the lessons from one case to another necessarily involves some form of abstraction. The problem is the avoidance of clarity in meaning. The solution is not simply to abstain from using certain words, or to substitute new jargon for old, but to do what we can to make our writing as clear as possible. We do that through the use of fresh imagery, of concrete detail, and by taking care to spell out precisely who and what we mean whenever we're tempted to invoke old spooks like "the people" or mystical processes like "struggle."

The point is not simply to describe the present state of anarchist writing but to reverse the trends that have brought us here. And while many of the examples in "Politics and the English Language" are now very much out of date, Orwell's advice remains sound. He offers one general principle, six rules, and six questions.

The principle is: "Let the meaning choose the word, and not the other way about."[4]

The rules are:

1. Never use a metaphor, simile or other figure of speech which you are used to seeing in print.
2. Never use a long word where a short one will do.
3. If it is possible to cut out a word, always cut it out.
4. Never use the passive [voice] where you can use the active.
5. Never use a foreign phrase, a scientific word or a jargon word if you can think of an everyday English equivalent.
6. Break any of these rules sooner than say anything outright barbarous.[5]

Were there a contemporary anarchist style guide, nearly all of these rules would be reversed: *Only* use figures of speech that you are used to seeing in print; *never* use a short word if a long word is available; If it is possible to add a word, *always* add it in; *never* use the active voice where you might use the passive; *always* use a foreign phrase or jargon word if the everyday English word can be avoided; and *write barbarously* rather than violate any of these rules.

No one has formalized such commandments, and no one has had to. The slow drift of the language, and the overall cloudiness of our thought, allows us to adopt such practices without trying and often without recognizing it. To break such habits, however, requires a conscious effort.

Orwell's advice, put as succinctly as possible, might be summarized: Think before you write. Specifically:

> A scrupulous writer, in every sentence that he writes, will ask himself at least four questions, thus: What am I trying to say? What word will express it? What image or idiom will make it clearer? Is this image fresh enough to have an effect? And he will probably ask himself two more: Could I put it more shortly? Have I said anything that is avoidably ugly?[6]

This approach assumes, of course, that the writer has some definite idea of what he intends to convey to the reader, that it is not his aim simply to cycle through the fashionable platitudes in order to represent the right line or to rehearse stock phrases for some imaginary debate.

The purpose of anarchist writing, I believe, is—or should be—not to demonstrate how radical we are, or to dazzle our friends with our erudition, but to improve the quality of anarchist thought, to give our ideas a broader circulation, and to use those ideas to help reshape the world. But in its present state our writing, taken as a whole, seems ill-suited to every one of these aims. It produces, instead, hazy thinking, political and intellectual insularity, and ultimately, irrelevance.

I don't mean to suggest that the only thing standing in the way of revolution is bad prose. But it is possible that a great deal of the nonsense could be shaken out of anarchism if we would commit ourselves to the clear expression of our ideas and if we would demand the same from the publications that we read. It is very difficult to write clearly unless one is also thinking clearly. And if a sentence cannot be translated from anarcho-English into plain English, there is a very good chance that it is meaningless.

Chapter Nine

The Tower of Babel and Other Confusions
A Reply to CrimethInc

My essay "Political Writing is Bad Writing" originally appeared in a pamphlet alongside a response from the anarchist collective CrimethInc, titled "English and the Anarchist Language."[1] Their reply is not so much a counterargument as a series of reservations, some of which fail to connect to any point that I actually raised. However, the misunderstanding itself is illuminating and may help to show where our politics differ.

CrimethInc's argument moves through three main points: first, that "language is not neutral; it incarnates the power relations of

the society that produced it."[2] The conventions of the language re-
produce the conventions of society and limit the range of meanings
that it is possible to communicate without also altering the language.
Therefore, "we shouldn't focus only on properly *designating* our ideas
via language, but on *destabilizing* the language itself—showing how it
is enemy territory and opening new points of departure."[3]

Second, and following from the previous argument: "A strict focus
on accuracy alone would never produce a Lewis Carroll or a Kathy
Acker."[4] And for that matter, CrimethInc asks:

> What is Orwell himself remembered for today—his
> essays, or his novels? His logic or his neologisms? His
> politics or his thoughtcrime? If not for the vitality of
> his imagination, his realism would never have reached
> us. He invented Newspeak to portray how language
> can be used to limit thought, but paradoxically he
> needed *new language* to convey this idea.[5]

They go on to observe the paradox of "bad writing that is *better* than
good writing" and to say that "the cheerful excesses of youth will always outshine more prudent prose."[6] They then move on to a defense
of "nonrepresentational expression," irony, ambiguity, and in general, plurality of meaning: "the more widely diverging [the readers']
responses, the better."[7] All of which is to say—part of what makes
anarchist writing *anarchist* is that it "must not establish new norms,
but open up spaces of free play and uncertainty."[8]

Third and finally, CrimethInc concludes that *rules* are not especially useful for communication, that some rules are worth violating,
and that sometimes the very thing "that makes it *worth* violating the
rules" is precisely what "makes it worth writing at all." In closing
they advise, "in defiance of Orwell and our own better judgement":
"*Write barbarously!*"[9]

This is not a bad argument, exactly, but it misses its target by a
wide measure. Neither Orwell nor I inveigh against imaginative writing, creative language, or multiplicity of meaning. In fact, Orwell's
argument in "Politics and the English Language," which I borrow *in*

toto for my essay, is expressly *in favor* of "fresh, vivid, home-made" language, as opposed to "a lifeless, imitative style."[10] And elsewhere Orwell, like CrimethInc, expresses his admiration for "Nonsense Poetry"[11] and "Good Bad Books."[12] In fact, CrimethInc praises "the vitality of his imagination" in service of his "realism," but they fail to register that it is precisely Orwell's realism—the careful description of concrete detail—that makes the imaginative vision so vital. Their dramatic close, urging us to "write barbarously" rather than worry about a bunch of boring rules, is not the clever inversion that it first seems, since Orwell advised us to "*Break* any of these rules sooner than say anything barbarous."[13] Orwell's guidelines end (as sound advice often does) by imploring us to trust our own best judgment.

This sort of problem is endemic to the CrimethInc essay and, I suspect, inherent to their entire approach to these questions. For while their argument is, as I said, not bad (even if misapplied), the appeal of CrimethInc has never been with the power of their analysis and argumentation, but with their aesthetics, with the force of their rhetoric, with their poetics. (Who can help but admire a title like *Days of War, Nights of Love*?) But that is also their greatest weakness. For many of their metaphors, allusions, and sly jokes badly misfire if we stop to think them through.

For example, their question, "Which anarchists are most widely read outside the anarchist milieu?"[14] is never answered, suggesting that it is meant rhetorically. But as such it fails twice. First, because the question does not suggest its own answer. I honestly do not know whom they have in mind (if anyone). And second: in the world of fact, the answer would not seem to support their argument. If we understand the question as "which anarchists, living or dead…" I can think of no better candidate than Tolstoy, whose sober realism might be thought to epitomize the kind of prose CrimethInc argues against. If we take the question to mean "which *living* anarchist" the answer is demonstrably Noam Chomsky, who rejects rhetorical appeals on principle.[15] "I don't trust good speakers," he told one interviewer. "We don't want to be swayed by superficial eloquence, by emotion and so on. What we ought to ask for is the opportunity to think things through for ourselves."[16]

A similar blunder occurs at the end of the essay, when the CrimethInc authors urge, "Topple the Tower of Babel, the imperial project of imposing a unitary logic on language and thought."

Now, I don't know what CrimethInc uses for a Bible, but the King James tells us (Genesis 11:1–9):

> (1) And the whole earth was of one language, and of one speech....
>
> (4) And they said, Go to, let us build us a city and a tower, whose top may reach unto heaven....
>
> (5) And the Lord came down to see the city and the tower, which the children of men builded.
>
> (6) And the Lord said, Behold, the people is one, and they have all one language; and this they begin to do: and now nothing will be restrained from them, which they have imagined to do.
>
> (7) Go to, let us go down, and there confound their language, that they may not understand one another's speech.
>
> (8) So the Lord scattered them abroad from thence upon the face of all the earth: and they left off to build the city.
>
> (9) Therefore is the name of it called Babel; because the Lord did there confound the language of all the earth.

In this story, all of humanity decides to build a tower to heaven—as good a metaphor for the anarchist project that I know of. God, realizing that "the people united will never be defeated" and feeling their effort as a threat to his authority, decides to stop them. He performs this act of divine repression through a kind of divide-and-rule, specifically by *"confound[ing] their language, that they may not understand one another's speech."*

CrimethInc, here, sides with the ultimate authority against a united humanity and their dreams of heaven. Of course—and this is precisely my point—that is probably not what they mean to be saying. It's just that they have not attended very carefully to the way that their metaphor is supposed to work, and as a result their own allusion undercuts their argument. No divine intervention is required; CrimethInc confounds *their own* language. As Orwell noted, the "lack of precision" makes it so that a "writer either has a meaning and cannot express it, or he inadvertently says something else."[17] That is the trap that CrimethInc falls into—except that they cannot even recognize it as a trap.

What Orwell intended—in fact, what he "most wanted to do"— was "to make political writing into an art."[18] CrimethInc tries to go a step further, to elevate it to the level of the mythopoetic. They therefore frame our disagreement not simply in terms of clarity versus obscurity in language and thought but as an incarnation of "a centuries-old debate" between rationalism and romanticism. "Do we side with the lucid prose of William Godwin, or the incandescent poetry of Percy Shelley?" they ask,[19] forgetting that Godwin was to Shelley both "a luminary too dazzling for the darkness which surrounds him" and "the regulator and former of my mind."[20] Without *Political Justice*, there is no *Mask of Anarchy*.[21]

CrimethInc presents us with a Nietzschean choice between "Apollonian argumentation that frames anarchism as the culmination of the Enlightenment, or the Dionysian romance of an assault on Western civilization."[22] Yet again their metaphor betrays their cause, because Nietzsche spoke of "two interwoven artistic impulses, *the Apollonian and the Dionysian*"[23]—antagonistic, but equally necessary. In the very first paragraph of *The Birth of Tragedy* he compares them to a quarrelsome couple:

> [The] continuous development of art is bound up with the *Apollonian* and *Dionysian* duality—just as procreation depends on the duality of the sexes, involving perpetual strife with only periodically intervening reconciliations.... Through Apollo and Dionysus, the two art deities of the Greeks, we come to recognize that in the Greek world there existed a tremendous opposition, in origin and aims, between the Apollonian art

of sculpture, and the nonimagistic, Dionysian art of music. These two tendencies run parallel to each other, for the most part openly at variance; and they continually incite each other to new and more powerful births, which perpetuate an antagonism, only superficially reconciled by the common term "art"; till eventually, by a metaphorical miracle of the Hellenic "will," they appear coupled with each other, and through this coupling ultimately generate an equally Dionysian and Apollonian form of art—Attic tragedy.[24]

Nietzsche later switches metaphors and describes "the intricate relation of the Apollonian and the Dionysian" as "a fraternal union of the two deities: Dionysius speaks the language of Apollo; and Apollo, finally the language of Dionysus; and so the highest goal of tragedy and of all art is attained."[25] The philosopher Walter Kaufmann, who translated much of Nietzsche's *oeuvre*, offers this gloss:

Apollo represents ... the power to create harmonious and measured beauty; the strength to shape one's own character no less than works of art; the principle of individuation; the form-giving force, which reached its consummation in Greek sculpture. Dionysus ... is the symbol of that drunken frenzy which threatens to destroy all forms and codes; the ceaseless striving which apparently defies all limitations; the ultimate abandonment we sometimes sense in music.

In *The Birth of Tragedy*, Nietzsche did not extol one at the expense of the other; but if he favors one of the two gods, it is Apollo. His thesis is that it took both to make possible the birth of tragedy, and he emphasizes the Dionysian only because he feels that the Apollonian genius of the Greeks cannot be fully understood apart from it.... Beauty is the monument of Apollo's triumph over Dionysus.[26]

Nietzsche therefore comes close to answering the broadest of the questions raised by CrimethInc's essay, concerning "the alchemy that sets good writing apart from merely serviceable."[27] For Nietzsche the highest peak of artistic creation is reached neither by suppressing the Dionysian chaos, nor by surrendering to it, but by harnessing and directing it with an Apollonian discipline.

CrimethInc can only view constraints—even purely formal constraints, like those governing language—as impediments to free expression. They cannot see that the structure is the very thing that makes expression possible *at all*. That is true even of the avant-garde violation of those same constraints. As the actor Stephen Fry observes, there is a great difference between John Cage's "works requiring ball bearing and chains to be dropped on to prepared pianos" and children banging, however enthusiastically, upon the keys. Part of the difference, surely, is related to the fact that "Cage's first pieces were written in the Western compositional tradition" just as "Picasso's early paintings are flawless models of figurative accuracy."[28] Noam Chomsky argues along similar lines, responding to an interviewer's curiosity about the relationship between language and freedom:

> I think that anyone's political ideas or their ideas of social organization must be rooted ultimately in some concept of human nature and human needs. Now my own feeling is that the fundamental human capacity is the capacity and the need for creative self-expression, for free control of all aspects of one's life and thought. One particularly crucial realization of this capacity is the creative use of language as a free instrument of thought and expression.... [At the same time,] I think that true creativity means free action within the framework of a system of rules. In art, for instance, if a person just throws cans of paint randomly at a wall, with no rules at all, no structure, that is not artistic creativity, whatever else it may be. It is a commonplace of aesthetic theory that creativity involves action that takes place within a framework of rules, but is not narrowly

determined either by the rules or by external stimuli. It is only when you have the combination of freedom and constraint that the question of creativity arises.[29]

For CrimethInc, it is the (Dionysian) passion for rebellion, not the (Apollonian) clarity of ideas, on which the anarchist movement is built. That is, I think, to a very large degree, correct. And our differing assessments of that fact point to our most serious political disagreements. Again, CrimethInc's rhetoric betrays their purpose. They write: "Most people are drawn to the anarchist project by the desire for the wild and mysterious, for something ineffable."[30] Notice that the sentence goes wrong from the very first word: *Most* people are not drawn to the anarchist project at all! Most people remain either entirely unaware of its existence or else regard it as a form of lunacy. The reasons for that attitude are certainly numerous, but a style of discourse that seeks to make politics "mysterious" and "ineffable" must surely be counted among them.

Broadly speaking, the failure of anarchism to make itself attractive—or even intelligible—to very large numbers of people indicates either that some immutable element of human nature is repelled by the ideals of freedom and equality, or else, as a matter of contingent historical fact, we anarchists have simply not found a way to make those ideals seem both desirable and attainable. If the former, then the entire project needs to be reconsidered. But if it is the latter, then by persisting with our present rhetorical strategies we are not, as CrimethInc advises, "concentrat[ing] on our strengths" but to the contrary, succumbing to our weaknesses.[31]

Chapter Ten

"All but Hopeless"
Pessimism in Politics

Modern Times

THIS IS NOT A GOOD MOMENT FOR OPTIMISM. DISASTER APPROACHES from several sides—climate change, resource scarcity, increasing inequality, war. By almost any objective measure our prospects are bad.[1]

The Left's recent history offers little if any reason to think that this situation might be remedied. In the past twenty years we've seen popular movements—anti-globalization, anti-war, Occupy, Black Lives Matter—blossom and wither with astonishing speed, rarely producing fruit. Instead, each rebellion has pulled in enormous numbers of people, many total neophytes, then stoked their hopes and thrown them into a flurry of activity with little regard for the eventual outcome. Some years, or merely weeks, later—when the teargas has cleared, a few militants have been jailed, and some of the more ambitious leaders have settled into jobs with progressive nonprofits or the Democratic Party—perhaps a few minor victories have been won, but the ultimate aims seem as remote as ever.

The people who had entered the movement in droves drift away in ones and twos—a slow bleed, but, with nothing to staunch the flow, ultimately fatal. Having joined eagerly, full of hope and energy and raw idealism, they leave exhausted, disappointed, bitter. Some will look back at this period wistfully, as a youthful adventure, others with resentment, thinking it a kind of swindle. Some *won't* leave but will gloom around the margins of the Left for years, feeling cheated or betrayed and casting blame in all directions. And there are those others who will cling on with a desperate and touching devotion, insisting that, like Tinkerbell, a social movement can be saved if we all just *believe* hard enough. Perhaps some—and we never know how many—will patiently wait for another opportunity, then roll up their sleeves and try again. But more—I'm afraid, *many* more—will take from their experience the lesson that struggle is pointless, that nothing ever changes, and that their energy is better spent just trying to make the best of circumstances as they find them, looking for satisfaction in their private lives, their families and careers, and pursuing such pleasures as they can afford. Of these, the most idealistic will turn their attention inwards—with therapy, spirituality, poetry, or a commitment to "sustainable living"—and persuade themselves that they are, in their own small way, keeping alive the flame that, a short while before, had been burning brightly in the streets. And finally there are those people who will make a new cause of their own disillusionment and turn against the Left altogether.

The Temptations of Pessimism

George Orwell was no stranger to disappointment. Writing in 1940, he remarked, "every *positive* attitude has turned out a failure. Creeds, parties, programmes of every description have simply flopped, one after another. The only 'ism' that has justified itself is pessimism."[2]

But pessimism is not an answer. It is the question. And once it is asked, we must find some way to respond.

Orwell considered three types of reply: misanthropy, irresponsibility, and mysticism, as professed by Jonathan Swift, Henry Miller, and Arthur Koestler, respectively.[3]

The first of these produces politics that are conservative, if not purely negative.[4] Jonathan Swift, as Orwell describes him, "is a Tory anarchist, despising authority while disbelieving in liberty, and preserving the aristocratic outlook while seeing clearly that the existing aristocracy is degenerate and contemptible."[5] Swift was an "anarchist" in that he was opposed to the existing society, and a "Tory" in that he was suspicious of any effort to change it. Obviously there is something about the combination with which Orwell could sympathize.[6] He sometimes referred to himself, too, as "a Tory Anarchist," though in a different sense—a "Tory," in that he saw himself as acting within an established tradition, whether that be characterized as Christian morality, English liberty, Western civilization, or simple decency, and an anarchist, not in sectarian terms, but where it counts: in his almost instinctual opposition to all types of tyranny.[7]

Gulliver's Travels, Orwell stated frankly "has meant more to me than any other book ever written," and "a year has never passed without my re-reading at least part of it."[8] Still, he felt that the novel's view of the world was "peculiarly unacceptable" and even "diseased," because Swift's variety of pessimism was a product of misanthropy, rather than the other way around.[9] In Swift's view, human beings were inherently selfish, foolish, and physically disgusting; any notion of progress would ultimately run up against our lower nature. "He couldn't see what the simplest person sees, that life is worth living and human beings, even if they're dirty and ridiculous, are mostly decent."[10] The difference between this attitude and Orwell's is not merely a matter of opinion but of basic outlook. As Herbert Read put it, "Fundamental to Swift is a certain *disgust* of humanity and *despair* of life; fundamental to Orwell is a *love* of humanity and a passionate desire to live in freedom."[11] Orwell can see the value in human life, where Swift finds only appalling absurdity.

Compared to Swift, Henry Miller comes across as a rather cheerful nihilist. He has no grudge against humanity, though he also feels no obligation to it:

> he believes in the impending ruin of western civilization much more firmly than the majority of "revolutionary" writers; only he does not feel called upon to do anything about it. He is fiddling while Rome is burning, and, unlike the enormous majority of people who do this, fiddling with his face toward the flames.[12]

This kind of deliberate irresponsibility also has its attractions—to be indifferent to society, untouched by the tragedy unfolding, unconcerned with the future. It brings a kind of peace. Orwell reflects, "*Tropic of Cancer* ends with an especially Whitmanesque passage, in which, after the lecheries, the swindles, the fights, the drinking bouts and the imbecilities, he simply sits down and watches the Seine flowing past in a sort of mystical acceptance of the thing-as-it-is." One may well envy such beatific calm. "Only," Orwell asks at once, "*what* is he accepting? . . . To say 'I accept' in an age like our own is to say that you accept concentration camps, rubber truncheons, Hitler, Stalin, bombs, aeroplanes, tinned food, machine guns, spies, *provocateurs*, press censorship, secret prisons, aspirins, Hollywood films and political murders."[13]

Miller can, Orwell cannot. Orwell recalled meeting Miller in 1936, "when I was passing through Paris on my way to Spain," and discovering that the older man "felt no interest in the Spanish war whatever." Miller did not even try to dissuade Orwell from his mission but "merely told me in forcible terms that to go to Spain at that moment was the act of an idiot." Miller could understand going "from purely selfish motives" or "out of curiosity," but "to mix oneself up in such things *from a sense of obligation* was sheer stupidity," and the political ideas underlying such a decision—"combating Fascism, defending democracy, etc etc"—"were all boloney." So far as Miller could tell, "Our civilization was destined to be swept away and replaced by something so different that we should scarcely regard it has human—a prospect that did not bother him, he said."[14]

It *does* bother Orwell, and he believes that it *should* bother us, even if there are moments when, like Jonah—the reluctant prophet who tried to flee his responsibilities and thus endured a brief sojourn inside a whale—we wish that it did not.[15] The difference, again, is not at the level of opinion but at that of psychology and perhaps even fundamental nature. Miller cannot be made to feel that the fate of civilization particularly matters, while Orwell cannot help but to feel that it does. Yet Miller, unlike Swift, does at least retain his sense of human sympathy. As Orwell departed for Spain, Miller sent him with a thick corduroy jacket to keep him warm in the trenches.[16]

The third writer, Arthur Koestler, takes a more ambiguous view, and one in many respects closer to Orwell's own. Koestler was a former Communist who described himself as a "short-term pessimist,"[17] implying that he might yet remain a long-term optimist. The form this optimism takes, however, is somewhat paradoxically a sense of resignation, renouncing any efforts to improve the world while privately holding on to a kind of idealism and preserving a fantasy image of the Utopia to come:

> As an ultimate objective he believes in the Earthly Paradise.... But his intelligence tells him that the Earthly Paradise is receding into the far distance and that what is actually ahead of us is bloodshed, tyranny, and privation.... So you get the quasi-mystical belief that for the present there is no remedy, all political action is useless, but that somewhere in space and time human life will cease to be the miserable brutish thing it is now.[18]

Orwell suggests that this ambivalence results from a profound disappointment in the Russian Revolution, "the central event in Koestler's life." As Orwell reminds us, "a quarter of a century ago it was confidently expected that the Russian Revolution should lead to Utopia." Koestler shared in that expectation at the time, and now he is "too acute" to see the subsequent events as anything but a disaster, and "too sensitive not to remember the original objective." He therefore refuses the usual consolations, and instead "draws the conclusion: This is what revolutions lead to"—secret police and show trials; not more freedom, but less. Practically, then, the only course open to him is "to be a 'short-term pessimist,' i.e. to keep out of politics, make a sort of oasis within which you and your friends can remain sane, and hope that somehow things will be better in a hundred years."[19] Koestler, in other words, preserves his idea of Utopia, but to do so he surrenders the possibility of political action. Utopia will arrive, sometime and somehow, but there is nothing that he can do to bring it about, or even to facilitate the process. This, of course, is precisely the Christian attitude toward the Kingdom of God. It is politics transmuted into faith—a quietist politics, a passive faith.

No Way Out

Koestler, Miller, and Swift were very different writers and lived very different lives. But in each case, the logical outcome of their views would be a withdrawal from political life. They could only recommend that you stay out of trouble, tend to your garden, raise your children, and write books, if at all, from a purely literary point of view. Such a course may well seem alluring, with its promise of a quiet life and the personal satisfaction that comes from unmediated private pursuits, whether stamp-collecting, bird-watching, woodworking, or crosswords. And of course it is safer—in the short term. Yet it can only be a fantasy.

George Bowling, Orwell's antihero in *Coming Up for Air*, tries briefly to realize this fantasy, returning to Lower Binfield, the village where he was raised, for a stolen day of fishing. All he wants is a brief respite from his work, his wife, and the long shadow of impending war. The peace he longs for is, in his mind, mixed up with the England of his boyhood, with the feel of the sun in the summertime, and of course, with fishing: "As soon as you think of fishing you think of things that don't belong to the modern world. The very idea of sitting all day under a willow tree beside a quiet pool—and being able to find a quiet pool to sit beside—belongs to the time before the war, before the radio, before aeroplanes, before Hitler."[20]

Bowling is not a rebel, but neither is he a fool. He sees what is coming and does not imagine that he can change it. He does not want to *fight*, he wants to *escape*. And so when the young men of the Left Book Club ask him, "If war broke out and we had the chance to smash Fascism once and for all, wouldn't you fight?," Bowling is blunt in his refusal: "You bet I wouldn't.... There's been enough smashing done already, if you ask me."[21] He goes on, more sympathetically, "Listen, son.... In 1914 *we* thought it was going to be a glorious business. Well, it wasn't. It was just a bloody mess.... You don't feel like a hero. All you know is that you've had no sleep for three days, you stink like a polecat, you're pissing your bags with fright and your hands are so cold you can't hold your rifle." He tells the boys firmly, with echoes of Miller's advice to Orwell a few months before, "If it comes again, you keep out of it. Why should you get your body plugged full of lead? Keep it for some girl."[22]

Yet, unlike Miller, George Bowling knows, though he hates to admit it, that when the war arrives, there will be no way to keep out of it:

> *It's all going to happen.* All the things you've got at the back of your mind, the things you're terrified of, the things that you tell yourself are just a nightmare or only happen in foreign countries. The bombs, the food-queues, the rubber truncheons, the barbed wire, the coloured shirts, the slogans, the enormous faces, the machine-guns squirting out of bedroom windows. It's all going to happen.... There's no escape. Fight against it if you like, or look the other way and pretend not to notice, or grab your spanner and rush out to do a bit of face-smashing along with the others. But there's no way out.[23]

Bowling is, in his fashion, the counterpoint to Miller. Miller, as Orwell describes him is "a willing Jonah," not trapped so much as hiding "inside the whale": "He has performed the essential Jonah act of allowing himself to be swallowed, remaining passive, *accepting*."[24] Orwell recognizes that it is "probably a very widespread fantasy":

> For the fact is that being inside a whale is a very comfortable, cosy, homelike thought.... There you are, in the dark, cushioned space that exactly fits you, with yards of blubber between yourself and reality, able to keep up an attitude of the completest indifference, no matter what *happens*.... Short of being dead, it is the final, unsurpassable stage of irresponsibility.

Bowling sought a similar comfort, a break from responsibility, if only for a moment. He did not seek solace with Miller among the dilettantes and expatriates of the Latin Quarter but beside a quiet fishing hole by a perfectly ordinary English town. What he found instead was that the pool had been drained and used as a dump, and the village transformed out of all recognition. At the end, he is forced to recognize that he was only fleeing the inevitable: "The old life's finished, and to go about looking for it is just a waste of time. There's no way back to Lower Binfield, you can't put Jonah back into the whale."[25]

The Doctor's Dilemma

Orwell himself felt that "there is no such thing as 'keeping out of politics.'"[26] With fascism and socialism battling one another, "the times are growing harsher, the issues are clearer,"[27] and the stakes are higher. Besides which, in an age of military conscription and concentration camps, you can try to avoid politics if you like, but politics may very well find you regardless. It is the nature of totalitarianism to eliminate private life, to abolish the individual, and the development of nuclear weapons presents further difficulties (for Koestler's view, among other things) since it threatens to annihilate the future as well.

Described this way, the situation must sound impossible: All action is futile, but inaction is suicidal. Those who live by the sword die by the sword; but "If you throw away your weapons, some less scrupulous person will pick them up."[28]

What, then, can one do?

Orwell's answer: We do what we must.

The model he offers is that of "a doctor treating an all but hopeless case." At a superficial level, his actions seem pointless or even contradictory: "As a doctor, it is his duty to keep the patient alive, and therefore to assume that the patient has at least a chance of recovery." However: "As a scientist, it is his duty to face the facts, and therefore to admit that the patient will probably die." Likewise, left-wing political activity can only "have meaning if we assume that Socialism *can* be established, but if we stop to consider what probably *will* happen, then we must admit, I think, that the chances are against us."[29]

There are specific features of the physician's predicament deserving of notice: First, the case is a bad one, but it is just possible that the patient may survive. The job of the doctor, then, is to make the most of whatever meager chances do exist. And because medicine is a science and not merely a collection of techniques, his ability to save the patient depends on his knowledge of the disease. Therefore his recognition of the facts, his understanding of just how grim the prognosis really is, does not interfere with his efforts to save the patient: it is part of what makes possible the care that the physician offers.

Second, it is not hope that propels the doctor's action, but a sense of duty. (*Hope* appears only once in the lines quoted above, and in extremely circumscribed form; *duty*, twice, and in direct declaration.) The doctor's emotions—whether enthusiasm, despair, pity, or disgust—are not allowed to enter into his decisions. So long as a cure remains a technical possibility, however remote, it is his responsibility to pursue it. And so he does.[30]

A Nightmare Paradise

Then again, how hopeless is the case, after all? Humanity's doom may yet be relative.

Koestler's despair, Orwell argued, was a product of his idealism. Utopia may never arrive, but perhaps the search for Utopia is part of the problem: "We are living in a nightmare precisely *because* we have tried to set up an earthly paradise."[31]

Orwell's pessimism is of a different sort, tied to his conservative disposition. Because he thought the Earthly Paradise neither attainable nor desirable, he was never tempted by the sort of Left Machiavellianism that would find in utopian ideals the justification for atrocities.[32] By the same token, he was also somewhat inured to the sense of radical despair even once it became fashionable. His more modest hopes produced less crushing defeats: having never been enamored of the Bolsheviks, he did not have to suffer a period of disillusionment with the USSR. Never being drawn to perfection—as a goal or even as a standard of measurement—Orwell could recognize progress where it occurred, without being burdened by the naive expectation that it be total or occur all at once.[33]

This type of realism demands that we reconcile ourselves, not to the world as it is but at least to the world as it must be—that is, not to existing social conditions, but to the human condition. Orwell assumed, and in a way he even hoped, that after the revolution, the drama of life would go on, with masses of people spending their time "working, breeding, and dying"[34] as they always have. Even in a classless society, life would be a struggle, often characterized by pointless suffering and disappointment.[35] People would still race bicycles, fall in love, write poetry, raise their children, drink wine, rest on the beach—and likewise, they will undoubtedly endure accidents, heartbreak, embarrassment, grief, arguments, hangovers, sunburn, illness, and death. The difference is that they would do these things, foolish or painful as they may be, under conditions of relative equality, without the fear of bankruptcy, homelessness, and starvation, without having to rely on the boss's good will and the landlord's fastidiousness, without being called on to trade away some portion of their dignity in exchange for their life's needs.

Orwell writes soberly, tentatively, but with a strangely encouraging tone: "Perhaps some degree of suffering is ineradicable from human life, perhaps even the choice before man is always a choice of evils, perhaps even the aim of Socialism is not to make the world perfect but to make it better."[36]

Second Thoughts on Airstrip One

Maybe, then, Orwell's reputation for pessimism is overstated. Much of it traces back to *1984* and specifically to a misapprehension of the novel's purpose.[37] The book is not a prophesy but a warning. Orwell bluntly declared in a press release after the book's publication: "*The moral is: Don't let it happen. It depends on you.*"[38] He elaborated in a letter to the UAW's Francis Henson: "I do not believe that the kind of society I describe necessarily *will* arrive, but I believe … that something resembling it *could* arrive."[39]

One person who *did* believe in the irresistible rise of something like oligarchical collectivism was the former Trotskyist and future neoconservative James Burnham, author of *The Managerial Revolution* and *The Machiavellians*. Orwell summarized Burnham's views:

> Capitalism is disappearing, but Socialism is not replacing it. What is now arising is a new kind of planned, centralised society which will be neither capitalist nor, in any accepted sense of the word, democratic. The rulers of this new society will be the people who effectively control the means of production: that is, business executives, technicians, bureaucrats and soldiers, lumped together by Burnham, under the name of "managers." These people will eliminate the old capitalist class, crush the working class, and so organise society that all power and economic privilege remain in their own hands. Private property rights will be abolished, but common ownership will not be established. The new "managerial" societies will not consist of a patchwork of small, independent states, but of great super-states grouped round the main industrial centres in Europe, Asia, and America. These super-states will fight among themselves for possession of the remaining uncaptured portions of the earth, but will probably be unable to conquer one another completely. Internally, each society will be hierarchical, with an aristocracy of talent at the top and a mass of semi-slaves at the bottom.[40]

The influence on Orwell is obvious.[41] Burnham supplies the vision for the world of *1984*, and Orwell fills in the details, elaborates the fantasy at the level of daily life, and shows us what it would be like for an ordinary person living in a society of that sort.

The difference is that Burnham thought that this new world was inevitable and, furthermore, desirable. Orwell counters that Burnham thought it inevitable *because* it was what he desired: "his theory, for all its appearance of objectivity, is the rationalisation of a wish." Burnham's prediction does not reveal "anything about the future," but "merely tells us what kind of world the 'managerial' class themselves . . . would like to live in."[42]

Remember that *1984*'s most famous and unsettling line—"If you want a picture of the future, imagine a boot stamping on a human face—forever"—does not represent Orwell's view, but that of the Inner Party inquisitor, O'Brien.[43] The image is borrowed from Jack London's *Iron Heel*: "We will grind you revolutionists down under our heel, and we shall walk upon your faces."[44] Both books depict authoritarian societies arising in the aftermath of revolution. Yet they also suggest, not in the main action of the stories they tell, but at the edges, that the boot does *not* crash down indefinitely: The appendix of *1984* and the foreword to *The Iron Heel* each extend the narrative beyond the period of repression.[45] They are written from the perspective of the still-more-distant future, and refer to the novels' events as occurring in the remote past.[46] The reign of the Oligarchs, and that of the Inner Party, has ended. Dystopias, it seems, do not last forever. Even totalitarian systems never quite manage to be *total*. There are always gaps, blindspots, fault lines, interstices, where other possibilities develop. Hope survives at the margins.[47]

The Future is Unwritten

Orwell was a great believer in possibilities. He believed in socialism and democracy not merely as ideals but as workable systems. He believed in the possibility of revolution, even in quiet, peaceable England. And he believed in the danger of counter-revolution—especially a counter-revolution proceeding under the revolutionary banner.

He had seen something like that happen in Spain, when the Communists reversed the gains of the revolutionary period and liquidated their left-wing opponents.[48] He recounts that experience in *Homage to Catalonia*, and its lessons show up again in *Animal Farm* and *1984*. All three books tell stories of revolutions gone wrong; but none of them suggests that revolutions *must* go wrong. Rather, they warn against certain types of mistakes, in the hope that better mistakes may yet be possible: "All revolutions are failures," Orwell confessed, "but they are not all the same failure."[49]

Chapter Eleven

"The Struggle Would Continue, the Idea Would Survive"

The Spanish Civil War and the Cultural Imagination[1]

Symbolic Deaths

THERE ARE TWO DEATHS AT THE END OF GUILLERMO DEL TORO'S FILM *Pan's Labyrinth*.[2] One is that of Ofelia, a young girl who tries to escape her abusive stepfather by entering an enchanted fairyland. She returns there, absorbed by the magic, as the blood runs out of her body.

The second death is that of the girl's stepfather, Captain Vidal, the fascist commander responsible for suppressing the guerrillas in the nearby hills. In the end he is captured by the resistance fighters. He offers his last words: "Tell my son ... Tell him what time his father died. Tell him that I—"

But he is interrupted by guerrillas: "No. He won't even know your name." They shoot him, and he falls.

Seventy-five years after the fascist generals declared their victory over the democratic Republic, the Spanish Civil War is still being fought. It is being fought in movies, books, and comics. It has become a battle of historical memory and cultural imagination.

Party Lines

Outside of anarchist circles, the war is remembered now less for its politics than for its literature.[3] Partly that is because the history of the conflict has always been so distorted by ideological concerns. In his essay, "Looking Back on the Spanish War," George Orwell writes:

> [In] Spain, for the first time, I saw newspaper reports which did not bear any relation to the facts, not even the relationship which is implied in an ordinary lie. I saw great battles reported where there had been no fighting, and complete silence where hundreds of men had been killed. I saw troops who had fought bravely denounced as cowards and traitors, and others who had never seen a shot fired hailed as the heroes of imaginary victories.... I saw, in fact, history being written not in terms of what happened but of what ought to have happened according to various "party lines."[4]

Within Spain itself, the grasp on the facts was weakened even further after the fascist victory. Under Franco, Spanish society was blanketed with a sort of silence about the war. There was an official story—enforced through censorship and secrecy, promoted through propaganda—of brave military heroes saving civilization from the reds. But this story necessarily left out more than it explained. And on both sides, most people adopted a prudent reticence: To confess to being a "red," or even just to have failed to support the military coup, would be tantamount to admitting to treason. But to say too much about the process of victory—the denunciations, the disappearances, the torture and brutality—that would be shameful as well.

Internationally, the war's memory proved just as embarrassing to just as many people: There were atrocities on all sides, the western democracies refused to defend an elected government against a fascist putsch, and the Soviet Union came forward as the agent of counter-revolution.

But the war's cultural legacy has been a lasting one. In 2003, the US State Department insisted that Pablo Picasso's painting *Guernica*—which symbolically represents the aerial bombardment of the Basque city during the Civil War—be hidden from view as Colin Powell addressed the United Nations Security Council to urge support for the invasion of Iraq. The painting, it seems, remains a potent indictment against military aggression and the diplomats worried about the effect it would have if it appeared as the backdrop for Powell's speech.[5]

Absent Friends

In 2008, NBM released the third and final installment of Vittorio Giardino's graphic novel *No Pasarán!*[6] Set in late 1938, the series centers on the disappearance of Guido Treves, a Republican militiaman, and his friend Max Friedman's efforts to find him. The two men had served together in the International Brigades, and when Treves stopped writing to his wife, she turned to Max for help. Reluctantly, Friedman returns to Spain and begins asking uncomfortable questions, unsure of whom he can trust.

Such mysteries were not strictly the stuff of fiction. The American writer John Dos Passos found himself playing a similar role in a prelude to the Communist Party's takeover of the revolutionary government. In the fall of 1936, Dos Passos's friend and translator, José Robles, had been arrested at his home by armed men in plain clothes. They did not identify themselves or their agency. Robles was Spanish by birth, but had been living in the United States and teaching at Johns Hopkins. He was on vacation in Spain when the war broke out, felt compelled to stay, and soon found himself working closely with Russian advisors at the Ministry of War. Dos Passos had been mustering support for the Republican cause overseas, and was in Spain to work on a film, *The Spanish Earth*, along with Ernest Hemingway.

Robles's wife pleaded with Dos Passos to help find her husband, and for weeks he made increasingly desperate inquiries. The answers he received were maddeningly inconsistent. Some officials assured him "that the charges against José Robles were not serious and that he was in no danger." But at the same time, a conscience-stricken functionary in the propaganda office privately informed the family that Robles was dead. "The general impression that the higher-ups in Valencia tried to give," Dos Passos later recalled, "was that if Robles was dead he had been kidnapped and shot by anarchist 'uncontrollables.'"[7] Meanwhile, a rumor was circulating—concocted by Communist agents with the assistance of Josephine Herbst, and then propagated by Hemingway—that Robles was a traitor. Hemingway clung to this story seemingly as an article of faith, later claiming, "I happened to know that the man had been shot two weeks before as a spy after a long and careful trial in which all charges against him had been proven."[8]

Hemingway urged Dos Passos to back off, saying that asking too many questions would only appear suspicious. "Think nothing of it," he advised. "People disappear every day."[9] Hemingway's attitude was not hard realism but cheap sadism. He was not simply resigned to the existence of secret prisons and summary executions; he was enthusiastic about them and eager to show himself to be tougher and more manly than his grief-stricken friend.[10]

It wasn't until weeks later that Dos Passos had it authoritatively confirmed—by the Chief of Police in Madrid—that Robles was dead. *Why?* he demanded. The police official replied abstractly, "Dos, we are living in terrible times. To overcome them, we have to be terrible ourselves."[11]

Of course there had been no trial. There were no charges, and nothing had been proven. The truth was, Robles had been serving as an adjunct to General Vladmir Gorey, whose mission in Spain was to orchestrate the Communist control of the government. Robles had been murdered simply as a precaution to obscure the machinations leading up to the Communist government's attack on their left-wing rivals in May of 1937. Dos Passos's questions brought unwanted attention to this minor incident in the sectarian struggle, and so it became necessary to discredit and marginalize him—a job Hemingway accomplished, if half-unwittingly, with a combination of gossip and bullying. The confrontation destroyed their friendship and, with it, Dos Passos's faith in the Left.[12]

Meanwhile, as the Communists took hold of the Spanish government, disappearances became distressingly common. Orwell reports: "The tales of arrests went on, extending over months, until the number of political prisoners, not counting Fascists, swelled into thousands." People were held without charges, many incommunicado, some in secret prisons, their families unable to learn where, why, or even *if* they were in custody.

> A typical case is that of Kurt Landau and his wife. They were arrested about 17 June, and Landau immediately "disappeared." Five months later his wife was still in jail, untried and without news of her husband. She declared a hunger-strike, after which the Minister of Justice sent word to assure her that her husband was dead.[13]

Military officials, likewise, were imprisoned without notice to their superiors, and seemingly without a thought to the possible consequences for the war effort. George Kopp, for example, was apprehended while transporting documents from the Ministry of War to the head of operations at the Eastern Front. "I admit I was angry when I heard of Kopp's arrest," Orwell wrote.

> He was my personal friend, I had served under him for months, I had been under fire with him, and I knew his history. He was a man who had sacrificed

everything—family, nationality, livelihood—simply to come to Spain and fight against Fascism.... He had been in the line since October 1936, had worked his way up from militiaman to major, had been in action I do not know how many times, and had been wounded once.... And all they could do in return was to fling him into jail.[14]

No doubt the case held a special urgency for Orwell, since that same day he learned of Kopp's arrest he had also received news of another friend, Bob Smillie, dying in a Communist jail. "I know that in the middle of a huge and bloody war it is no use making too much fuss over an individual death," Orwell reflected. "But what angers one about a death like this is its utter pointlessness. To be killed in battle—yes, that is what one expects; but to be flung into jail, not even for any imaginary offence, but simply owing to dull blind spite, and then left to die in solitude—that is a different matter."[15] Though wanted by the police himself, and in the midst of arranging for his departure from Spain, Orwell resolved to do everything in his power to win Kopp's freedom.[16]

Orwell, Dos Passos, and the fictional Friedman all make essentially the same decision: to focus on a single death among thousands, to risk safety and freedom for the sake of a friend, all the while knowing that the effort would almost certainly prove useless—but feeling, nonetheless, that one cannot do otherwise.

Orwell failed, but Kopp survived.[17] Friedman, like Dos Passos, was more successful in his search, but ultimately less fortunate. When Max discovers Treves's fate, it is too late to help him. He had already been dead for weeks. All that is left for Max was to bury his friend and write to the widow.

Hopeless Causes

Since the war, the international volunteers have held a special place in popular culture, as the symbol of defeated idealism. A Spanish Civil War backstory has often served as a quick way to establish a character as a certain sort of hero—a man who has given up on "causes" not out of cowardice but out of disgust, who has seen his humanitarian ideals crash up against the realities of war and collapse as a result. *Casablanca's* Rick Blaine (Humphrey Bogart) is the most famous case, an idealist who has turned to cynicism as a kind of self-defense. "I stick my neck out for nobody," he lies. "I'm not fighting for anyone anymore except myself. I'm the only cause I'm interested in."[18]

There are plenty of other examples available for anyone who wants to find them. For instance: Michael O'Hara (Orson Welles) in *The Lady from Shanghai*,[19] the Marvel Comics superhero Wolverine,[20] and Kit McKittrick from Dorothy B. Hughes's novel, *The Fallen Sparrow*. Captured and tortured, McKittrick despairs:

> Let them win. They'd won anyway. He was too small to halt the juggernaut. He was too tired, too hot, too parched, his body too agonized, to dare any longer. Even the changeless truths that had sent him with gay heart and arrogant passion to join the International Brigade had gone in heat and dark and bestiality. He couldn't defend these any longer.[21]

McKittrick escapes, but he carries the bitterness and despair with him like scars. Back in New York, he considers the change: "It was difficult to remember that once there was a Black Irish youth with passion for truth and justice and beauty, for the integrity of spiritual values.... His ideals had been left behind in a prison in Spain."[22] What replaced them was the feeling that "might was right; by the strong alone was victory deserved. Only by accepting the validity of the methods of the new order could the prophets of the new order be conquered."[23] That, at any rate, is what he tells himself. Yet, in the course of the novel, he finds himself still fighting the fascists, still defending the ideals that he had renounced—"decency and beauty and truth."[24] His motives are confused. He is driven by loyalty, vengeance, jealousy, masculine pride, and even blood-lust, but at the end he has to recognize the hold his old values have on him still: "Ideals had roots. If they were granted you, they could not be eradicated no matter to what ordeal they led."[25]

Max Friedman, too, witnessed the brutalizing effects of war, and worried that the means employed would tarnish the ends. His crisis came earlier, however, and took a very different form. He remembers an exchange with Treves, after executing a fascist sympathizer:

> "Stop thinking about it, Max, [Treves says.] It was necessary.... He would have done the same thing in our shoes."
>
> "Exactly. You know, Guido, I'm beginning to think we're becoming like them."...
>
> "It's the war that's cruel, Max. That's why we have to end it as soon as possible. No one is innocent, but our reasons are on the right side."
>
> "Of course. But sometimes, thinking you're right may not be enough reason to shoot someone."[26]

Looking back on this incident, Max reflects: "Blood nausea, that's what it was. It doesn't matter how right the cause is, you just come to the conclusion that you can't kill any more."[27]

Despite everything, Friedman somehow preserved his conscience, his sense of decency. It was, of course, his reason for fighting; and then, equally, his reason to stop fighting; and finally, again, his reason to return to Spain. The war may be lost, the revolution betrayed, failure nearly certain—but all the more reason not to abandon a friend.

Dying for What One Loves

As literary figures, the Republican heroes are disillusioned and defeated, some of them have been corrupted and compromised, but they remain—secretly and sometimes even against their will—idealists. *Casablanca's* Rick defines the type. He presents himself as cynical and self-interested, but at the crucial moment he steps forward to take risks and make sacrifices to help a Resistance leader escape the Nazis. Whether he acts for love or politics is unclear, and unimportant.

Likewise, in Albert Camus's novel *The Plague*—which is often read as an allegory of the Nazi occupation and French resistance—one character, Rambert, a journalist stranded in the quarantine zone, wants to escape and reunite with the woman he loves, rather than stay and enlist in the sanitary crews fighting the epidemic.

> I don't think it's that I'm afraid to risk my skin again, [he says].... I took part in the Spanish Civil War.... I know now that man is capable of great deeds. But if he isn't capable of a great emotion, well, he leaves me cold.... I've seen enough of people who die for an idea. I don't believe in heroism. I know it's easy and I've learned it can be murderous. What interests me is living and dying for what one loves.[28]

Rambert doesn't realize that Rieux—a doctor treating those infected with the plague—faces a similar predicament: his wife is in a sanatorium a hundred miles away. When Rambert discovers this fact, something in him shifts and he decides to work with the doctor until arrangements can be made for his escape. Much later, then, on the eve of his departure, he gives up the plan, determined to stay until the end.

This resolve to fight, to suffer, to face death—not morbidly but, on the contrary, because life is worth living—is one of the features of the figure of the Spanish War hero. At the end of *For Whom the Bell Tolls*, Hemingway's hero Robert Jordan decides to die fighting rather than abandon his mission. Injured, alone, and waiting for the enemy troops to get within range, he thinks to himself: "If we win here we will win everywhere. The world is a fine place and worth fighting for and I hate very much to leave it."[29]

Orwell did not reflect so philosophically about the prospect of his own demise. Yet after he was shot in the throat, he did observe that "[the] whole experience of being hit by a bullet is very interesting.... Roughly speaking it was the sensation of being *at the centre* of an explosion." There was "a loud bang and a blinding flash of light," but fortunately "no pain." His legs gave out, his arms fell limp, and he could only barely squeak out the words to ask where he was hit. "As soon as I knew that the bullet had gone clean through my neck I took it for granted that I was done for." Laying on the stretcher, roughly bandaged and waiting to die, "My first thought, conventionally enough, was for my wife." And then: "My second was a violent resentment at having to leave this world which, when all is said and done, suits me so well."[30]

He later reflected:

> This war, in which I played so ineffectual a part, has left me with memories that are mostly evil, and yet I do not wish that I had missed it. When you have had a glimpse of such a disaster as this ... the result is not necessarily disillusionment and cynicism. Curiously enough the whole experience has left me with not less but more belief in the decency of human beings.[31]

So, too, in *The Plague*, the narrator concludes: "We learn in time of pestilence: that there are more things to admire in men than to despise."[32]

Neither Orwell nor Camus is famous for his optimism. And it is not self-deception but its opposite—courage—that allows them to retain this faith in humanity and their hopes for the future.

After Defeat

For Orwell, Spain remained a symbol of hope even after the Republic had fallen.

"The choice before us," he wrote of Britain's standoff with Nazi Germany a couple of years later, "is not so much between victory and defeat as between revolution and apathy." To surrender to the Germans would be worse than to be forcibly conquered, because surrender would mean that "the thing we are fighting for"—freedom, justice, decency—"will have been destroyed partly by our own act." However, he argues, "We cannot be *utterly* defeated if we have made our revolution beforehand." Even if the Nazis occupy the country—with everything that would entail—"another process, ultimately deadly to the German power-dream, will have started." He points to Spain as a model: "The Spanish people were defeated, but the things they learned during those two and a half memorable years will one day come back upon the Spanish Fascists like a boomerang."[33]

There are things, he insists, that can withstand a defeat but that cannot endure surrender. Even if England is conquered, "the struggle would continue, the *idea* would survive."[34]

The Spanish poet Antonio Machado felt similarly. "To strategists, politicians, and historians," he acknowledged, "it will all be clear: we lost the war. Speaking personally, I am not so sure. Perhaps we won."[35]

History did not stop in 1939. Franco marched into Madrid. He imprisoned, tortured, and killed the best elements of Spanish society. He ruled Spain almost by decree for an entire generation, and fascism survived on the Iberian Peninsula for a quarter-century after the end of World War II. But even dictators die.

Franco died an unjustly peaceful death in 1975. His successor, King Juan Carlos, immediately began the transition back to parliamentary democracy. He legalized the Spanish Socialist Workers' Party, and later the Communist Party. He called for elections and instituted a new constitution, under which he relinquished his absolute power. And, in 1981, the king—backed by parliament and popular sentiment—successfully faced down an attempted military coup.

Spain is slowly starting to face its past. In 2004, the Socialist government created a Memorial Commission to absolve those suppressed by the fascist regime. In 2007, the government took the further step of de-memorializing Franco, ordering the removal of all street names, statues, monuments, and public symbols associated with his rule. However, the Catholic Church—which still maintains the most prominent memorial, "The Valley of the Fallen"—strenuously objected, and the subsequent government (controlled by the conservative Popular Party) all but halted the process. Though technically illegal, streets bearing Franco's name and statues depicting his image remain.[36]

It's a truism that the victors write the history; but after seventy-five years, it still isn't clear who the victors are. Looking at Spain today, from the perspective of 1936 it can only seem a disappointment. But looking at it from the perspective of 1940 it must seem like a kind of miracle. I don't mean to suggest that electoral victories and modest reforms—liberalized divorce, same-sex marriage, and increased regional autonomy—provide the happy ending to a disastrous war, a failed revolution, and a bloody dictatorship. But these later developments do show how tentative historical "endings" necessarily are, and how little can be guaranteed by violence. And so today it is the dream of the revolution, not the brutality of the dictatorship, that endures.

We can see here, after slow, painful decades of fascist oppression, a kind of victory—though a victory that only guarantees further struggle.

Appendix

Reading Orwell
A Study Plan

BELOW IS A SHORT OUTLINE RELATING SELECTIONS FROM THE four-volume *Collected Essays, Journalism and Letters* to Orwell's books. I have arranged the listings chrono-thematically, so that Orwell's thinking on various subjects can be seen to develop over time. Thus the guide begins with Orwell's experience in Burma, though his novel on the subject was published slightly later. From there it tracks his career by following the trail of his novels. That pattern holds until Section Seven, after which the essays become increasingly prominent, with units centering on Orwell's attitudes about war, England, the aftermath of war, propaganda and literature, and the role of the writer.

With such a quantity of material, not every item will hold the same interest. I have adopted a comprehensive rather than exhaustive approach and thus tried to include the most important and interesting items, while recognizing that the process of selection is necessarily somewhat subjective. Each section centers on a small number of major works (the titles of which appear in **bold**), followed by related or supporting material. Most letters, reviews, and poems have been omitted.

The length of each section is such that a small group could meet at intervals of two or four weeks and discuss the reading. Following such a plan, they should have a good grasp of Orwell's overall work in six months or a year.

Preparation: Biography

It may be helpful to begin by reading a short biography. Peter Lewis's *George Orwell: The Road to 1984* would be well suited to this purpose. In addition to providing a good overview of Orwell's life, it is short, readable, and thoroughly illustrated with interesting and often quite rare photographs.

Peter Lewis, *George Orwell: The Road to 1984* (New York: Harcourt Brace Jovanovich, 1981).

Section One: Burmese Days

Burmese Days (1934)
from *Collected Essays, Journalism and Letters, Volume I*:
12. A Hanging
59. My Epitaph by John Flory
68. [On Kipling's Death]
88. Shooting an Elephant
118. Review: *Trials in Burma* by Maurice Collis
153. Marrakech
155. Not Counting Niggers
from *Collected Essays, Journalism and Letters, Volume II*:
30. Rudyard Kipling

Section Two: Down and Out

Down and Out in Paris and London (1933)
from *Collected Essays, Journalism and Letters, Volume I*:
11. The Spike
15. Hop-Picking
25. Clink
27. Common Lodging Houses
37. Introduction to the French edition of *Down and Out in Paris and London*
from *The Collected Essays, Journalism and Letters, Volume IV*:
58. How the Poor Die

Section Three: Déclassé Novels

A Clergyman's Daughter (1935)
Keep the Aspidistra Flying (1936)
from *Collected Essays, Journalism and Letters, Volume I*:
89. Bookshop Memories
from *Collected Essays, Journalism and Letters, Volume IV*:
119. George Gissing

Section Four: Wigan Pier

The Road to Wigan Pier (1937)
from *Collected Essays, Journalism and Letters, Volume I*:
74. *The Road to Wigan Pier* Diary
95. Your Questions Answered
132. Why I Joined the Independent Labour Party

Section Five: Spain

Homage to Catalonia (1938)
from *Collected Essays, Journalism and Letters, Volume I*:
100. Spilling the Spanish Beans
105. Letter to Geoffrey Gorer (September 15, 1937)
113. Letter to the Editor of *Time and Tide* (February 5, 1938)

Section Eight: The English People

Section Eleven: Propaganda and Literature

from *Collected Essays, Journalism and Letters, Volume II*:

1. **New Words**
14. The Proletarian Writer
20. **The Frontiers of Art and Propaganda**
21. **Tolstoy and Shakespeare**
22. The Meaning of a Poem
23. **Literature and Totalitarianism**
38. BBC Internal Memorandum
43. W.B. Yeats
45. Pamphlet Literature
47. Literature and the Left
55. Mark Twain—The Licensed Jester
56. Poetry and the Microphone

from *Collected Essays, Journalism and Letters, Volume III*:

35. Propaganda and Demotic Speech
68. Arthur Koestler
69. Tobias Smollett: Scotland's Best Novelist
72. A Controversy: Orwell: Agate

from *The Collected Essays, Journalism and Letters, Volume IV*:

16. **The Prevention of Literature**
25. **Decline of the English Murder**
36. In Front of Your Nose
38. **Politics and the English Language**

Section Twelve: Dystopia

1984 (1949)

from *Collected Essays, Journalism and Letters, Volume II*:

2. Review: *Mein Kampf* by Adolf Hitler
8. Review: *The Totalitarian Enemy* by Franz Borkenau
11. **Prophecies of Fascism**
25. Wells, Hitler, and the World State

from *The Collected Essays, Journalism and Letters, Volume IV*:

7. **Introduction to *Love of Life and Other Stories* by Jack London**

17. Review of *We*
19. Pleasure Spots

Section Thirteen: Why I Write

from *Collected Essays, Journalism and Letters, Volume I*:
1. Why I Write
91. In Defense of the Novel
from *Collected Essays, Journalism and Letters, Volume II*:
7. [Autobiographical Note]
from *The Collected Essays, Journalism and Letters, Volume IV*:
6. Good Bad Books
13. Nonsense Poetry
23. Books v. Cigarettes
40. Some Thoughts on the Common Toad
44. A Good Word for the Vicar of Bray
47. Confessions of a Book Reviewer
54. The Cost of Letters
57. Politics vs. Literature: an Examination of *Gulliver's Travels*
63. Riding Down from Bangor
76. Lear, Tolstoy and the Fool
118. Review: *The Soul of Man Under Socialism* by Oscar Wilde
129. Review: *Notes towards the Definition of Culture* by T.S. Eliot
150. The Question of the Pound Award
167. Extracts from a Manuscript Note-book

Endnotes

Introduction

1   George Orwell, "Rudyard Kipling," in *The Collected Essays, Journalism and Letters of George Orwell, Volume II: My Country Right or Left, 1940–1943*, eds. Sonia Orwell and Ian Angus (New York: Harcourt Brace Jovanovich, 1968), 192–93.

2   George Orwell, "You and the Atom Bomb," in *The Collected Essays, Journalism and Letters of George Orwell, Volume IV: In Front of Your Nose, 1945–1950*, eds. Sonia Orwell and Ian Angus (New York: Harcourt Brace Jovanovich, 1968), 9. Confirmed as first use by *Oxford English Dictionary*, OED.com, accessed September 17, 2016.

3   I realize that, properly speaking, the title should be rendered *Nineteen Eighty-Four*. But the Signet paperback that I bought in high school, and have read and reread since then, has it as *1984*. Then again, that is the same edition that advertises itself as containing a "Special Preface" by Walter Cronkite—but does not. George Orwell, *1984* (New York: Signet, 1984).

4   For an examination of the competing, conflicting, contradictory uses of Orwell as a figure, see: John Rodden, *The Politics of Literary Reputation: The Making and Claiming of "St. George" Orwell* (New York: Oxford University Press, 1989).

5   Josef Schneider, in conversation, 2004.

6   Quoted in Sarah Peters, "Justice Breyer Warns of Orwellian Government," *The Hill*, November 8, 2011, thehill.com/blogs/blog-briefing-room/news/192445-justice-breyer-warns-of-orwellian-government, accessed September 2, 2016.

7   Alana Abramson, "Sales of Orwell's *1984* Increase as Details of NSA Scandal Emerge," *ABC News*, June 11, 2013, http://abcnews.go.com/blogs/headlines/2013/06/sales-of-orwells-1984-increase-as-details-of-nsa-scandal-emerge/, accessed September 2, 2016.

8   Kimiko de Freytas-Tamura, "George Orwell's *1984* is Suddenly a Best-Seller," *The New York Times*, January 25, 2017, https://www.nytimes.com/2017/01/25/books/1984-george-orwell-donald-trump.html?_r=3, accessed May 2, 2017.

9   Delaney Strunk, "Theaters are Screening *1984* to Protest Trump," CNN.com, April 4, 2017, http://www.cnn.com/2017/04/04/us/1984-theater-protest-trnd/, accessed May 2, 2017.

10 George Orwell, "Why I Write," in *The Collected Essays, Journalism and Letters of George Orwell, Volume I: An Age Like This, 1920–1940*, eds. Sonia Orwell and Ian Angus (New York: Harcourt Brace Jovanovich, 1968), 5. Emphasis in original.

11 Orwell put this observation in negative terms, suggesting that "a bird's eye view is as distorted as a worm's eye view." George Orwell, "War-Time Diary: 14 March 1942–15 November 1942," in *Collected, Vol. II*, 430. Ellipses in original.

12 He explains: "For some months I lived entirely in coal-miners' houses. I ate my meals with the family, I washed at the kitchen sink, I shared bedrooms with miners, drank beer with them, played darts with them, talked to them by the hour together. But though I was among them, and I hope and trust they did not find me a nuisance, I was not one of them, and they knew it even better than I did. However much you like them, however interesting you find their conversation, there is always that accursed itch of class-difference, like the pea under the princess's mattress. It is not a question of dislike or distaste, only of difference, but it is enough to make real intimacy impossible. Even with miners who described themselves as Communists I found that it needed tactful maneuverings to prevent them from calling me 'sir'; and all of them, except in moments of great animation, softened their northern accents for my benefit. I liked them and hoped they liked me; but I went among them as a foreigner, and both of us were aware of it." George Orwell, *The Road to Wigan Pier* (San Diego: Harcourt, 1958), 156.

13 George Orwell, *Homage to Catalonia* (San Diego: Harcourt Brace and Company, 1952), 4–5.

14 Orwell wrote to Cyril Connolly from Barcelona, "I have seen wonderful things & at last really believe in Socialism, which I never did before.... On the whole, though I am sorry not to have seen Madrid, I am glad to have been on a comparatively little-known front among Anarchists & Poum people instead of in the International Brigade, as I should have been if I had come here with CP credentials instead of ILP ones." Orwell, "Letter to Cyril Connolly (June 8, 1937)," in *Collected, Vol. I*, 269.

15 Orwell, "Writers and Leviathan," in *Collected, Vol. IV*, 412–13.

16 Orwell, "Why I Write," in *Collected, Vol. I*, 4.

17 Ibid., 4–5.

18 George Woodcock, "George Orwell, 19th Century Liberal," in *George Orwell: The Critical Heritage*, ed. Jeffrey Meyers (London: Routledge & Kegan Paul, 1975), 235.

19 Quoted in Rodden, *The Politics of Literary Reputation*, 91.

20 That is the main theme of his novel *Coming Up for Air* (London: Secker & Warburg, 1963).

21 Orwell, "Why I Write," in *Collected, Vol. I*, 7.

22 George Orwell, "As I Please (August 4, 1944)," in *The Collected Essays, Journalism and Letters of George Orwell, Volume III: As I Please, 1943–1945*, eds. Sonia Orwell and Ian Angus (New York: Harcourt Brace Jovanovich, 1968), 199.

23 That should not be confused with any effort to bring Orwell "up to date." As a writer he belonged to his time as definitely as he belonged to his native language. Nor is it an attempt to "claim" Orwell for any ideological camp or to defend him from his various critics and detractors. Christopher Hitchens already wasted too much ink defending Orwell's honor from insults which otherwise may well have been forgotten. And who, we may ask, will save Orwell from Hitchens? Christopher Hitchens, *Why Orwell Matters* (New York: Basic Books, 2002).

24 John Rodden is right to insist that "questions about a man's posthumous politics are manifestly absurd," and his study assembles the evidence that illustrates the point. Rodden, *The Politics of Literary Reputation*, 263.

25 George Orwell, "Letter to Humphrey House (April 11, 1940)," in *Collected, Vol. I*, 131.

26 For those so inclined, however, a study guide is included as an appendix.

27 George Orwell, "Letter to the Duchess of Atholl (November 15, 1945)," in *Collected, Vol. IV*, 30.

28 The difference between critique and dismissal was brought to my attention by Kevin Van Meter, in conversation, 2016. He makes a related set of points in: Kevin Van Meter, "Freely Disassociating: Three Stories on Contemporary Radical Movements," Institute for Anarchist Studies, June 8, 2015, https://anarchist studies.org/2015/06/08/freely-disassociating-three-stories-on-contemporary -radical-movements-by-kevin-van-meter/, accessed September 30, 2016.

29 George Orwell, "London Letter to *Partisan Review* (December 1944)," in *Collected, Vol. III*, 295.

30 It will be observed, here and in the essays that follow, that in my criticisms of the Left I generally omit specific examples. The reasons for this choice are two: First, the problems I point to are long-standing, but fashions change very quickly. Any example I offer, therefore, will likely seem dated inside of two years and the fact that the particular example may have expired ought not to mislead us to conclude that the problem has been overcome. Second, the failings I discuss are so common that even a representative sample of recent instances would quickly prove tiresome, but the selection of one or two must be arbitrary and may seem like I am singling out specific individuals or groups while sparing others. In general, then—with the exception of my direct response to CrimethInc—I have foregone direct quotation or the citing of specific cases. I trust that anyone passingly familiar with contemporary left-wing politics will recognize the problems as I describe them.

31 George Orwell, "In Front of Your Nose," in *Collected, Vol. IV*, 124.

32 Orwell, "Why I Write," in *Collected, Vol. I*, 1.

Chapter One

1   *George Orwell, Diaries*, ed. Peter Davison (Liveright Publishing Corporation, 2012); and, *George Orwell: A Life in Letters*, ed. Peter Davison (New York: Liveright, 2013). Portions of this essay appeared previously in Kristian Williams, "Don't Forget: A Review of George Orwell's Diaries," *Toward Freedom*, https://towardfreedom.com/archives/special-reports-archives/dont-forget-a-review-of-george-orwells-diaries/, May 13, 2013; and, Kristian Williams, "Orwell's Defeats," *In These Times*, http://inthesetimes.com/article/15468/a_man_in_dialogue_with_his_time, August 16, 2013.

2   Orwell, "To Steven Runciman (August? 1920)," in *Life in Letters*, 6.

3   Of course, obsessive scholars will find the occasional gem. For example, a brief note about two children being bitten by rats—"in the face, as usual"—would seem to foreshadow Winston Smith's torture in Room 101. And the attentive reader can learn of Orwell's single experiment with marijuana: "Unpleasant taste &—so far as I am concerned—no effect." Orwell, *Diaries*, 493 and 106.

4   Orwell, "Benefit of Clergy: Some Notes on Salvador Dali," in *Collected, Vol. III*, 156.

5   Julian Symons wrote of Orwell: "He always tells the truth—as he sees it. He has remarkably few prejudices, theories or preconceived notions about anything. He simply observes and records; and the truth he records is often very different from that recorded by statisticians and philosophers. They know what should happen: George Orwell tells you what is happening, according to the evidence of his eyes and ears." Quoted in Rodden, *The Politics of Literary Reputation*, 307.

6   Orwell, *Diaries*, 418.

7   Ibid., 478–79.

8   Orwell, "To David Astor (September 5, 1949)," in *Life in Letters*, 485.

9   Orwell, "To John Middleton Murry (April 28, 1948)," in Ibid., 402.

10 Orwell, *Diaries*, 537–38.

11 Ibid., 536–37. The book in process was, of course, *1984*. Orwell wrote his last and most lasting novel practically as an invalid and did revisions while in the hospital. In the end, he was ambivalent about the result: "I am not pleased with the book but I am not absolutely dissatisfied.... I think it is a good idea but the execution would have been better if I had not written it under the influence of TB." (Orwell, "To Fredric Warburg (October 22, 1948)" in *Life in Letters*, 418.) It is curious to observe that his frustration itself may have worked its way into the novel, a major theme of which is the reduction of thought to hollow slogans.

12 As he advised in "Politics and the English Language": "When you think of something abstract you are more inclined to use words from the start, and ... the existing dialect will come rushing in.... Probably it is better to put off using words as long as possible and get one's meaning as clear as one can through pictures and sensations." Orwell, "Politics and the English Language," in *Collected, Vol. IV*, 138–39.

13 Orwell, "Looking Back on the Spanish War," in *Collected, Vol. II*, 249.

14 Orwell, "Why I Write," in *Collected: Vol. I*, 6.

15 Orwell, *Diaries*, 323.

16 Ibid., 333.

17 Ibid., 280. Capitalization in original.

18 Ibid., 229.

19 Ibid., 362.

20 Ibid., 333.

21 Ibid., 337.

22 Graduate researchers, please take note.

23 Orwell, "In Front of Your Nose," in *Collected, Vol. IV*, 125. Contrariwise: "One way of feeling infallible is not to keep a diary." Orwell, "As I Please (December 17, 1943)," in *Collected, Vol. III*, 59.

24 Orwell, *1984*, 9.

25 Orwell, "As I Please (December 17, 1943)," in *Collected, Vol. III*, 59.

26 Orwell, *Diaries*, 281. Emphasis in original.

27 Orwell, "To Celia Kirwan (April 6, 1949)," in *Life in Letters*, 457.

28 For an excellent overview of the incident, see: Timothy Garton Ash, "Orwell's List," *New York Review of Books*, September 25, 2003, http://www.nybooks.com/articles/2003/09/25/orwells-list/, accessed March 11, 2016.

29 *The Daily Telegraph* lamented, "it was as if Winston Smith had willingly cooperated with the Thought Police." Quoted in Christopher Hitchens, *Why Orwell Matters* (New York: Basic Books, 2002), 155.

30 Ash, "Orwell's List."

31 Ibid.

32 Ibid.

33 Hitchens, *Why Orwell Matters*, 159–60.

34 Orwell, "To Sir Richard Rees (May 2, 1949)," in *Life in Letters*, 470.

35 Gordon Bowker, *Inside George Orwell* (New York: Palgrave Macmillan, 2003), 421–22.

36 Orwell, "Why I Write," in *Collected, vol. I*, 5. Emphasis in original.

37 Jacintha Buddicom, "A Letter from Jacintha Buddicom (May 4, 1972)" in *Life in Letters*, 9.

38 Jacintha Buddicom, *Eric and Us: A Remembrance of George Orwell* (London: Leslie Frewin, 1974), 87.

39 Ibid., 70.

40 Ibid., 71.

41 Ibid.

42 Ibid., 117.

43 Ibid.

44 Dione Venables, "Postscript to Eric and Us," in *Eric and Us: A Remembrance of George Orwell* by Jacintha Buddicom (Chichester: Finlay, 2006) 182. Capitalization in original.

45 Ibid. Capitalization in original.

46 Ibid.

47 Buddicom, *Eric and Us*, 145.

48 "What a wonderful thing to have a kid of one's own," he wrote to Rayner Heppenstall in congratulations on the birth of his daughter. "I've always wanted one so." Orwell, "To Rayner Heppenstall (April 16, 1940)," in *Life in Letters*, 177.

49 Quoted in Venables, "Postscript," 186.

50 For example: "One sometimes gets the impression that the mere words 'Socialism' and 'Communism' draw towards them with magnetic force every fruit-juice drinker, nudist, sandal-wearer, sex-maniac, Quaker, 'Nature Cure' quack, pacifist and feminist in England." Orwell, *The Road to Wigan Pier*, 174.

51 Quoted in Bernard Crick, *George Orwell: A Life* (Boston: Little, Brown and Company, 1980), 13. The same image occurs in *Keep the Aspidistra Flying*: "This woman business! What a bore it is! What a pity we can't cut it right out, or at least be like the animals—minutes of ferocious lust and months of icy chastity. Take a cock pheasant, for example. He jumps up on the hens' backs without so much as a with your leave or by your leave. And no sooner it is over than the whole subject is out of his mind. He hardly even notices his hens any longer; he ignores them, or simply pecks them if they come too near his food. He is not called upon to support his offspring, either. Lucky pheasant!" George Orwell, *Keep the Aspidistra Flying* (New York: Harcourt, Brace and Company, 1956), 102.

52 "'I hated the sight of you,' he said. 'I wanted to rape you and then murder you afterwards. Two weeks ago I thought seriously of smashing your head in with a cobblestone.'" Orwell, *1984*, 101.

53 "She gets what I've finally decided is a definite pleasure out of rocking herself to and fro with her arms across her breast, and glooming at me, 'But George, it's very *serious*! I don't know where the money's coming from!'" Orwell, *Coming Up for Air*, 11. Emphasis in original.

54 "He was a man of independent income, calling himself a painter—he produced about half a dozen mediocre landscapes every year—and he had come to Knype Hill two years earlier and bought one of the new villas behind the Rectory. In appearance he was a fine, imposing-looking man, though entirely bald (he was at great pains to conceal this), and he carried himself with such a rakish air as to give the impression that his fairly sizable belly was merely a kind of annex to his chest. His age was forty-eight, and he owned to forty-four. People in the town said that he was a 'proper old rascal'; young girls were afraid of him, not without reason." George Orwell, *A Clergyman's Daughter* (New York: Harcourt, Brace and Company, 1960), 45.

55 Ibid., 49.

56 Peter Davison, "[Note on] A Letter for Jacintha Buddicom (May 4, 1972)," in *Life in Letters*, 10.

"'But why couldn't they leave you *alone*?' Dorothy thinks afterward. 'Why did they always have to kiss you and maul you about? They were dreadful when they kissed you—dreadful and a little disgusting, like some large, furry beast that rubs itself against you, all too friendly and yet liable to turn dangerous at any moment. And beyond their kissing and mauling there lay always the suggestion of those other, monstrous things (*'all that'* was her name for them) of which she could hardly even bear to think."" Orwell, *A Clergyman's Daughter*, 91–92. Emphasis in original.

57 Quoted in Buddicom, *Eric and Us*, 147.

58 Orwell, "To Jacintha Buddicom ([February 15,] 1949)," in *Life in Letters*, 445.

59 Buddicom, "A Letter from Jacintha Buddicom (May 4, 1972)," in *Life in Letters*, 9.

Chapter Two

1 Orwell, "Letter to George Woodcock," in *Collected, Vol. IV*, 369–70.

2 Orwell, *The Road to Wigan Pier*, 33.

3 Orwell, "Letter to Jack Common," in *Collected, Vol. I*, 216.

4 Orwell, "Letter to the Editor of the New English Weekly," in *Collected, Vol. 1*, 332. On the complexities of Orwell's views on homosexuality, see Bowker, *Inside George Orwell*, 431. For (inconclusive) evidence of his own homosexual tendencies, see: Orwell, "Extract from a Letter to Cyril Connolly (Easter 1921)," in *Life in Letters*, 7–8.

5 Orwell, "Review: *The Soul of Man Under Socialism* by Oscar Wilde," in *Collected, Vol. IV*, 428.

6 George Woodcock, *The Crystal Spirit: A Study of George Orwell* (New York: Schocken Books, 1984), 41.

7 Peter Stansky and William Abrahams, *The Unknown Orwell* (New York: Alfred A. Knopf, 1972), 125.

8 Orwell, *Road to Wigan Pier*, 127.

9 Orwell, "Letter to George Woodcock," *Collected, Vol. IV*, 370.

10 Ibid.

11 Bowker, *Inside George Orwell*, 431. He may have read "De Profundis" earlier. Recalling his experiences at boarding school, Orwell says he learned there that "Whatever happened was right." (Orwell, "Such, Such Were the Joys," in *Collected, Vol. IV*, 359.) Wilde, in "De Profundis," wrote that prison taught him that "whatever is realised is right." Oscar Wilde, "De Profundis': 'Epistola: In Carcere et Vinculis' (January–March 1897)," in *Collins Complete Works of Oscar Wilde* (Glasgow: Harper Collins, 2003), 1056.

12 Orwell, "'Lady Windermere's Fan': A Commentary by George Orwell," in *Orwell: The Lost Writings*, ed. W.J. West (New York: Arbor House, 1985), 170.

13 Orwell, "Review: *Landfall* by Nevil Shute[…]," in *Collected, Vol. II*, 45. Compare: "a man who admires innocence must be immensely corrupt." Oscar Wilde, note on Orig. MS. First Draft, *A Woman of No Importance* (British Library, Add. 81622 3019A), 71.

14 Orwell, "Review: *Angel Pavement* by J.B. Priestley," in *Collected, Vol. II*, 25. Wilde: "All bad art is the result of good intentions." Wilde, "De Profundis," 1044; "The artist is the creator of beautiful things.... No artist has ethical

sympathies. An ethical sympathy in an artist is an unpardonable mannerism of style." Wilde, *The Picture of Dorian Gray*, in *Collins Complete Works*, 17.

15   Orwell, "To G.H. Bantock (Late 1945–Early 1946)," in *Life in Letters*, 276. Wilde: "Disobedience ... is man's original virtue. It is through disobedience that progress has been made, through disobedience and through rebellion." Wilde, "The Soul of Man Under Socialism," in *Collins Complete Works*, 1176.

16   Orwell, *Road to Wigan Pier*, 146–47.

17   Wilde, "Soul of Man," 1193.

18   Ibid., 1181.

19   Ibid., 1182.

20   Ibid., 1194. In "Why I Write," Orwell observed: "The great mass of human beings are not acutely selfish. After the age of about thirty they abandon individual ambition—in many cases, indeed, they almost abandon the sense of being individuals at all—and live chiefly for others or are simply smothered under drudgery." (Orwell, "Why I Write," in *Collected, Vol. I*, 3). Again, he directly echoes "The Soul of Man": "Socialism would relieve us from that sordid necessity of living for others.... Socialism itself will be of value simply because it will lead to Individualism." Wilde, *Soul of Man*, 1174–75. (Orwell quotes from the "sordid necessity" line in his review of "The Soul of Man Under Socialism." Orwell, "Review: *The Soul of Man*," in *Collected, Vol. IV*, 427.)

21   Susan Wolf, "Moral Saints," in *Ethics*, ed. Peter Singer (Oxford: Oxford University Press, 1994), 346.

22   Ibid., 361.

23   Runes's *Dictionary of Philosophy* says the word morals "is used to designate the codes, conduct, customs of individuals or of groups"; aesthetics deals "with beauty or the beautiful, especially in art, [and] with taste and standards of value in judging art"; and, politics is both the "normative science" covering the "organization of social goods" and the "branch of civics concerned with government and state affairs." Dagobert D. Runes, *The Dictionary of Philosophy* (New York: Philosophical Library, 1942), 202, 6, and 242.

24   Peter Singer writes of the difference in the introduction to his excellent anthology *Ethics*: "What is ethics? The word itself is sometimes used to refer to the set of rules, principles, or ways of thinking that guide, or claim authority to guide, the actions of a particular group; and sometimes it stands for the systematic study of reasoning about how we ought to act.... 'Morality' brings with it a particular, and sometimes inappropriate, resonance today. It suggests a stern set of duties that require us to subordinate our natural desires—and our sexual desires get particular emphasis here—in order to obey the moral law. A failure to fulfill our duty brings with it a heavy sense of guilt. Very often, morality is assumed to have a religious basis. These connotations of 'morality' are features of a particular conception of ethics, one linked to the Jewish and Christian traditions, rather than an inherent feature of any ethical system." Singer, "Introduction," in *Ethics*, 4–5.

25   Bernard Williams writes: "By origin, the difference between the two is that

between Latin and Greek, each relating to a word meaning *disposition* or *custom*. One difference is that the Latin term from which 'moral' comes emphasizes rather more the sense of social expectation, while the Greek favors that of individual character." Bernard Williams, *Ethics and the Limits of Philosophy* (Cambridge, MA: Harvard University Press, 1985), 6. Emphasis in original.

26 This crucial difference was brought to my attention by Emily-Jane Dawson, in conversation, November 23, 2016.

27 Wolf, "Moral Saints," 350.

28 I have it on good authority—from the novice master at the largest Benedictine monastery in Europe—that among monks it is widely understood that "nobody wants to live with a saint." Father Otto Betler, in conversation, October 23, 2016.

29 Wilde wrote of himself, "I am a born antinomian. I am one of those who are made for exceptions, not for laws"; and of Christ, "For him there were no laws: there were exceptions merely." Wilde, "De Profundis," 1019 and 1035.

Orwell's biographers recall: "Blair and his friends ... as 'Antinomians,' claimed the right to set standards of their own." (Stansky and Abrahams, *Unknown Orwell*, 122.) However, Orwell later criticized his Etonian chum Connolly for admiring a "kind of sluttish antinomianism—lying in bed till four in the afternoon and drinking pernod." Orwell, "Review: *The Rock Pool* by Cyril Connolly[...]" in *Collected, Vol. I*, 226.

Always heretical and usually pejorative, the term is defined by *Webster's* as: "1- one who holds that under the gospel dispensation of grace the moral law is of no use or obligation because faith alone is necessary to salvation;" and "2- one who rejects a socially established morality." *Webster's Ninth New Collegiate Dictionary* (Springfield, MA: Merriam-Webster Inc., 1987).

The Catholic Encyclopedia tells us, further, that the term was first coined during the Protestant Reformation, and has been associated with the doctrines of Johannes Agricola, Anne Hutchinson, the Anabaptists of Munster, the Plymouth Brethren, and retroactively, with some of the Gnostics. It has been consistently condemned by theologians and suppressed by religious authorities, both Catholic and Protestant. Francis Aveling, "Antinomianism," *The Catholic Encyclopedia, Vol. 1* (New York: Robert Appleton Company, 1907), http://www.newadvent.org/cathen/01564b.htm, accessed June 16, 2014.

30 Orwell, "Lady Windermere's Fan," 168.

31 For an exhaustive reading of Wilde along these lines, see: Neil McKenna, *The Secret Life of Oscar Wilde* (New York: Basic Books, 2005).

32 Wilde, "The Critic as Artist," in *Collins Complete Works*, 1114.

33 Oscar Wilde, "The Cenci," in *Selected Journalism*, ed. Anya Clayworth (Oxford: Oxford University Press, 2004), 61.

34 Wilde, *Picture of Dorian Gray*, 17.

35 For a defense of morality's supremacy, see: Iris Murdock, "The Sovereignty of Good Over Other Concepts," in *The Sovereignty of Good* (London: Routledge, 1991). On the place of art in particular, see pages 85–90.

36 Sartre said of Wilde, "his 'Beautiful' is an engine of war with which to destroy the Good.... The aesthete's Beauty is Evil disguised as value." Jean-Paul Sartre, *Saint Genet: Actor and Martyr*, trans. Bernard Frechtman (New York: George Braziller, 1963), 373.

37 Wilde, "Critic as Artist," 1154.

38 Wilde wrote, in response to criticisms of *Dorian Gray*, "If a man sees the artistic beauty of a thing, he will probably care very little for its ethical import. If his temperament is more susceptible to ethical than to aesthetic influences, he will be blind to questions of style, treatment, and the like." Oscar Wilde, "To the Editor of the Scots Observer (August 13, 1890)," in *The Complete Letters of Oscar Wilde*, eds. Merlin Holland and Rupert Hart-Davis (New York: Henry Holt and Company, 2000), 446.

39 Oscar Wilde, "The English Renaissance of Art," in *The Uncollected Oscar Wilde*, ed. John Wyse Jackson (London: Fourth Estate, 1995), 21. Contrast with these lines from the "Sermon on the Mount," where Jesus says, "But seek ye first the kingdom of God, and his righteousness; and all these things shall be added unto you." Matthew 6:33.

40 Wilde, "English Renaissance of Art," in *Uncollected*, 25.

41 Orwell, "The Frontiers of Art and Propaganda," in *Collected, Vol. II*, 125.

42 Orwell, "Inside the Whale," in *Collected, Vol. I*, 505. Born in 1903, Orwell was himself one of those men, too young to fight, for whom Housman's brand of frustrated hedonism had such appeal.

43 Ibid., 508.

44 Orwell, "Looking Back on the Spanish War," in *Collected, Vol. II*, 258–59.

45 Orwell, "Frontiers of Art and Propaganda," in Ibid., 126.

46 Orwell, "Inside the Whale," in *Collected, Vol. I*, 510.

47 Ibid,, 512. He quotes as evidence Edward Upward's *Marxist Interpretation of Literature*: "no book written *at the present time* can be 'good' unless it is written from a Marxist or near-Marxist viewpoint." Quoted in Orwell, "Inside the Whale," in Ibid., 522. Emphasis in original.

48 See, for example, his review of Philip Henderson's *The Novel Today*, which serves as a first draft from many of the ideas, and even some of the lines, from "Inside the Whale" and "Politics vs. Literature." There he rejects both "propagandist critic[ism]" and "the notion of art for art's sake" within a single paragraph. Orwell, "Review: *The Novel Today* by Philip Henderson," in *Collected, Vol. I*, 257.

49 Orwell, "Frontiers of Art and Propaganda," in *Collected, Vol. II*, 126. Interestingly, Orwell and Wilde voiced exactly the same criticisms of Charles Reade. Orwell described Reade as "one of those writers ... who squander their talents on 'showing up' some local and temporary abuse which will probably have disappeared of its own accord within a few years." (Orwell, "Bernard Shaw," in *The Lost Writings*, 120.) Wilde wrote that Reade "wrote one beautiful book ... and wasted the rest of his life in a foolish attempt to be modern, to draw public attention to the state of our convict prisons, and the management of our private lunatic

asylums…. Charles Reade, an artist, a scholar, a man with a true sense of beauty, raging and roaring over the abuses of contemporary life like a common pamphleteer or a sensational journalist, is really a sight for the angels to weep over." Wilde, "The Decay of Lying," in *Collins Complete Works*, 1077.

50   Orwell, "Charles Dickens," in *Collected, Vol. I*, 448.

51   Orwell, "Politics and the English Language," in *Collected, Vol. IV*, 139.

52   Orwell, "The Question of the Pound Award," in *Collected, Vol. IV*, 491.

53   Orwell, "Benefit of Clergy: Some Notes on Salvador Dali," in *Collected, Vol. III*, 161.

54   Ibid.

55   Orwell, "As I Please (January 28, 1944)," in *Collected, Vol. II*, 85.

56   Orwell, "Benefit of Clergy," in *Collected, Vol. III*, 161.

57   Both writers, in their handling of the topic, owe a debt to Thomas De Quincey. De Quincy wrote: "Everything in this world has two handles. Murder, for instance, may be laid hold of by its moral handle (as it generally is in the pulpit, and at the Old Bailey); and *that*, I confess, is its weak side; or it may also be treated *aesthetically*, as the Germans call it—that is, in relation to good taste." Thomas De Quincey, "On Murder Considered as One of the Fine Arts," in *The Collected Writings of Thomas De Quincey, Volume XIII: Tales and Prose Phantasies*, ed. David Masson (Edinburgh: Adam and Charles Black, 1890), 13. Emphasis in original.

Wilde repeatedly cites De Quincy's essay on Wainewright, and elsewhere borrowed a joke from the first line of "On Murder, Considered as One of the Fine Arts," saying that he wished to found a Society for the Suppression of Virtue. Richard Ellmann, *Oscar Wilde* (New York: Alfred A. Knopf, 1988), 9. Compare to De Quincey, "On Murder," 9.

58   Wilde, "Pen, Pencil and Poison," in *Collins Complete Works*, 1093.

59   Ibid., 1106.

60   Wilde, "Phrases and Philosophies for the Use of the Young," in *Collins Complete Works*, 1244. Of course, he also stated the contrary view: "All crime is vulgar, just as all vulgarity is crime." Wilde, *Picture of Dorian Gray*, 152.

61   Orwell, "Decline of the English Murder," in *Collected, Vol. IV*, 99–100. Orwell here echoes De Quincey in his evaluation of murder: "For the final purpose of murder, considered as a fine art, is precisely the same as that of tragedy, in Aristotle's account of it; viz., 'to cleanse the heart by means of pity and terror.'" De Quincey, "On Murder," 54.

62   Orwell, "Decline of the English Murder," in *Collected, Vol. IV*, 100.

63   Ibid., 101. In "Raffles and Miss Blandish," Orwell makes a similar observation about the war's effects on the public's taste for crime fiction. Orwell, "Raffles and Miss Blandish," in *Collected, Vol. III*.

64   Orwell, "Decline of the English Murder," in *Collected, Vol. IV*, 101.

65   Orwell, *Coming Up for Air*, 26–27.

66   Ibid., 53–54. Emphasis in original.

67   Orwell, "Inside the Whale," in *Collected, Vol. I*, 505–6.

68 Orwell, "Politics vs. Literature: An Examination of Gulliver's Travels," in *Collected, Vol. IV*, 221.

69 Ibid., 1154.

70 For more on Wilde's aesthetic basis for ethics, see: Kristian Williams, "Dorian Gray and the Moral Imagination," *The Common Review* 8, No. 3 (Winter 2010): 26.

71 Wilde, *Picture of Dorian Gray*, 28.

72 Ibid., 66.

73 Wilde, "Critic as Artist," 1154.

74 In his annual report of 1943, the Director of Indian Services at the BBC wrote of Orwell: "I have the highest opinion of his moral, as well as of his intellectual capacity. He is transparently honest, incapable of subterfuge, and, in early days, would have either been canonised—or burnt at the stake!" Quoted in Peter Davison, "1941–1943," in *Life in Letters*, 195–96.

On later descriptions of Orwell as a secular saint, see: Rodden, *The Politics of Literary Reputation*, especially section 19, "'St. George,' The Halfway Saint," 322–36.

75 Orwell, *1984*, 52.

76 Orwell, "Will Freedom Die with Capitalism?" in *The Complete Works of George Orwell, Volume 12: A Patriot After All, 1940–41*, ed. Peter Davison, *et al.* (London: Secker and Warburg, 1998), 460.

77 Orwell, *1984*, 52. Emphasis in original. Winston's rebellion is partly aesthetic. On a whim, he buys a paperweight—a piece of coral embedded in glass—and reflects: "It's a beautiful thing.... doubly attractive because of its apparent uselessness." (Orwell, *1984*, 81.) Later he adds, "I don't think it was ever put to any use. That's what I like about it." (Ibid., 12.) ("All art is quite useless," Wilde wrote, approvingly, in his preface to *The Picture of Dorian Gray* [17].)

The rebellion is also explicitly anti-moral: "I hate purity. I hate goodness. I don't want any virtue to exist anywhere. I want everyone to be corrupt to the bones." Orwell, *1984*, 104.

78 Wilde, "Soul of Man," 1197.

79 Orwell, "London Letter to *Partisan Review* (December 1944)," in *Collected, Vol. III*, 298.

80 Orwell, "Lear, Tolstoy and the Fool," in *Collected, Vol. IV*, 300.

81 Orwell, *Homage to Catalonia*, 78.

82 Orwell, "Some Thoughts on the Common Toad," in *Collected, Vol. IV*, 144–45.

83 Orwell, "The British Crisis: London Letter to *Partisan Review* (8 May 1942)," in *Collected, Vol. II*, 216.

84 Orwell, "Wartime Diary: 18 May 1940–28 August 1941," in *Collected, Vol. II*, 385.

85 Orwell was also concerned with the "persecution of scientists" in his own time. Orwell, "To Dr C.D. Darlington (19 March, 1947)," in *Life in Letters*, 346; and Orwell, "To Roger Senhouse (26 December 1948), in Ibid., 427.

86 Orwell, *1984*, 209. Orwell likewise points to a number of "analogies between

Communism and Roman Catholicism" in *The Road to Wigan Pier* (177–78 and 181–82). Finally, see also his letter of August 26, 1947 to Richard Usborne, reprinted in Davison, "Introduction," in *Life in Letters*, xi.

87   Orwell, *Coming Up for Air*, 176–77.

88   Orwell, "Some Thoughts on the Common Toad," in *Collected, Vol. IV*, 144.

89   Orwell, *Coming Up for Air*, 176–77.

90   Orwell, *1984*, 99–100.

91   Dorothy's surname may also, for Orwell, carry some association with spring, given the repeated mention of "hares" in the above passages.

92   Orwell, *1984*, 272.

93   Ibid., 105.

94   "We control life, Winston, at all its levels. You are imagining that there is something called human nature which will be outraged by what we do and will turn against us. But we create human nature. Men are infinitely malleable." Ibid., 222.

95   Ibid., 245.

96   The fact that the language of the Declaration of Independence—quoted on the last page of the book—has survived despite being "impossible to render ... into Newspeak while keeping the sense of the original" underscores the point. Ibid., 256.

97   "Lear, Tolstoy and the Fool" represents a direct continuation of the discussion in "The Frontiers of Art and Propaganda," where Orwell offered his fullest discussion of Art for Art's Sake. "Frontiers" was originally a talk broadcast by the BBC Overseas Service on April 30, 1941. Orwell, "Frontiers of Art and Propaganda [note]," in *Collected, Vol. II*, 127.

The very next week, on May 7, 1941, Orwell broadcast "Tolstoy and Shakespeare," which begins: "Last week I pointed out that art and propaganda are never quite separable.... But one cannot infer from that that there is no such thing as an aesthetic judgment, that every work of art is simply and solely a political pamphlet and can be judged only as such.... And in illustration of this I want to examine one of the greatest pieces of moral, non-aesthetic criticism—anti-aesthetic criticism, one might say—that have ever been written: Tolstoy's essay on Shakespeare." Orwell, "Tolstoy and Shakespeare," *Collected, Vol. II*, 127. "Lear, Tolstoy and the Fool" refines and expands the ideas Orwell first explored in this BBC broadcast.

98   Orwell, "Lear, Tolstoy and the Fool," in *Collected, Vol. IV*, 289.

99   Ibid., 301.

100   Ibid., 298–99.

101   Orwell, "Reflections on Gandhi," in *Collected, Vol. IV*, 467. Orwell himself noted that "the essay on Tolstoy ... really connects up with the Gandhi article" and "some of what I said in it I also said appropos [*sic*] of Gandhi." Orwell, "To Sir Richard Rees (March 31, 1949)," in *Life in Letters*, 456; and, Orwell, "To Sir Richard Rees (June 1, 1949)," in Ibid., 474.

102   Orwell, "Reflections on Gandhi," in *Collected, Vol. IV*, 467.

103 Ibid., 466.

104 Orwell, "Lear, Tolstoy and the Fool," in *Collected, Vol. IV*, 294.

105 Orwell, "Reflections on Gandhi," in *Collected, Vol. IV*, 467. Emphasis in original.

106 Orwell, "Lear, Tolstoy and the Fool," in *Collected, Vol. IV*, 298.

107 In 1984, Orwell describes the good Party member as a kind of political saint: "A Party member is expected to have no private emotions and no respites from enthusiasm." (Orwell, *1984*, 174.)

It is in this spirit that Winston Smith fabricates an account of "a certain Comrade Ogilvy ... [a] humble, rank-and-file Party member whose life and death he [Big Brother] held up as an example worthy to be followed.... He was a total abstainer and nonsmoker, had no recreations except a daily hour in the gymnasium, and had taken a vow of celibacy.... He had no subjects of conversation except the principles of Ingsoc, and no aim in life except the defeat of the Eurasian enemy and the hunting-down of spies, saboteurs, thought-criminals, and traitors generally." Comrade Ogilvy died much as he lived: "Pursued by enemy jet planes while flying over the Indian Ocean with important despatches, he had weighted his body with his machine gun and leapt out of the helicopter into deep water, despatches and all—an end, said Big Brother, which it was impossible to contemplate without feelings of envy." Ibid., 42.

Of course this is a disgusting account, and any system of thought that would present Ogilvy as an example to be admired or emulated could only be understood as a sort of perversion. Ogilvy's life is wasted, and it would be wasted even if he did not die young, and even if he devoted himself to some better cause. There is a sense in which Ogilvy does not register as an individual even, but as a sort of puppet for duty. It is fitting that Smith does not even try to make him a realistic character, for anything that might make him seem plausibly human— any non-prescribed interest, any glimmer of personality—must necessarily detract from "his purity and single-mindedness." In these features—and in his peculiar lack of features—Ogilvy resembles, very closely, the moral saint. (For more on this comparison, see: Ruth Ann Lief, *Homage to Oceania: The Prophetic Vision of George Orwell* [Ohio State University Press: 1969], 56–57.)

It may be significant that Comrade Ogilvy drowns. He does not, in other words, get his "nose above water" or "come up for air."

108 Orwell, "The Art of Donald McGill," *Collected, Vol. II*, 163. Is it a version of this duality, a skepticism about the claims of sainthood, or simple, profane, mischievousness that we detect in this letter of 1932? "I have promised to paint one of the church idols (a quite skittish-looking B.V.M. [Blessed Virgin Mary], half life-size, & I shall try & make her look as much like one of the illustrations in *La Vie Parisienne* as possible)." Orwell, "To Eleanor Jaques (June 14, 1932)," in *Life in Letters*, 16.

109 Orwell, "Art of Donald McGill," in *Collected, Vol. II*, 164.

110 Ibid., 165. In support of this view, Orwell quotes from Ecclesiastes: "Be not righteous over much; neither make thyself over wise; why shouldst thou

destroy thyself?" Quoted in Orwell, "The Art of Donald McGill," in *Collected, Vol. II*, 165

111 Wilde, "An Ideal Husband," in *Collins Complete Works*, 561.

112 Wilde, *Picture of Dorian Gray*, 39.

113 He explains that it is "less fine" because it "contents itself usually, by some strange perversity, with all that is inferior in art and song." Wilde, "To Rebecca Smith (July 1883?)," in *Complete Letters*, 215.

114 He had also proposed translating Flaubert's *La Tentation de St. Antoine*. See Wilde, "To W.E. Henley ([December? 1888])," *Complete Letters*, 372, note 2.

115 Wilde, "La Sainte Courtisane, or The Woman Covered with Jewels," in *Collins Complete Works*, 738.

116 Wilde, "Salomé," trans. Lord Alfred Douglas, in *Collins Complete Works*, 589–91.

117 Ibid., 590. A later translation gives the line more force: "I hear only the word of God." Wilde, "Salomé: A Tragedy in One Act," trans. Joseph Donohue (Charlottesville: University of Virginia Press, 2011), 28.

118 One is reminded of Wilde's moral from Dorian Gray: "All excess, as well as all renunciation, brings its own punishment," Wilde, "To the Editor of the St James's Gazette (June 26 [1890]), in *Complete Letters*, 430.

119 I owe this observation to Guy Willoughby, *Art and Christhood: The Aesthetics of Oscar Wilde* (Rutherford: Fairleigh Dickinson University Press, 1993), 80.

120 Wilde, "Soul of Man," 1180–81.

121 Wilde, "De Profundis," 1036–37.

122 Wilde, "Soul of Man," 1194.

123 "Yes: There was to be, as Lord Henry had prophesied, a new Hedonism that was to recreate Life, and to save it from that harsh, uncomely Puritanism that is having, in our day, its curious revival. It was to have its service of the intellect, certainly; yet, it was never to accept any theory or system that would involve sacrifice of any mode of passionate experience. Its aim, indeed, was to be experience itself, and not the fruits of experience, sweet or bitter as they might be. Of that asceticism that deadens the senses, as of the vulgar profligacy that dulls them, it was to know nothing. But it was to teach man to concentrate himself upon the moments of a life that is itself but a moment." Wilde, *Picture of Dorian Gray*, 99–100.

124 For detailed criticisms of Edwards, Bentham, and Kant, especially as their systems relate to human sympathy or one's attachments to one's own projects, see: Jonathan Bennett, "The Conscience of Huckleberry Finn," in *Ethics*; Bernard Williams, "A Critique of Utilitarianism" in J.J.C. Smart and Bernard Williams, *Utilitarianism, For and Against* (Cambridge: Cambridge University Press, 1973); and Rae Langton, "Maria von Herbert's Challenge to Kant," in *Ethics*.

125 Wolf, "Moral Saints," 352.

126 Imperfection, too: "Morality does not help me…," Wilde wrote from prison. "But while I see that there is nothing wrong in what one does, I see that there is something wrong in what one becomes. It is well to have learned that." Wilde, "De Profundis," 1019–20.

127 Wilde, "Soul of Man," 1180. As Wilde wrote to his friend Robbie Ross, "you are a little saint, not, I am glad to say, in conduct, which is nothing, but in soul, which is all." Wilde, "To Robert Ross (April 27, 1900)," in *Complete Letters*, 1185.

128 As Wilde wrote in "The Critic as Artist": "To know anything about oneself one must know all about others. There must be no mood with which one cannot sympathise, no dead mode of life that one cannot make alive." (Wilde, "Critic as Artist," 1137). He concluded, from prison, "Whatever happens to another happens to oneself." Wilde, "De Profundis," 1027.

129 Wilde, "Soul of Man," 1181.

Wolf offers an almost Wildean aphorism: "a person may be *perfectly wonderful* without being *perfectly moral*." Wolf, "Moral Saints," 358. Emphasis in original.

130 Wilde, "De Profundis," 1029.

131 Ibid., 1027. Wilde writes of Jesus: "That which is the very keynote of romantic art was to him the proper basis of actual life." Wilde, "De Profundis," 1035.

"Wilde's Christ … achieves a series of reconciliations, each of which overlaps with and complements the others. Ethics dissolves into aesthetics; piety is absorbed into practice; Hebraism and Hellenism combine; the gap closes between life and art." Willoughby, *Art and Christhood*, 112–13.

132 Wilde, "De Profundis," 1036.

133 Ibid., 1035.

134 Another idea I've borrowed from Willoughby, *Art and Christhood*, 139.

135 Wilde, "Soul of Man," 1181.

136 Ibid., 1180–81.

137 Wilde, "Phrases and Philosophies," 1244. It is a theme Wilde returned to repeatedly: In his poem "Humanitad," he urges us "To make the Body and the Spirit one / with all right things." Oscar Wilde, "Humanitad," in *Collins Complete Works*, 825.

138 "To be really medieval one should have no body. To be really modern one should have no soul. To be really Greek one should have no clothes." Oscar Wilde, "A Few Maxims for the Instruction of the Over-Educated," in *Collins Complete Works*, 1242.

139 Wilde, "De Profundis," 1029.

140 I am grateful to Jerusha McCormack for this observation.

141 "Father Damien was Christ-like when he went out to live with the lepers, because in such service he realised fully what was best in him. But he was not more Christ-like than Wagner, when he realised his soul in music; or than Shelley, when he realised his soul in song." Wilde, "Soul of Man," 1181.

142 Wilde, "To Mrs Lathbury (Summer 1890?)," in *Complete Letters*, 437.

143 "The Philistine may, of course, object that to be absolutely perfect is impossible. Well, that is so: but then it is only the impossible things that are worth doing nowadays!" Wilde, "Mrs Langtree as Hester Grazebook," in *Uncollected*, 70.

144 Quoted in George Woodcock, *Oscar Wilde: The Double Image* (Montréal: Black Rose Books, 1989), 195–96.

145 Wilde, "De Profundis," 1017.
146 Ibid., 1018.
147 Ibid., 1024.
148 Ibid., 1020.
149 Ibid., 1024–25.
150 "Of course all this is foreshadowed and prefigured in my art. Some of it is in 'The Happy Prince': some of it in 'The Young King,' ... a great deal of it is hidden away in the note of Doom that like a purple thread runs through the gold cloth of *Dorian Gray*: in 'The Critic as Artist' it is set forth in many colours: in *The Soul of Man* it is written down simply and in letters too easy to read: it is one of the refrains whose recurring motifs make *Salomé* so like a piece of music and bind it together as a ballad: in the prose-poem of the man who from the bronze of the image of the 'Sorrow that abideth for Ever' it is incarnate. It could not have been otherwise." Wilde, "De Profundis," 1026.
151 Wilde, "To H.C. Marillier ([Postmark 12 December 1885])," in *Complete Letters*, 272.
152 Orwell, "Lear, Tolstoy and the Fool," in *Collected, Vol. IV*, 293. Emphasis in original.
153 "It is the feet of clay that makes the gold of the image precious." Wilde, *Picture of Dorian Gray*, 131.
154 Orwell, *1984*, 112.
      Defeat, as Orwell said repeatedly, is preferable to surrender. For example: Orwell, "The Lion and the Unicorn: Socialism and the English Genius," in *Collected, Vol. II*, 108; Orwell, "Looking Back on the Spanish War," in *Collected, Vol. II*, 263; Orwell, *Homage to Catalonia*, 180–81; and Orwell, *Diaries*, 285–86 and 331.
155 Orwell, *1984*, 138. Emphasis in original.
156 Orwell, "Inside the Whale," in *Collected, Vol. I*, 524.
157 Orwell, *1984*, 135.
158 Ibid., 136.
159 Ibid., 137.
160 Alasdair MacIntyre, *After Virtue: A Study in Moral Theory* (Notre Dame: University of Notre Dame Press, 1984), 124.
161 Orwell, *1984*, 136.
162 Ibid.
163 Ibid., 27–29.
164 Ibid., 29.
165 Ibid.
166 As he wrote in "The Soul of Man Under Socialism": "Progress is the realization of Utopias." Wilde, "Soul of Man," 1184.
167 Orwell, "Wells, Hitler and the World State," in *Collected, Vol. II*, 142–43.
168 Orwell, "Politics vs. Literature," in *Collected, Vol. IV*, 215–16. This idea recurs in *1984*: "nothing was illegal, since there were no longer any laws"; yet "He had committed ... the essential crime that contained all others in itself. Thoughtcrime, they called it." Orwell, *1984*, 9 and 19.

169 Orwell notes that Swift's Utopia is not populated by human beings, but by horses called Houyhnhnms: "They are unattractive because the 'Reason' by which they are governed is really a desire for death. They are exempt from love, friendship, curiosity, fear, sorrow and—except in their feelings toward the Yahoos, who occupy rather the same place in their community as the Jews in Nazi Germany—anger and hatred." (Orwell, "Politics vs. Literature," in *Collected, Vol. IV*, 218). Interesting for our purposes here, Orwell specifically compares Swift's attitude with that of "another disbeliever in the possibility of happiness," Tolstoy: "In both men you have the same anarchistic outlook covering an authoritarian cast of mind ... and in both cases a sort of horror of the actual process of life." Orwell, "Politics vs. Literature," 217.

170 Orwell, "Lear, Tolstoy and the Fool," in *Collected, Vol. IV*, 299.

171 Orwell, "Art of Donald McGill," 162.

172 Wilde, "Soul of Man," 1184.

Chapter Three

1 Orwell, "The English People," in *Collected, Vol. III*, 13.

2 Bertrand Russell came close: "Orwell had too much human sympathy to imprison himself in a creed." Bertrand Russell, "[Obituary,] *World Review*, June 1950," in *George Orwell: The Critical Heritage*, 300.

3 On this point, see: Orwell, "Letter to Humphry House (April 11, 1940)," in *Collected, Vol. I*, 531–32.

4 Gordon Bowker describes Orwell's idea of decency as "Christian morality minus the dogma." Bowker, *Inside George Orwell*, 421.

5 Orwell, "Letter to Humphry House (April 11, 1940)," in *Collected, Vol. I*, 530.

6 Orwell, "The English People," in *Collected, Vol. III*, 6.

7 Ibid., 7.

8 Ibid., 8.

9 Ibid., 7–8.

10 Ibid., 30. Emphasis in original.

11 Orwell, "Editorial to Polemic [May 1946]," in *Collected, Vol. IV*, 154–59. For more on this contrast, see: Orwell, "The Prevention of Literature," in *Collected, Vol. IV*, 70–72.

12 Orwell, "Editorial to Polemic," in *Collected, Vol. IV*, 159–60.

13 George Orwell, *Burmese Days* (New York: Harcourt, Brace and Company, 1950), 69.

14 Orwell, *A Clergyman's Daughter*, 23.

15 Ibid., 249.

16 Ibid., 251.

17 Orwell, *Burmese Days*, 94.

18 "But now it was precisely from decency that he wanted to escape. He wanted to go down, deep down, into some world where decency no longer mattered; to cut the strings of his self-respect, to submerge himself—to *sink*." Orwell, *Keep*

the Aspidistra Flying, 203. Emphasis in original.

19   Ibid., 38, 114, 210, and 229.

20   Ibid., 214.

21   Ibid., 42 and 94.

22   Ibid., 212.

23   Ibid., 90.

24   Ibid., 82.

25   Ibid., 239.

26   Orwell, *Burmese Days*, 22.

27   Ibid., 47.

28   Ibid., 23.

29   Orwell, *Coming Up for Air*, 110.

30   Ibid., 110–11.

31   Ibid., 152.

32   Orwell, elsewhere: "With all its injustices, England is still the land of habeas corpus, and the overwhelming majority of English people have no experience of violence or illegality. If you have grown up in that sort of atmosphere it is not at all easy to imagine what a despotic regime is like." Orwell, "Inside the Whale," in *Collected, Vol. I*, 515.

33   Orwell, *Coming Up for Air*, 163.

34   Orwell, *1984*, 31.

35   George Orwell, *Down and Out in Paris and London* (San Diego: Harcourt, Brace and Company, 1961), 39, 52, 88, and 105.

36   Of course social expectations necessarily intruded: "he had to speak roughly when there was anyone else present, for it does not do for a waiter to be friendly with plongeurs." Orwell, *Down and Out*, 66.

37   "Being a beggar, he said, was not his fault, and he refused either to have any compunction about it or to let it trouble him. He was … quite ready to take to crime if he saw a good opportunity. He refused on principle to be thrifty … spending his surplus earnings on drink.... He was ready to extract every penny he could from charity, provided that he was not expected to say thank you … [or] to sing hymns for buns." Orwell, *Down and Out*, 166.

38   He goes on, with a sentimentality rivaling Dickens's: "Especially on winter evenings after tea, when the fire glows in the open range and dances mirrored in the steel fender, when Father, in shirt-sleeves, sits in the rocking chair at one side of the fire reading the racing finals, and Mother sits on the other with her sewing, and the children are happy with a pennorth of mint humbugs, and the dog lolls roasting himself on the rag mat—it is a good place to be in." Orwell, *The Road to Wigan Pier*, 116–17.

39   Ibid., 60.

40   Ibid., 58.

41   Ibid., 70.

42   "The evil of poverty is not so much that it makes a man suffer as that it rots him physically and spiritually," he wrote. Therefore, in addition to the purely economic

aspects, "The problem is how to turn the tramp from a bored, half alive vagrant into a self-respecting human being." Orwell, *Down and Out*, 204–6.

43 Orwell, *Homage to Catalonia*, 105.
44 Ibid., 5–6.
45 Ibid., 6.
46 Ibid., 104.
47 Ibid., 105.
48 Ibid., 112.
49 Ibid., 220–23.
50 Ibid., 3–4.
51 Orwell, "Looking Back on the Spanish War," in *Collected, Vol. II*, 266.
52 Later Orwell appealed to a group of Civil Guards, asking that they give evidence in Kopp's defense. They said they could not help, but one of them knew him by reputation: "Kopp was *buen chico* (a good fellow)." Orwell knew of course that "it was all useless." Even if there was a trial, the evidence wouldn't matter. And if Kopp were shot "that will be his epitaph: the *buen chico* of the poor Civil Guard who was part of a dirty system but had remained enough of a human being to know a decent action when he saw one." Orwell, *Homage to Catalonia*, 225–26.
    Against all probability, Kopp was released after eighteen months. See: Chapter Eleven, "'The Struggle Would Continue, The Idea Would Survive,'" in this volume.
53 As Orwell wrote to Humphry House, in a correspondence about Dickens: "The thing that frightens me about the modern intelligentsia is their inability to see that human society must be based on common decency, whatever the political and economic forms may be.... I don't believe that capitalism, as against feudalism, improved the actual quality of human life, and I don't believe that Socialism *in itself* need work any real improvement either.... I believe that these economic advances merely provide the opportunity for a step forward which, as yet, hasn't happened.... All we have done is to advance to a point at which we *could* make a real improvement in human life, but we shan't do it without the recognition that common decency is necessary." Orwell, "Letter to Humphry House (April 11, 1940)," in *Collected, Vol. I*, 531–32. Emphasis in original.
54 See, for example: Orwell, "Literature and Totalitarianism," in *Collected, Vol. II*.
55 Reviewing *1984* for the *Marxist Quarterly*, James Walsh accuses Orwell of harboring a "depressing hatred of everything approaching progress." James Walsh, "[*1984*,] *Marxist Quarterly*, January 1956," in *George Orwell: The Critical Heritage*, 287.
56 Orwell recalls guilt-leveraging lectures from his headmistress: "'I don't think it's awfully decent of you to behave like this, is it? Do you think it's quite playing the game by your mother and father to go on idling your time away, week after week, month after month? Do you *want* to throw all your chances away? You know your people aren't rich, don't you? You know they can't afford the same things as other boys' parents. How are they to send you to a public school if you don't win a scholarship? I know how proud your mother is of you. Do you *want*

to let her down?'" Orwell, "Such, Such Were the Joys," in *Collected, Vol. IV*, 341. Emphasis in original.

57 "My chief hope for the future is that the common people have never parted company with their moral code." Orwell, "Letter to Humphry House (April 11, 1940)," in *Collected, Vol. I*, 532.

58 Orwell, "Charles Dickens," in *Collected, Vol. I*, 459.

59 Orwell, "Film Review: *The Great Dictator*," in *All Art is Propaganda: Critical Essays*, ed. George Packer (Boston: Mariner Books, 2009), 146.

60 Orwell, "Charles Dickens," in *Collected, Vol. I*, 459.

61 Orwell, "The English People," in *Collected, Vol. III*, 8.

62 Orwell, "Charles Dickens," in *Collected, Vol. I*, 459.

63 Orwell, "Great Dictator," 146–47.

64 Ibid., 146.

65 Orwell, "Letter to Humphry House (April 11, 1940)," in *Collected, Vol. I*, 532.

66 Orwell, "Charles Dickens," in *Collected, Vol. I*, 416–17. Emphasis in original.

67 Ibid., 457–58.

68 Ibid., 458.

69 Ibid., 427. George Woodcock, in his essay, "George Orwell, 19th Century Liberal," notes that the core of Orwell's description of Dickens could equally apply to Orwell himself. Woodcock, "George Orwell, 19th Century Liberal," in *George Orwell: The Critical Heritage*, 246.

70 Orwell, "*Great Dictator*," 145. The critics have not tended to agree with Orwell. Established opinion has tagged the speech "a major error" (Dilys Powell, "*The Great Dictator*," 234), "a bad case of overwriting" (Otis Ferguson, "Less Time for Comedy," 237), "dreadful ... a hoary collection of disorganized platitudes, belligerently delivered" (Walter Kerr, "The Lineage of Limelight," 292), and "feeble and fatuous" (Richard Schickel, "Introduction: The Tramp Transformed," 31)— all in Richard Schickel, ed., *The Essential Chaplin: Perspectives on the Life and Art of the Great Comedian* (Chicago: Ivan R. Dee, 2006).

71 *The Great Dictator*, Charles Chaplin, dir. (Irvington, New York: The Criterion Collection, 2011).

72 It is interesting that the aspects that make the speech most compelling—the break from character, the direct form of address, the plain language, and the simple message—are precisely those that the critics find objectionable. See again: Schickel, "Introduction," 31; Powell, "*The Great Dictator*," 234; Ferguson, "Less Time for Comedy," 237; and, Kerr, "The Lineage of Limelight," 292.

73 Orwell, "*The Great Dictator*," 145.

Chapter Four

1 Orwell, "Looking Back on the Spanish War," in *Collected, Vol. II*, 267.

2 Orwell, "War-time Diary: 28 May 1940–28 August 1941," in *Collected, Vol. II*, 360.

3   Ibid.

4   Ibid.

5   Ibid.

6   Orwell, "Decline of the English Murder," in *Collected, Vol. IV*, 101.

7   Orwell, *Homage to Catalonia*, 47.

8   Orwell, "War-time Diary, 14 March 1942–15 November 1942," in *Collected, Vol. II*, 440.

9   Orwell, *1984*, 11.

10   Ibid.

11   Ibid.

12   Orwell, "Who Are the War Criminals?" in *Collected, Vol. II*, 321; and, Orwell, "Raffles and Miss Blandish," in *Collected Vol. III*, 224.

13   Orwell, "As I Please (August 4, 1944)," in *Collected, Vol. III*, 199.

14   Ibid., 199–200.

15   Orwell, *1984*, 15.

16   Ibid., 16. Later he witnesses just such a change: The speaker at a demonstration "was haranguing the crowd," vehemently condemning Eurasia. "His voice, made metallic by the amplifiers, boomed forth an endless catalogue of atrocities, massacres, deportations, lootings, rapings, torture of prisoners, bombing of civilians, lying propaganda, unjust aggressions, broken treaties. It was almost impossible to listen to him without being first convinced and then maddened. At every few moments the fury of the crowd boiled over and the voice of the speaker was drowned by a wild beast-like roaring that rose uncontrollably from thousands of throats." After about twenty minutes, "a messenger hurried on to the platform and a scrap of paper was slipped into the speaker's hand. He unrolled and read it without pausing in his speech. Nothing altered in his voice or manner, or in the content of what he was saying, but suddenly the names were different. Without words said, a wave of understanding rippled through the crowd. Oceania was at war with Eastasia! … The Hate continued exactly as before, except that the target had been changed." Ibid., 149–50.

17   "[To] do anything that suggested a taste for solitude, even to go for a walk by yourself, was always slightly dangerous. There was a word for it in Newspeak: ownlife, it was called, meaning individualism and eccentricity." Ibid., 70.

18   Orwell, *1984*, 220.

19   Orwell, "War-time Diary: 28 May 1940–28 August 1941," in *Collected, Vol. II*, 389.

20   Ibid. Emphasis in original.

21   Ibid.

22   Ibid. Emphasis in original.

23   Orwell, "As I Please (March 31, 1944)," in *Collected, Vol. III*, 115; and, Orwell, "In Defense of P.G. Wodehouse," in *Collected, Vol. III*, 354.

24   Orwell, *Diaries*, 331.

25   Orwell, "War-time Diary: 14 March 1942–15 November 1942," in *Collected, Vol. II*, 450.

26 Orwell, "An Unpublished Letter to the Editor of *The Times*," in *Collected, Vol. II*, 243–44. Those chains show up in a small way in *1984*: "A long line of trucks, with wooden-faced guards armed with sub-machine guns standing upright in each corner, was passing slowly down the street. In the trucks little yellow men in shabby greenish uniforms were squatting, jammed close together. Their sad, Mongolian faces gazed out over the sides of the trucks utterly incurious. Occasionally when a truck jolted there was a clank-clank of metal: all the prisoners were wearing leg-irons. Truck-load after truck-load of the sad faces passed." Orwell, *1984*, 96.

27 Orwell, "As I Please (March 31, 1944)," in *Collected, Vol. III*, 115.

28 Ibid.

29 Orwell, "Revenge is Sour," in *Collected, Vol. IV*, 3–4.

30 "It is absurd to blame any German or Austrian Jew for getting his own back on the Nazis. Heaven knows what scores this particular man may have had to wipe out; very likely his whole family had been murdered; and, after all, even a wanton kick to a prisoner is a very tiny thing compared with the outrages committed by the Hitler regime." Ibid., 4.

31 Ibid. Emphasis in original.

32 Orwell, "Revenge is Sour," in *Collected, Vol. IV*, 5.

33 Orwell, "As I Please (September 8, 1944)," in *Collected, Vol. III*, 230–31. Orwell returned to these photographs, and similar ones showing the execution of German prisoners by Russians, in his "Notes on Nationalism" (*Collected, Vol. III*, 369–70).

34 [Friedrich] Nietzsche, *Thus Spoke Zarathustra: A Book for All and None*, trans. Walter Kaufmann (New York: Penguin, 1978), 100.

35 Ibid., 99.

36 Part of this section originally appeared as Kristian Williams, "'Two Wasted Years': Orwell at the BBC," *In These Times*, http://inthesetimes.com/article/13785/two_wasted_years_orwell_at_the_bbc, September 6, 2012.

37 Orwell, "Notes on Nationalism," in *Collected, Vol. III*, 371. Emphasis in original.

38 Orwell, *1984*, 204.

39 Orwell, "Letter to Philip Rahv (December 9, 1943)" in *Collected, Vol. III*, 53.

40 Orwell, "BBC Internal Memorandum (October 15, 1942)," in *Collected, Vol. II*, 244–45.

41 W.J. West, "Introduction," in *Orwell: The Lost Writings*, 21 and 53

42 Orwell, "Letter to L.F. Rushbrook-Williams (September 24, 1943)," in *Collected, Vol. II*, 316.

43 Orwell, "War-time Diary: 14 March 1942–15 November 1942," in *Collected, Vol. II*, 411.

44 Orwell, "As One Non-Combatant to Another (A Letter to 'Obadiah Hornbooke' [Alex Comfort]," in *Collected, Vol. II*, 302.

45 Still, Orwell may not have been entirely satisfied with his own justifications. As he made his plans to resign, he wrote to Rayner Heppenstall: "Re cynicism, you'd be cynical yourself if you were in this job. However I am definitely leaving

it probably in abt 3 months. Then by some time in 1944 I might be near-human again & able to write something serious. At present I'm just an orange that's been trodden on by a very dirty boot." Orwell, "Letter to Rayner Heppenstall (August 24, 1943)," in *Collected, Vol. II*, 305.

46   Orwell, "Writers and Leviathan," in *Collected, Vol. IV*, 412–13.

47   Ibid., 413–14.

Chapter Five

1   Eric Blair, "Awake! Young Men of England," in *George Orwell: The Complete Poetry*, ed. Dione Venables (Finlay Publisher, 2015), 1.

2   Orwell, *Homage to Catalonia*, 231–32.

3   Orwell, *Coming Up for Air*, 25.

4   See: George Orwell, "To Charles Doran (November 26, 1938)," in *Life in Letters*, 138; Orwell, "Letter to Geoffrey Gorer (September 15, 1937)," in *Collected, Vol. 1*, 284; and, Orwell, "Letter to Herbert Read (March 5, 1939)," in *Collected, Vol. I*, 387.

5   Orwell, "My Country Right or Left," in *Collected, Vol. I*, 538–39. A short time before, Orwell had written in "The Limit to Pessimism," "it is all very well to be 'advanced' and 'enlightened', to snigger at Colonel Blimp and proclaim your emancipation from all traditional loyalties, but a time comes when the sand of the desert is sodden red and what have I done for thee, England, my England?" Orwell, "The Limit to Pessimism," in *Collected, Vol. I*, 535.

6   Orwell wrote to Herbert Read from Marrakech: "I believe it is vitally necessary for those of us who intend to oppose the coming war to start organising for illegal anti-war activities. It is perfectly obvious that any open and legal agitation will be impossible not only when war has started but when it is imminent, and that if we do not make ready *now* for the issue of pamphlets etc. we shall be quite unable to do so when the decisive moment comes.... It seems to me that the commonsense thing to do would be to accumulate the things we should need for the production of pamphlets, stickybacks, etc, lay them by in some unobtrusive place and not use them until it becomes necessary." Orwell, "Letter to Herbert Read (January 4, 1939)," in *Collected, Vol. I*, 377–78. Emphasis in original.

7   He wrote to Jack Lehmann in July 1940: "What is so terrible about this kind of situation is to be able to do nothing. The govt won't use me in any capacity, not even a clerk, and I have failed to get into the army because of my lungs. It is a terrible thing to feel oneself useless and at the same time on every side to see halfwits and profascists filling important jobs." Orwell, "Letter to John Lehmann (July 6, 1940)," in *Collected, Vol. II*, 29.

8   See: Peter Davison, "The Home Guard and Orwell ... With Some Personal Reflections," *The Orwell Society Journal* 8 (May 2016).

9   W.J. West, "Introduction," in *Orwell: The Lost Writings*.

10   Orwell, "The Lion and the Unicorn," in *Collected, Vol. II*, 94.

11   The same line appears in Orwell, "The Lion and the Unicorn," in *Collected,*

Vol. II, 90; Orwell, *Homage to Catalonia*, 61; and George Orwell, "Patriots and Revolutionaries," in *The Betrayal of the Left*, ed. Victor Gollancz (London: Victor Gollancz Ltd., 1941), 238. In *Homage to Catalonia*, Orwell paraphrased the POUM's line: "It is nonsense to talk of opposing Fascism by bourgeois 'democracy.' Bourgeois 'democracy' is only another name for capitalism, and so is Fascism; to fight against Fascism on behalf of 'democracy' is to fight against one form of capitalism on behalf of a second which is liable to turn into the first at any moment. The only real alternative to Fascism is workers' control. If you set up any less goal than this, you will either hand the victory to Franco, or, at best, let in Fascism by the back door." (Orwell, *Homage to Catalonia*, 60–61.) Compare that summation with his own position, outlined in a letter to Geoffrey Gorer in 1937: "After what I have seen in Spain I have come to the conclusion that it is futile to be 'anti-Fascist' while attempting to preserve capitalism. Fascism after all is only a development of capitalism, and the mildest democracy, so-called, is liable to turn into Fascism when the pinch comes.... If one collaborates with a capitalist-imperialist government in a struggle 'against Fascism,' i.e. against a rival imperialism, one is simply letting Fascism in by the back door." Orwell, "Letter to Geoffrey Gorer (September 15, 1937)," in *Collected, Vol. I*, 284.

12   "In England such concepts as justice, liberty and objective truth are still believed in. They may be illusions, but they are very powerful illusions. The belief in them influences conduct, national life is different because of them.... Even hypocrisy is a powerful safeguard." Orwell, "The Lion and the Unicorn," in *Collected, Vol. II*, 63.

13   Ibid., 109.

14   See especially: Orwell, "The English People," in *Collected, Vol. III*; and, Orwell, "The Lion and the Unicorn," in *Collected, Vol. II*.

15   Orwell, "Lear, Tolstoy and the Fool," in *Collected, Vol. IV*, and Orwell, "Charles Reade" in *Collected, Vol. II*.

16   Orwell, "Raffles and Miss Blandish" in *Collected, Vol. III*; and, Orwell, "The Art of Donald McGill," in *Collected, Vol. II*.

17   Orwell, "In Defense of English Cooking," in *Collected, Vol. III*; Orwell, "Review: *The Pub and the People* by Mass Observation," in *Collected, Vol. III*; Orwell, "'The Moon Under Water,'" in *Collected, Vol. III*; and, Orwell, "A Nice Cup of Tea," in *Collected, Vol. III*.

18   Orwell, "The English People," in *Collected, Vol. III*, 2. It is not always pleasant to observe one's own people from the outside. On Easter 1949, as he lay dying in a sanatorium, Orwell recorded in his diary the strange effect "of hearing large numbers of upper-class English voices" after two years in Scotland. "And what voices! A sort of over-fedness, a fatuous self-confidence, a constant bah-bahing of laughter abt nothing, above all a sort of heaviness & richness combined with a fundamental ill-will—people who, one instinctively feels, without even being able to see them, are enemies of anything intelligent or sensitive or beautiful. No wonder everyone hates us so." Orwell, "Extracts from a Manuscript Note-book," in *Collected, Vol. IV*, 515.

19   Orwell, "The English People," in *Collected, Vol. III*, 2–3.

20   Orwell, "Author's Preface to the Ukrainian Edition of Animal Farm," in *Collected, Vol. III*, 405.

21   Orwell, "The Lion and the Unicorn," in *Collected, Vol. II*, 90.

22   Ibid., 102.

23   Ibid., 109.

24   Ibid., 102–3.

25   He explores these errors in Orwell, "London Letter to the *Partisan Review* [December 1944]," in *Collected, Vol. III*, 293–99.

26   As radical historian Howard Zinn remarked, "Revolutionary change does not come as one cataclysmic moment (beware of such moments!) but as an endless succession of surprises, moving zig-zag towards a decent society." Howard Zinn, *You Can't Be Neutral on a Moving Train: A Personal History of Our Times* (Boston: Beacon Press, 2002), 208.

27   Orwell, "Notes on Nationalism," in *Collected, Vol. III*, 362. Emphasis in original. What Orwell meant by the essentially "defensive" character of patriotism may be inferred from a simple statement drawn from one of his "London Letters" to the *Partisan Review*: "I hate to see England either humiliated or humiliating anybody else." (Orwell, "London Letter to the *Partisan Review* (December 1944)," in *Collected, Vol. III*, 297.) The nationalist, in contrast, does long to see his own country humiliate its enemies.

28   Orwell, "Notes on Nationalism," in *Collected, Vol. III*, 362.

29   Orwell, "The Sporting Spirit," in *Collected, Vol. IV*, 43.

30   Orwell, *1984*, 174–75.

31   Ibid.

32   Orwell, "Notes on Nationalism," in *Collected, Vol. III*, 363. Emphasis in original.

33   Ibid., 372–76.

34   As Seymour Hersh, winner of the Orwell Award, concluded at the time: "There are many who believe George Bush is a liar, a President who knowingly and deliberately twists facts for political gain. But lying would indicate an understanding of what is desired, what is possible, and how best to get there. A more plausible explanation is that words have no meaning for this President beyond the immediate moment, and so he believes that his mere utterance of the phrases makes them real." Seymour M. Hersh, *Chain of Command: The Road from 9/11 to Abu Ghraib* (New York: HarperCollins, 2004), 367.

35   Examining a minor campaign misstep (mispronouncing *Nevada*), James Fallows argues that Trump's intellectual style is characterized by "toxic mixture of ignorance, certitude, and bullying": "Trump is totally wrong.... [He] *doesn't know he's wrong*, or care that he might be.... And still he is *a bully and a jerk about it*." James Fallows, "Trump Time Capsule #129: 'Nobody Says It the Other Way,'" theatlantic.com, October 6, 2016, https://www.theatlantic .com/notes/2016/10/trump-time-capsule-129-nobody-says-it-the-other-way/503117/. Emphasis in original. accessed November 23, 2016

36   Scott Wilson and John Cohen, "Poll Finds Broad Support for Obama's

Counterterrorism Policies," *Washington Post*, February 8, 2012, https://www
.washingtonpost.com/politics/poll-finds-broad-support-for-obamas-counterterrorism
-policies/2012/02/07/gIQAFrSEyQ_story.html, accessed July 11, 2016.

37 Glenn Greenwald, "Repulsive Progressive Hypocrisy," *Salon.com*, February 8,
2012, http://www.salon.com/2012/02/08/repulsive_progressive_hypocrisy/,
accessed July 11, 2016. For Greenwald's earlier warning that neoconservatism
was degenerating into "a personality cult … impervious to reasoned argument
and … [based entirely on] loyalty to the leader," see: Glenn Greenwald, "Do Bush
Followers Have a Political Ideology?" *Unclaimed Territory*, February 12, 2006,
http://glenngreenwald.blogspot.com/2006/02/do-bush-followers-have-political
.html, accessed July 11, 2016.

38 On the lineage of these politics and some of the persistent difficulties, see:
Michael Staudenmaier, "Brave Motherfuckers: Reflections on Past Struggles
to Abolish White Supremacy," in *Taking Sides: Revolutionary Solidarity and the
Poverty of Liberalism*, ed. Cindy Milstein (Oakland: AK Press, 2015); and, Mike
S[taudenmaier], "The White Skin Privilege Concept: From Margin to Center
of Revolutionary Politics," [2007], https://kasamaarchive.org/2011/05/12/
white-skin-privilege-its-place-in-revolutionary-politics/, May 12, 2011, accessed
July 10, 2016.

39 Writing in 1979, the Sojourner Truth Organization warned against a growing
"confusion" among the anti-imperialist Left, between "unconditional support for
national liberation" and "an uncritical identification with positions taken by the
national liberation leadership." They explained: "Unconditional support involves
a conscious subordination of political differences for definite political reasons.…
This has nothing to do with any attribution of infallibility and omniscience. We
do liberation movements no favor by disguising disagreements, or, still worse, by
evading questions which must be of concern to all revolutionaries." They end by
reminding their readers of "the disastrous consequences" that resulted "when genuinely revolutionary forces all over the world abandoned responsibility for all major political questions to the Soviet leadership." Sojourner Truth Organization,
"'Unconditional Support' and 'Follow Third World Leadership': An Editorial,"
Urgent Tasks 6 (Fall 1979), http://www.sojournertruth.net/ut6editorial.html, accessed April 29, 2017.

40 Orwell thought that such partnerships were inherently fraudulent, and usually
fragile: "There can be no real alliance on the basis of 'Stalin is always right.' The
first step towards a real alliance is the dropping of illusions." Orwell, "As I Please
(September 1, 1944)," in *Collected, Volume III*, 227.

41 It is, of course, a slogan taken from *Animal Farm*. George Orwell, *Animal Farm*
(New York: Signet, 1946), 40.

42 Spencer Sunshine, "Left Antisemitism" (Anti-Racist Action conference; Portland,
Oregon, 2010), https://soundcloud.com/rosecityantifa2/spencer-sunshine-left-1,
accessed April 20, 2017.

43 Orwell, "Notes on Nationalism," in *Collected, Vol. III*, 363.

44 Orwell, "The Freedom of the Press," in *Animal Farm* (New York: Alfred A

Knopf, 1993), 106.

45   Orwell, "Notes on Nationalism," in *Collected, Vol. III*, 366–70.

46   Orwell, "Through a Glass, Rosily," in *Collected, Vol. IV*, 34–36. At this stage, Orwell still believed that "the advantages of a lie are always short-lived," and in the long term the suppression of "inconvenient facts" must be self-defeating. At the level of pure tactics, "The trouble is that if you lie to people, their reaction is all the more violent when the truth leaks out, as it is apt to do in the end." But more fundamentally (at least for the political Left), "genuine progress can only happen through increasing enlightenment, which means the continuous destruction of myths." (Ibid., 35–37.) Orwell here did not yet grasp how distinctly unlikely such arguments were to persuade the sort of people who write letters to the newspapers demanding less information.

47   Orwell, "As I Please (December 8, 1944)," in *Collected, Vol. III*, 289.

48   Nietzsche parodied this thinking as "saying 'the wretched alone are the good; the poor, impotent, lowly alone are the good; the suffering, deprived, sick, ugly alone are pious, alone are blessed by God, blessedness is for them alone— and … the powerful and the noble, are on the contrary the evil, the cruel, the lustful, the insatiable, the godless … [and therefore] the unblessed, accursed, and damned!'" [Friedrich] Nietzsche, "On the Genealogy of Morals," in *Basic Writings of Nietzsche*, trans. and ed. Walter Kaufmann (New York: The Modern Library, 1992), 470.

     His prophet Zarathustra therefore accused the professors of this morality: "your most secret ambitions to be tyrants thus shroud themselves in words of virtue." Nietzsche, *Thus Spoke Zarathustra*, 100.

49   Orwell, "War-time Diary: 14 March 1942–15 November 1942," in *Collected, Vol. II*, 423.

50   Orwell, "Review: *The Vicar of Wakefield* by Oliver Goldsmith," in *Collected, Vol. III*, 371–72. Emphasis in original.

51   Ibid., 371.

52   Orwell, "Looking Back on the Spanish War," in *Collected, Vol. II*, 258.

53   Orwell, *1984*, 205. Emphasis in original.

54   Ibid., 69.

55   Ibid., 207.

56   For his advice on writing, see Orwell, "Politics and the English Language," in *Collected, Vol. IV*.

57   Orwell, "Notes on Nationalism," in *Collected, Vol. III*, 380. Emphasis in original.

58   Orwell, "Why I Write," in *Collected, Vol. I*, 1.

59   Orwell, *1984*, 26.

60   Nazia Parveen and Harriet Sherwood, "Police Log Fivefold Rise in Race-Hate Complaints Since Brexit Result," *theguardian.com*, June 30, 2016, https://www.theguardian.com/world/2016/jun/30/police-report-fivefold-increase-race-hate-crimes-since-brexit-result, accessed July 12, 2016.

61   Human Rights Watch, "Syria: Events of 2015," in *World Report 2016*, https://www.hrw.org/world-report/2016, accessed July 14, 2016.

62 Danielle Allen traces the causal line from Iraq to Syria to the refugee crisis to Brexit. Danielle Allen, "U.S. Bears Some Responsibility for Brexit," *Washington Post*, June 24, 2016, https://www.washingtonpost.com/opinions/global-opinions/us-bears-some-responsibility-for-brexit/2016/06/24/09df-79ba-39fd-11e6-8f7c-d4c723a2becb_story.html, accessed July 11, 2016.

63 Paul Krugman reminds us, "The fraudulence of the case for war was actually obvious even at the time: the ever-shifting arguments for an unchanging goal were a dead giveaway. So were the word games—the talk about W.M.D [*sic*] that conflated chemical weapons (which many people did think Saddam had) with nukes, the constant insinuations that Iraq was somehow behind 9/11." Paul Krugman, "Errors and Lies," *New York Times*, May 18, 2015, https://www.nytimes.com/2015/05/18/opinion/paul-krugman-errors-and-lies.html?_r=0, accessed July 14, 2016.

64 "Full Text: Bin Laden's 'Letter to America'," *theguardian.com*, November 24, 2002, https://www.theguardian.com/world/2002/nov/24/theobserver, accessed July 14, 2016.

65 Regarding the least well known of these examples, see Orwell, "Marrakech," in *Collected, Vol. I.*

66 Orwell, "As I Please (May 12, 1944)," in *Collected, Vol. III*, 146.

67 Compare: Orwell, "As I Please (November 15, 1946)," in *Collected, Vol. IV*, 237–38; and, Orwell, "As I Please (January 24, 1947)," in *Collected, Vol. IV*, 272–74.

68 Orwell, "The Sporting Spirit," in *Collected, Vol. IV*, 41. Orwell may have seen this effect up close. In Burma he played on the police football team, center-forward. Alok Raj, *Orwell and the Politics of Despair: A Critical Study of the Writings of George Orwell* (Cambridge: Cambridge University Press, 1990), 60–61.

69 Orwell, "The Lion and the Unicorn," in *Collected, Vol. II*, 109.

70 Orwell, "Toward European Unity," *Collected, Vol. IV*, 372.

71 Ibid., 373–74. It is this anti-imperialist provision which most sharply distinguishes Orwell's proposal from Clarence Streit's plan for the merger of the existing democracies, which Orwell critiqued in his essay "Not Counting Niggers." Nonetheless one comment Orwell made concerning Streit's plan applies equally well to his own: "Of course it is not going to happen, nothing advocated by well-meaning literary men ever happens." Orwell, "Not Counting Niggers," in *Collected, Vol. I*, 396.

72 Orwell, "Looking Back on the Spanish War," in *Collected, Vol. II*, 267.

73 Orwell, "Patriots and Revolutionaries," 244.

74 Ibid., 245.

Chapter Six

1 Originally published as Kristian Williams, "'Strict Discipline Combined with Social Equality': Orwell on Leadership in the Spanish Militias," *Perspectives on*

Anarchist Theory (2014).

2   Orwell, "Looking Back on the Spanish War," in *Collected, Vol. II*, 255–56.

3   Orwell, "Notes on the Spanish Militias," in *Collected, Vol I*, 319.

4   Historical details in this chapter are drawn from numerous sources, most notably: Helen Graham, *The Spanish Civil War: A Very Short Introduction* (Oxford: Oxford University Press, 2005).

5   Orwell, "Review: *Red Spanish Notebook* by Mary Low and Juan Brea, *Heroes of the Alcazar* by T. Timmermans," in *Collected, Vol. I*, 287.

6   Orwell, *Homage to Catalonia*, 4–5.

7   Mexico deserves a special mention: a poor country, an ocean away, it did more for the Republic than anyone could have expected, sending arms and accepting refugees. Its contribution, modest though it was, should have been enough to shame the major democracies.

8   He later reflected, "Had I gone to Spain with no political affiliation at all I should probably have joined the International Column and should no doubt by this time have had a bullet in the back for being 'politically unreliable,' or at least have been in jail. If I had understood the situation a bit better I should probably have joined the Anarchists." Orwell, "Letter to Jack Common (October? 1937)," in *Collected, Vol. I*, 289.

9   Orwell, *Homage to Catalonia*, 26.

10 George Orwell, [Broadcast of May 16, 1932,] *Orwell: The War Commentaries*, ed. W.J. West (New York: Schocken Books, 1985), 94–95. Interestingly, this passage was blocked from broadcast by the censors.

11 Orwell, *Homage to Catalonia*, 27.

12 Ibid.

13 Orwell, "Notes on the Spanish Militias," in *Collected, Vol. I*, 318.

14 Orwell, *Homage to Catalonia*, 196.

15 Ibid., 29. It is an important point, because "Later it became the fashion to pretend that the faults which were due to lack of training and weapons were the result of the equalitarian system. Actually, a newly raised draft of militia was an undisciplined mob not because the officers called the privates 'Comrade' but because raw troops are *always* an undisciplined mob." Ibid., 27–28. Emphasis in original.

16 Ibid., 28.

17 Orwell, "Spilling the Spanish Beans," in *Collected, Vol. I,* 272.

18 "After what I have seen in Spain I have come to the conclusion that it is futile to be 'anti-Fascist' while attempting to preserve capitalism." Orwell, "Letter to Geoffrey Gorer (September 15, 1937)," in *Collected, Vol. I*, 284. For a defense of the Popular Army and a critique of the POUM line, see: Raymond Carr, "Orwell and the Spanish Civil War," in *The World of George Orwell*, ed. Miriam Gross (London: Weidenfeld and Nicolson, 1972), 67–69.

19 Orwell, *Homage to Catalonia*, 104–5.

20 Ibid., 27.

21 Ibid., 28.

22 Ibid., 27–28.

23 Orwell states that POUM militiamen were never pressured to join the Party. (Orwell, "Notes on the Spanish Militias," in *Collected, Vol. I*, 325.) Additionally, "there was very little heresy-hunting in the P.O.U.M ... [and] short of being a pro-Fascist no one was penalized for holding the wrong political opinions." Orwell, *Homage to Catalonia*, 71.

24 Orwell, "Notes on the Spanish Militias," in *Collected, Vol. I*, 319. Emphasis in original.

25 Orwell, "The Lion and the Unicorn," in *Collected, Vol. II*, 86–87.

26 Orwell, "Looking Back on the Spanish War," in *Collected, Vol. II*, 250.

27 Orwell, *Homage to Catalonia*, 29.

28 Orwell, "Looking Back on the Spanish War," in *Collected, Vol. II*, 256.

29 Orwell, *Homage to Catalonia*, 67–70.

30 Orwell, "Spilling the Spanish Beans," in *Collected, Vol. I*, 275.

31 Orwell, *Homage to Catalonia*, 27.

32 In fact, Orwell himself "spent much of my time in the militia bitterly criticizing the P.O.U.M. 'line,' but I never got into trouble for it." Ibid., 71.

33 I describe the events surrounding these demonstrations in Kristian Williams, "Cop Killers and Killer Cops: Political Considerations," in *Fire the Cops! Essays, Lectures, and Journalism* (Montreal: Kersplebedeb, 2014).

34 Rose City Copwatch, "Decision-Making Processes, Meetings, and Facilitation," (December 4, 2005), on file with author.

35 See, for example: Emily, "Gender/Leadership," *Red Skies at Night* 1 (2013).

36 "Theoretically, promotion was done by election, but actually the officers and NCOs were appointed from above ... [but] this does not in practice make much difference." Orwell, "Notes on the Spanish Militias," in *Collected, Vol. I*, 318.

37 Ibid., 326.

38 I have focused in this essay on military-type activity precisely because it represents a hard case, where the stakes are highest, the need for discipline is clearest, and authoritarianism is most likely to creep in.

39 Orwell recalls that as a corporal "I made myself thoroughly unpopular" (Ibid., 319). Yet when his authority was challenged, a young recruit, whom he had personally offended, "sprang into the ring and began passionately defending me ... exclaiming, 'He's the best corporal we've got!'" Orwell, "Looking Back on the Spanish War," in *Collected, Vol. II*, 255.

40 Orwell, *Road to Wigan Pier*, 49. Emphasis in original.

41 "At the beginning one had to get orders obeyed (a) by appealing to party loyalty and (b) by force of personality.... It is extremely difficult to punish men who are already in the front line, because short of killing them it is hard to make them more uncomfortable than they are already. The usual punishment was double hours of sentry-go—very unsatisfactory because everyone is already short of sleep." Orwell, "Notes on the Spanish Militias," in *Collected, Vol. I*, 319–20.

42 Orwell, "To Dwight Macdonald (December 5, 1946)," in *Life in Letters*, 334. In a similar mood, Orwell wrote of Churchill during the Second World War:

"I'd gladly shoot him when the war is won, Or now, if there were someone to replace him." Orwell, "As One Non-Combatant to Another (A Letter to 'Obadiah Hornbooke')," in *Collected, Vol. II*, 301.

43   Mikhail Bakunin, *Bakunin on Anarchism*, trans. and ed. Sam Dolgoff (Montreal: Black Rose Books, 2002), 414–15. Paragraph break added for clarity.

Chapter Seven

1   Orwell, *Road to Wigan Pier*, 170.
2   Ibid., 171–73. Emphasis in original.
3   Ibid., 173.
4   Orwell, *Coming Up for Air*, 146.
5   Ibid., 148.
6   Ibid., 151–52. Emphasis in original.
7   Ibid., 148–49. Emphasis in original.
8   Ibid., 147–51.
9   Ibid., 149. In *Wigan Pier*, Orwell reports a similar impression of an Independent Labour Party meeting. In fact he uses the same word to describe both groups: "mingy" (Orwell, *Coming Up for Air*, 152): "I remember my sensations of horror on first attending an I.L.P. branch meeting in London.... Are these mingy little beasts, I thought, the champions of the working class? For every person there, male and female, bore the worst stigmata of sniffish middle-class superiority." Orwell goes on to wonder what would happen "If a real working man, a miner dirty from the pit, for instance, had suddenly walked into their midst." The official vanguard would, he surmises, "have been embarrassed, angry, and disgusted; some, I should think, would have fled holding their noses." Orwell, *Road to Wigan Pier*, 175.
10   Ibid., 182.
11   Ibid., 176.
12   Ibid., 221.
13   Ibid., 182.
14   Ibid. Emphasis in original.
15   Ibid., 176.
16   Kevin Van Meter first offered this formulation: "there is not a Yes to many, many No's reversing the call for 'One No, Many Yeses.'" Kevin Van Meter, "Insurgent Islands: A Continuing Conversation on Anarchism with Principles," *The Institute for Anarchist Studies*, November 9, 2015, https://anarchiststudies.org/2015/11/09/insurgent-islands-a-continuing-conversation-on-anarchism-with-principles-by-kevin-van-meter/, accessed December 23, 2016.
17   Orwell, "The Lion and the Unicorn," in *Collected, Vol II*, 63.
18   Orwell, "Inside the Whale," in *Collected, Vol I*, 516. Emphasis in original.
      Orwell had, as he noted, seen in person "the bodies of numbers of murdered men," as well as others killed in battle, and on one occasion he saw a

man hanged. He therefore had some conception of "what it means to destroy a healthy, conscious man ... the mystery, the unspeakable wrongness, of cutting a life short when it is in full tide," and had no patience for people who speak of the event lightly. (Orwell, "A Hanging," in *Collected, Vol. I*, 45.) But he may have responded with a special bitterness to this line of Auden's because it appears in a poem about Spain. Many of Orwell's friends and comrades there had found themselves among the victims of such "necessary murder."

19 Orwell, "Charles Dickens," in *Collected, Vol. I*, 460.

20 Orwell, "Letter to Jack Common (October 12, 1938)," in *Collected, Vol. I*, 357.

21 Orwell, "The Lion and the Unicorn," in *Collected, Vol. I*, 94.

22 In a 1997 editorial, the staff of *Z Magazine* considered the slow inversion of the phrase "the personal is political," which, when it "first took hold via the women's movement of the 1960s" expressed the insight that "the experiences, feelings, and possibilities of our personal lives were not just a matter of personal preferences and choices but were limited, molded, and defined by the broader political and social setting ... so that improving our personal experiences meant we must collectively address political relationships and structures." Over time however, this formulation was reversed and "turned into its opposite": "Others took the phrase to mean that the choices we make personally have political implications ... [so that] the political, the social, the economic, and the cultural derive from our personal choices." Rather than understanding our own circumstances as "largely a product of systemic relations," the "'personal is political' ... came to mean, instead, that all political phenomena arise from the accumulated personal choices of individuals." The focus of political action thus shifts, away from institutions and social systems, and toward "people's personal choices." Political action comes to consist more and more of making the best individual choices—and policing each other's: "Dress right, eat right, talk right, look right, consume right, so that one is the best person, politically, that one can hope to be." Z Staff, "The Personal is Political?!" *Z Magazine* (July/August 1997).

23 Orwell, *Road to Wigan Pier*, 221.

24 Much of this tendency toward self-isolation is driven, of course, by guilt—often guilt temporarily relieved by being projected onto other people. "It is strange," Orwell remarked, though of course he understood it only too well, "how easily almost any Socialist writer can lash himself into frenzies of rage against the class to which, by birth or by adoption, he himself invariably belongs." Ibid., 180.

25 For a good overview of the concept and its transfiguration, see: Douglas Williams, "Privilege," in *Keywords for Radicals: The Contested Vocabulary of Late-Capitalist Struggle*, eds. Kelly Fritsch, Clare O'Connor, and AK Thompson (Chico: AK Press, 2016).

26 The list is hardly a parody. The Wild Roots Feral Futures Collective defines oppression as "*any* conduct (typically along lines of institutionalized power and privilege) that demeans, marginalizes, rejects, threatens or harms any living being on the basis of ability, activist experience, age, class/income level, cultural background, education, ethnicity, gender, immigration status, language,

nationality, physical appearance, race, religion, self-expression, sexual orientation, species, status as a parent or other such factors." Quoted in Justin Podur, "Oppression," in *Keywords for Radicals*, 300. Emphasis in original.

27   As they explain: "This sense of guilt, coupled with the idea that the only ethical way to act is by taking direction from others, can make one feel powerless and debased. The model of ally politics puts the burden of racism exclusively onto white folks as an intentional flipping of the social hierarchies, while being clear that you can never escape this iniquity, but offering at least a partial absolution if you can follow the simple yet narrowly directed penance: Listen to people of color. Once you've learned enough from people of color to be a less racist white person, call out other white people on their racism. You will still be a racist white person, but you'll be a less racist white person, a more accountable white person. And at least you can gain the ethical high ground over other white people so you can tell them what to do." M., "A Critique of Ally Politics," in *Taking Sides*, 70.

28   Salar Mohandesi notes that identity politics "began as a critique of reductionism within socialist movements [but] has now fallen into the same conceptual error. " Salar Mohandesi, "Identity Crisis," *Viewpoint Magazine*, March 16, 2017, https://www.viewpointmag.com/2017/03/16/identity-crisis/, accessed March 16, 2017.

       Reflecting on the unintended consequences of a theory they had themselves advanced, Noel Ignatiev and John Garvey, two former editors of the journal *Race Traitor*, recently observed: "'Privilege politics' became a way of avoiding serious thought or political debate and a way of avoiding direct confrontations with the institutions that reproduce race and with the individuals responsible for the functioning of those institutions. The focus shifted to an emphasis on scrutinizing every inter-personal encounter between black people and whites to unearth underlying racist attitudes and to guide people in 'unlearning' them. This has developed into a tendency to strictly enforce the boundaries between the races." John Garvey and Noel Ignatiev, "Beyond the Spectacle," *Counterpunch*, June 22, 2015, http://www.counterpunch.org/2015/06/22/beyond-the-spectacle/, accessed June 22, 2015.

29   For an excellent analysis of the "ally" concept, see: Mab Segrest, "Allies," in *Keywords for Radicals*.

       The recent rhetorical shift from "allies" to "accomplices" signals a step in the right direction, since it at least implies mutual trust and shared risk. Too often, though, the difference is only rhetorical, not conceptual. The word changes, but the idea remains the same—though newly invested with a connotation of danger, adventure, and romantic criminality. On the differences between the two concepts, see: Indigenous Action Media, "Accomplices Not Allies: Abolishing the Ally Industrial Complex," in *Taking Sides*.

30   Orwell, *Animal Farm*, 123.

31   See, for example: Abbey Volcano, "Police at the Borders," in *Queering Anarchism: Addressing and Undressing Power and Desire*, eds. C.B. Daring, J. Rogue, Deric Shannon, and Abbey Volcano (Oakland: AK Press, 2012), 34–35.

32 In an interview with Chris Dixon, Tynan Jarrett reflects self-critically on the means employed in the campaign to transform the Women's Centre at Concordia University into the Centre for Gender Advocacy: "We used a lot of heavy-handed tactics to make people feel guilty, to lecture them, to do all these things that ultimately may change people's behavior but won't change their minds and will only make them resent you and are not positive things at all in the end. We just pushed, pushed a lot of people away. What we would have argued was that the space is either going to be safe for some people and unsafe for others, so we have to push away these middle-class white women who are racist and classist and ableist or else it's not going to be a safe space for other people. But I don't really think the world works like that, actually." Quoted in Chris Dixon, *Another Politics: Talking Across Today's Transformative Movements* (Oakland: University of California Press, 2014), 101.

33 Orwell, *Road to Wigan Pier*, 229.

34 Ibid., 228.

35 Orwell, "War-time Diary: 28 May 1940–28 August 1941," in *Collected, Vol. II*, 394. Orwell returned to this point repeatedly throughout his career. See also: Orwell, "London Letter to *Partisan Review* (August 15?, 1945)," in *Collected, Vol. III*, 396; and, Orwell, "Toward European Unity," in *Collected, Vol. IV*, 373–74.

36 Orwell, *Road to Wigan Pier*, 230.

37 Ibid., 231–32. In *Wigan Pier*, the focus is on class, but Orwell sees the situation as being "comparable to … race-difference, and experience shows that one *can* co-operate with foreigners, even with foreigners whom one dislikes, when it is really necessary." (Orwell, *Road to Wigan Pier*, 229. Emphasis in original.) Elsewhere Orwell cites an example of military necessity forcing the retirement of particular racial prejudices: "Until recently it was believed that the white races were much more liable to sunstroke that the coloured, and that a white man could not safely walk about in tropical sunshine without a pith helmet. There was no evidence whatever for this theory, but it served the purpose of accentuating the difference between 'natives' and Europeans. During the war the theory was quietly dropped and whole armies manoeuvred in the tropics without pith helmets." Orwell, "Notes on Nationalism," in *Collected, Vol. III*, 373–74.

38 Orwell, "Letter to Jack Common (September 29, 1938)," in *Collected, Vol. I*, 353.

39 A generation ago, Murray Bookchin complained of the "utter stupidity of the American 'left' during the late sixties in projecting a mindless 'politics of polarisation' and thereby wantonly humiliating so many middle-class—and, yes, let it be said: *bourgeois*—elements who were prepared to listen and to learn.… Insensible to the *unique* constellation of possibilities that stared it in the face, the 'left' simply fed its guilt and insecurities about itself and followed a politics of systematic alienation from all the authentic, radicalising forces in American society. This insane politics, coupled with a mindless mimicry of the 'third world,' a dehumanizing verbiage (the police as 'pigs,' opponents as 'fascists'), and a totally

dehumanizing body of values, vitiated all its claims as a 'liberation movement.'" The strategy, if that is the word, certainly had its effect: "The student strike that followed the Kent [State] murders revealed to the 'left' and the students alike that they had succeeded only too well in polarising American society, but that *they*, and not the country's rulers, were in the minority." Murray Bookchin, "On Spontaneity and Organization," in *Toward an Ecological Society* (Montreal: Black Rose Books, 1995), 256–57. Emphasis in original.

40 Orwell, *Road to Wigan Pier*, 217.
41 Ibid., 222.
42 Ibid., 220.
43 Ibid., 231.
44 Ibid., 216. Emphasis in original.
45 Orwell, *Coming Up for Air*, 155–56.
46 Orwell, "Review: *The Soul of Man Under Socialism* by Oscar Wilde," in *Collected, Vol. IV*, 428.

Chapter Eight

1   Originally published as Kristian Williams, "Anarchism and the English Language" in *Anarchism and the English Language/English and the Anarchists' Language* (CrimethInc Writers' Bloc, 2013). The title of this version is taken from Orwell, "Politics and the English Language," in *Collected, Vol. IV*, 135.
2   Orwell, "Politics and the English Language," in *Collected, Vol. IV*, 128.
3   Ibid., 130.
4   Ibid., 138.
5   Ibid., 139.
6   Ibid., 135.

Chapter Nine

1   Williams, "Anarchism and the English Language," and CrimethInc. Writers' Bloc, "English and the Anarchists' Language," both in *Anarchism and the English Language/English and the Anarchists' Language*.
2   CrimethInc, "English and the Anarchists' Language," 2.
3   Ibid., 3. Emphasis in original.
4   Ibid., 4.
5   Ibid. Emphasis in original.
6   Ibid. Emphasis in original.
7   Ibid., 5.
8   Ibid., 3.
9   Ibid., 6. Emphasis in original.
10 Orwell, "Politics and the English Language," in *Collected Vol. IV*, 135.
11 Orwell, "Nonsense Poetry," in *Collected, Vol. IV*.

12   Orwell, "Good Bad Books," in *Collected, Vol. IV*.

13   Orwell, "Politics and the English Language," in *Collected, Vol. IV*, 139. Emphasis added.

14   CrimethInc, "English and the Anarchists' Language," 5.

15   One study found that between 1974 and 1992, Chomsky was cited 11,619 times in publications listed in the Science Citation Index, and between 1972 and 1992, 7,449 times in the Social Science Citation Index—"likely the greatest number of times for a living person." Additionally, between 1980 and 1992 he was cited 3,874 times in the Arts and Humanities Citation Index, making him "the most cited living person in that period and the eighth most cited source overall." To give that some context, the Top Ten list would run: Marx, Lenin, Shakespeare, Aristotle, the Bible, Plato, Freud, Chomsky, Hegel, and Cicero. "Chomsky is Citation Champ," *MIT News*, April 15, 1992, http://news.mit. edu/1992/citation-0415, accessed December 12, 2016.

A 2005 readers' poll conducted by *Foreign Policy* and *Prospect* identified Chomsky as the world's top public intellectual. "Prospect/FP Top 100 Public Intellectual Results," *ForeignPolicy.com*, October 14, 2005, http://foreignpolicy .com/2005/10/15/prospectfp-top-100-public-intellectuals-results/, accessed December 12, 2016.

16   Quoted in "'False, False, False, and False': Noam Chomsky interviewed by Ray Suarez," *Talk of the Nation*, January 20, 1999, https://chomsky.info/19990120/, accessed December 12, 2016.

17   He does also identify a third option, which I do not believe applies in this particular case: "or he is almost indifferent as to whether his words mean anything of not." Orwell, "Politics and the English Language," in *Collected, Vol. IV*, 129.

18   Orwell, "Why I Write," in *Collected Vol. I*, 6.

19   CrimethInc, "English and the Anarchists' Language," 5.

20   Quoted in William St. Clair, *The Godwins and the Shelleys: The Biography of a Family* (New York: WW Norton & Company, 1989), 313 and 315.

21   I confess that here I have selected the poem simply for the title. Godwin's influence is more evident in *Queen Mab* and *The Revolt of Islam*. See: St. Clair, *The Godwins and the Shelleys*, 340–41 and 431, respectively.

22   CrimethInc, "English and the Anarchists' Language," 5.

23   Friedrich Nietzsche, "The Birth of Tragedy, or: Hellenism and Pessimism," in *Basic Writings of Nietzsche*, 81. Emphasis in original.

24   Ibid., 33. Emphasis in original.

25   Ibid., 130.

26   Walter Kaufmann, *Nietzsche: Philosopher, Psychologist, Antichrist* (Princeton: Princeton University Press, 1974), 128 and 130.

27   CrimethInc, "English and the Anarchists' Language," 1.

28   Stephen Fry, *The Ode Less Travelled: Unlocking the Poet Within* (New York: Gotham Books, 2006), xvii.

29   Noam Chomsky, "Linguistics and Politics (Spring 1969)," in *Language and Politics, Second Edition*, ed. C.P. Otero (Oakland: AK Press, 2004), 113.

30 CrimethInc, "English and the Anarchists' Language," 5–6.

31 Ibid., 5.

Chapter Ten

1 For an example showing how these problems are inter-related and mutually reinforcing, see: "Climate Change and Inequality are Driving War and Catastrophic Conflicts from Syria to Africa," *Democracy Now*, December 3, 2015, https://www.democracynow.org/2015/12/3/climate_change_and_inequality _are_driving , accessed November 5, 2016.

The *Bulletin of the Atomic Scientists'* Doomsday Clock, "an internationally recognized design that conveys how close we are to destroying our civilization with dangerous technologies of our own making," places us at "3 minutes to Midnight." ("Overview," *Bulletin of the Atomic Scientists*, 2016, http://thebulletin.org/overview, accessed November 6, 2016.) CNN notes, with unintentional symbolism, that the present setting is "the closest it has been to midnight since the Cold War days of 1984." Todd Leopold, "Doomsday Clock Stays at Three Minutes to Midnight," *CNN*, January 26, 2016, http://www.cnn.com/2016/01/26/us/doomsday-clock-feat/, accessed November 6, 2016.

2 Orwell, "The Limit to Pessimism," in *Collected, Vol. I*, 533. Emphasis in original.

3 For our purposes, it makes no difference whether Orwell's reading was the right one, or even a fair interpretation; the point is that this is how *he* understood their views, and responded accordingly. The quotations throughout are Orwell's, not the words of the authors he is discussing.

4 "Politically, Swift was one of those people who are driven into a sort of perverse Toryism by the follies of the progressive party of the moment." Orwell, "Politics vs. Literature: An Examination of *Gulliver's Travels*," in *Collected, Vol. IV*, 207.

5 Orwell, "Politics vs. Literature," *in Collected, Vol. IV*, 216–17.

6 Michael Sayers reports that Orwell "was sympathetic to the idea of change but didn't think it was possible to retain the values that make life worth living." Quoted in Gordon Bowker, *Inside George Orwell* (New York: Palgrave Macmillan, 2003), 174.

7 Quoted in Bowker, *Inside George Orwell*, 123 and 174.

8 Orwell, "Jonathan Swift: An Imaginary Interview," in *Orwell: The Lost Writings*, 113.

9 Orwell, "Politics vs. Literature," in *Collected, Vol. IV*, 221–22.

10 Orwell, "Jonathan Swift," in *Orwell: The Lost Writings*, 116. In "Politics vs. Literature," Orwell explains: "He remains permanently in a depressed mood which in most people is only intermittent, rather as though someone suffering from jaundice or the after-effects of influenza should have the energy to write books…. Swift falsifies his picture of the whole world by refusing to see anything in human life except dirt, folly and wickedness." Orwell, "Politics vs. Literature," in *Collected, Vol. IV*, 222.

11 Herbert Read, "[*1984*,] *World Review*, June 1950," in *George Orwell: The Critical*

Heritage, 283–84. Emphasis in original.

12   Orwell, "Inside the Whale," in *Collected, Vol. I*, 520. Emphasis in original.

13   Ibid., 499–500. Emphasis added.

Camus made the same complaint with regard to Nietzsche: "To say yes to everything supposes that one says yes to murder.... If the slave says yes to everything, he consents to the existence of a master and to his own sufferings.... If the master says yes to everything, he consents to slavery and to the suffering of others.... [In] the last analysis, to say yes to both [slave and master] was to give one's assent to the stronger of the two—namely, the master." Albert Camus, *The Rebel: An Essay on Man in Revolt*, trans. Anthony Bower (New York: Vintage International, 1984), 76–77.

14   Orwell, "Inside the Whale," *in Collected, Vol. I*, 519. Emphasis in original.

15   Ibid., 521.

16   Robert Colls, *George Orwell: English Rebel* (Oxford: Oxford University Press, 2013), 72.

17   Orwell, "Arthur Koestler," in *Collected, Vol. III*, 244.

18   Ibid., 243.

19   Ibid., 244.

20   Orwell, *Coming Up for Air*, 76.

21   Ibid., 154.

22   Ibid., 155. Emphasis in original.

23   Ibid., 227–28. Emphasis in original.

24   Orwell, "Inside the Whale," in *Collected, Vol. I*, 521. Emphasis in original.

25   Orwell, *Coming Up for Air*, 227.

26   Orwell, "Politics and the English Language," in *Collected, Vol. IV*, 137. See also: Orwell, "Why I Write," *in Collected, Vol. I*, 5–6; and, Orwell, "Notes on Nationalism," in *Collected, Vol. I*, 380.

27   Orwell, *Road to Wigan Pier*, 211.

28   Orwell, "Lear, Tolstoy and the Fool," in *Collected, Vol. IV*, 298. Alternately: "Those who take the sword perish by the sword, and those who don't take the sword perish by smelly diseases." Orwell, "Looking Back on the Spanish War," in *Collected, Vol. II*, 252.

29   Orwell, "Toward European Unity," in *Collected, Vol. IV*, 370. Emphasis in original.

Orwell had previously used the same analogy concerning even more bleak prospects: "When one considers how things have gone since 1930 or thereabouts, it is not easy to believe in the survival of civilization. I do not argue from this that the only thing to do is to abjure practical politics, retire to some remote place and concentrate either on individual salvation or on building up self-supporting communities against the day when the atom bombs have done their work. I think one must continue the political struggle, just as a doctor must try to save the life of a patient who is probably going to die." Orwell, "As I Please (November 29, 1946)," in *Collected, Vol. IV*, 248–49.

30   Noam Chomsky has made much the same point. Asked "What gives you hope?,"

he replies: "The short answer is that it doesn't really matter. How hopeful one or another of us may be is an insignificant matter of personal assessment of incalculable possibilities. We should do exactly the same things no matter what our subjective probabilities are. But when we see people all over the world struggling courageously under conditions of really terrible adversity, it seems to me not our business to pay much attention to our personal guesses, but rather to make use of the legacy of freedom and privilege that most of us enjoy." Noam Chomsky, "Language, Politics, and Propaganda," in David Jay Brown, *Conversations on the Edge of Apocalypse: Contemplating the Future with Noam Chomsky, George Carlin, Deepak Chopra, Rupert Sheldrake, and Others* (New York: St. Martin's Press, 2005), 38–39.

31   Orwell, "Notes on the Way," in *Collected, Vol. II*, 16. Emphasis in original.

32   Both Orwell and Koestler's views may be contrasted with what Orwell called "the Theory of Catastrophic Gradualism." According to this idea, "nothing is ever achieved without bloodshed, lies, tyranny and injustice, but on the other hand no considerable change for the better is to be expected as the result of even the greatest upheaval. History necessarily proceeds by calamities, but each succeeding age will be as bad, or nearly as bad, as the last. One must not protest against purges, deportations, secret police forces and so forth, because these are the price that has to be paid for progress: but on the other hand 'human nature' will always see to it that progress is slow or even imperceptible. If you object to dictatorship you are a reactionary, but if you expect dictatorship to produce good results you are a sentimentalist." Orwell, "Catastrophic Gradualism," in *Collected, Vol. IV*, 15–16.

33   "Progress is not an illusion, it happens, but it is slow and invariably disappointing. There is always a new tyrant waiting to take over from the old—generally not quite so bad, but still a tyrant." Orwell, "Charles Dickens," in *Collected, Vol. I*, 427.

34   Orwell, "Lear, Tolstoy and the Fool," in Collected, *Vol. IV*, 299.

35   "Most people get a fair amount of fun out of their lives, but on balance life is suffering, and only the very young or the very foolish imagine otherwise." Ibid.

36   Orwell, "Arthur Koestler," in *Collected, Vol. III*, 244. Camus, in his long treatise on the basis and the nature of rebellion, concludes: "man can master in himself everything that should be mastered. He should rectify in creation everything that can be rectified. And after he has done so, children will still die unjustly even in a perfect society. Even by his greatest effort man can only propose to diminish arithmetically the sufferings of the world. But the injustice and the suffering of the world will not cease to be an outrage.... Rebellion will die only with the last man." Camus, *The Rebel*, 303.

37   See: Rodden, *The Politics of Literary Reputation*, 244–50.

38   Quoted in Ibid., 246. Emphasis in original.

39   Orwell, "Letter to Francis A. Henson (extract)(June 16, 1949)," in *Collected, Vol. IV*, 502. Emphasis in original.

40   Orwell, "James Burnham and the Managerial Revolution," in *Collected, Vol. IV*,

160–61. Here, too, it is not important whether these *were* Burnham's views, only that Orwell thought they were.

41 On each point, Burnham's philosophy corresponds with the principles of Ingsoc—and with Emmanuel Goldstein's *Theory and Practice of Oligarchical Collectivism*. For instance: "War is Peace…. [The] conditions of life in all three super-states are very much the same…. Everywhere there is the same pyramidal structure, the same worship of semi-divine leader, the same economy existing by and for continuous warfare. It follows that the three super-states not only cannot conquer one another, but would gain no advantage by doing so. On the contrary, so long as they remain in conflict they prop one another up, like three sheaves of corn." Orwell, *1984*, 152–62.

42 Orwell, "James Burnham and the Managerial Revolution," in *Collected, Vol. IV*, 179.

43 Orwell, *1984*, 220.

44 Jack London, *The Iron Heel* (Chicago: Lawrence Hill Books, 1907), 63.

Orwell's treatment of the image fuses three tropes, each symbolic of authoritarian politics: first, the notion that "[the] autonomous individual is going to be *stamped* out of existence" by totalitarianism (Orwell, "Inside the Whale," in *Collected, Vol. I*, 525. Emphasis added); second, the fanatic's fantasy of "smashing people's faces in" (Orwell, *Coming Up for Air*, 151); third, the image of a *boot*, which Orwell first used in describing the chosen march of the Nazi armed forces: "The goose-step … is simply an affirmation of naked power; contained in it, quite consciously and intentionally, is the vision of a boot crashing down on a face." Orwell, "The Lion and the Unicorn," in *Collected, Vol. II*, 61–62.

45 Orwell, *1984*, 246–56; and, London, *Iron Heel*, 1–4

46 The Foreword to *The Iron Heal* refers to the "psychology of the persons that lived in that turbulent period embraced between the years 1912 and 1932—their mistakes and ignorance, their doubts and fears and misapprehensions, their ethical delusions, their violent passions, their inconceivable sordidness and selfishness. These are things that are so hard for us of this enlightened age to understand." London, *Iron Heel*, 1.

47 Ian Slater suggests that the Party's relative tolerance of verse and the habits of the proles—especially the English tradition of improvised song—might be one such weak point: "What the Party does not see is not only that this 'leniency' runs the risk that heretical thoughts will be spread through improvisation by unidentifiable authorship, but that the very form of the verse, that of the traditional English music hall song, is likely to recall older songs. Such recall is dangerous to the Party. Whether or not the words make sense, the verse *forms* remind the singer or singers of another time, and in so doing, constitute a threat to the state's supposed infallibility." Ian Slater, *Orwell: The Road to Airstrip One* (New York: WW Norton & Company, 1985), 213–14. Emphasis in original.

48 Orwell, "Letter to Geoffrey Gorer (September 15, 1937)," in *Collected, Vol. I*, 284.

49   Orwell, "Arthur Koestler," in *Collected, Vol. III*, 244.

Chapter Eleven

1   A different version of this essay appeared as Kristian Williams, "The Spanish Civil War, Cartooning, and the Cultural Imagination: *No Pasarán!*, *The Black Order Brigade*, and *Wolverine*," *The Comics Journal*, tcj.com, December 2009.

2   *El Laberinto del Fauno/Pan's Labyrinth*, dir. Guillermo del Toro (Madrid: Telecino, 2007).

3   For an overview, see: John M. Muste, *Say That We Saw Spain Die: Literary Consequences of the Spanish Civil War* (Seattle: University of Washington Press, 1966).

4   Orwell, "Looking Back on the Spanish War," in *Collected, Vol. II*, 256–57.

5   Maureen Dowd, "Powell Without Picasso," *New York Times*, February 5, 2003, http://www.nytimes.com/2003/02/05/opinion/powell-without-picasso.html, accessed December 10, 2016.

6   Vittorio Giardino, *No Pasarán!, Volume 1* (New York: NBM, 2000); Vittorio Giardino, *No Pasarán!, Volume 2* (New York: NBM, 2002); and, Vittorio Giardino, *No Pasarán!, Volume 3* (New York: NBM, 2008).

7   John Dos Passos, [Letter to *The New Republic* (July 1939),] in Stephen Koch, *The Breaking Point: Hemingway, Dos Passos, and the Murder of José Robles* (New York: Counterpoint: 2005), 271–72.

8   Quoted in Ibid., 258.

9   Quoted in Ibid., 124.

10   Hemingway even wrote a play titled *The Fifth Column*, lionizing the extra-legal executioners. One character is based on the real-life Commissar General of Investigation and Vigilance, Pepe Quintinilla, and another on Hemingway himself, recast as a spy and assassin. Stephen Koch comments: "*The Fifth Column* is an exceptionally nasty piece of work and the moral nadir of Hemingway's entire career." Koch, *Breaking Point*, 240.

11   Quoted in ibid., 160.

12   This story is detailed in Stephen Koch's *Breaking Point*. It is dramatized as a side story in the film *Hemingway & Gellhorn*, dir. Philip Kaufman (HBO Films, 2012).

13   Orwell, *Homage to Catalonia*, 207.

14   Ibid., 209–10.

15   Ibid., 217.

16   For details of Orwell's attempts to free Kopp, see Chapter Three, "On Common Decency."

17   Kopp languished in a Soviet-run prison for eighteen months, where he was treated horribly and "lost seven stone in weight" (ninety-eight pounds). But in January 1939, as arbitrarily as he was taken, he was released. He fled to England, where he was cared for by Laurence and Gwen O'Shaughnessy, Orwell's in-laws. He later went on to fight with the French Foreign Legion during World War

Two; he was "captured with two bullets in his chest & part of his left hand shot off," but nevertheless managed to escape. He later settled in Vichy France, where he worked as a spy for British Naval Intelligence. When he was discovered, he fled again to England, barely dodging the Gestapo. He died in 1951 from the injuries he sustained during the war. Kopp and Orwell remained friends for the rest of their lives.

Biographical information drawn from: *Collected, Vol. I*, 263, *n.1*. The "seven stone" quotation is from Orwell, "To Jack Common (December 26, 1938)," in *Life in Letters*, 152. The "captured" quote is from Eileen Blair, "Eileen to Norah Myles (c. December 5, 1940?)," in *Life in Letters*, 184.

18   *Casablanca*, dir. Michael Curtiz (Burbank: Warner Home Video, 2003).

19   *The Lady from Shanghai*, dir. Orson Welles (Burbank: Columbia Pictures, 2000).

20   In "Blood and Claws," Wolverine is pulled into a "time vortex" and transported into the past to write himself into the history of the Spanish Civil War. There he (impossibly) fights alongside both Orwell and Hemingway (who did not meet until the Second World War), *and* witnesses the bombing of Guernica. Unfortunately, he's pulled back to present-day British Columbia as abruptly as he left—which I suppose accounts for the fact that the good guys lose. Larry Hama, *et al.*, "Blood and Claws," *Wolverine* #35–37 (New York: Marvel Comics, 1991).

21   Dorothy B. Hughes, *The Fallen Sparrow* (New York: Bantam Books, 1979), 2.

22   Ibid., 81 and 127.

23   Ibid., 128.

24   Ibid., 196.

25   Ibid., 199.

26   Giardino, *No Pasarán!, Vol. 3*, 29–30.

27   Ibid.

28   Albert Camus, *The Plague*, trans. Stuart Gilbert (New York: Vintage International, 1991), 162–63. Emphasis in original.

29   Ernest Hemingway, *For Whom the Bell Tolls* (New York: Scribner, 1968), 467.

30   Orwell, *Homage to Catalonia*, 185–86. Emphasis in original.

31   Ibid., 230.

32   Camus, *The Plague*, 308.

33   Orwell, "The Lion and the Unicorn," in *Collected, Vol. II*, 108. Emphasis in original.

34   Ibid. Emphasis in original.

35   Quoted in Giardino, *No Pasarán!, Vol. 3*, 9.

36   Tobias Buck, "Facing Up to Franco: Spain 40 Years On," *Financial Times*, ft.com, May 8, 2015, accessed November 27, 2016.

Index

"Passim" (literally "scattered") indicates intermittent discussion of a topic over a cluster of pages.

A

aesthetics, 44–56 passim, 225n14, 226n23, 227n36, 230n77, 231n97
ally politics, 163, 251–52n27, 252n29
"alternative facts" (term), 1–2, 12
anarchists and anarchism, 150–51; Spain, 139, 248n8; Swift, 187; writing and, 168–84 passim
Animal Farm (Orwell), 4, 32, 117, 125, 150, 197
anti-civilization, 124, 158
antinomians, 44, 227n29
anti-war movement, 115, 242n6
Apollo and Dionysus, 181–84 passim
art for art's sake, 45–46, 47, 48, 228n48

Auden, W.H., 48, 159
authoritarianism, 79, 123, 131, 145, 196, 236n169. See also *1989* (Orwell); totalitarianism
authority, 42, 144–50 passim, 187, 249n39

B

Babel (biblical story). See Tower of Babel (biblical story)
bad writing. See writing, vague, shoddy, etc.
Bakunin, Mikhail, 150–51
BBC, 107, 115, 230n74, 231n97
beauty and ugliness. See aesthetics
betrayal, 71, 73
bias, 130, 147
"Big Brother" (term), 11, 12
The Birth of Tragedy (Nietzsche), 181–83
bombing of civilians, 97–98

AK Press is small, in terms of staff and resources, but we also manage to be one of the world's most productive anarchist publishing houses. We publish close to twenty books every year, and distribute thousands of other titles published by like-minded independent presses and projects from around the globe. We're entirely worker-run and democratically managed. We operate without a corporate structure–no boss, no managers, no bullshit.

The Friends of AK program is a way you can directly contribute to the continued existence of AK Press, and ensure that we're able to keep publishing books like this one! Friends pay $25 a month directly into our publishing account ($30 for Canada, $35 for international), and receive a copy of every book AK Press publishes for the duration of their membership! Friends also receive a discount on anything they order from our website or buy at a table: 50% on AK titles, and 20% on everything else. We have a Friends of AK ebook program as well: $15 a month gets you an electronic copy of every book we publish for the duration of your membership. You can even sponsor a very discounted membership for someone in prison.

Email friendsofak@akpress.org for more info, or visit the Friends of AK Press website: https://www.akpress.org/friends.html

There are always great book projects in the works–so sign up now to become a Friend of AK Press, and let the presses roll!